THE MAKING OF MURDOCH

THE MAKING OF MURDOCH

Power, politics and what shaped the man who owns the media

Tom Roberts

I.B. TAURIS
LONDON · NEW YORK · OXFORD · NEW DELHI · SYDNEY

I.B. TAURIS
Bloomsbury Publishing Plc
50 Bedford Square, London, WC1B 3DP, UK
1385 Broadway, New York, NY 10018, USA

BLOOMSBURY, I.B. TAURIS and the I.B. Tauris logo are trademarks of Bloomsbury Publishing Plc

Cover design by danileighdesign.com
Cover image © Bruce Milton Miller/Fairfax Media via Getty Images

A catalogue record for this book is available from the British Library.

A catalogue record for this book is available from the Library of Congress.

ISBN: HB: 978-1-7883-1511-1
        ePDF: 978-1-7883-1783-2
        eBook: 978-1-7883-1784-9

Typeset by RefineCatch Limited, Bungay, Suffolk
Printed and bound in Great Britain

To find out more about our authors and books visit www.bloomsbury.com
and sign up for our newsletters

CONTENTS

PROLOGUE

'THERE'S ONLY ONE RUPERT'

London, 19 July 2011. Keith Rupert Murdoch, the most powerful media proprietor the world has ever known, had been called to account for the actions of his tabloid *News of the World*. Some commentators got ahead of themselves, claiming 'The Twilight of the Gods' – that we were witnessing 'the fast fall of the house of Murdoch'.

As the committee of British MPs questioned the eighty-year-old about the hard facts of the phone-hacking scandal, viewers around the world saw a father with apparently shaky knowledge defer to his son James again and again on detail. His resolve suddenly strengthened, however, as he defended the 'family business' – a corporation that girdled the earth with 52,000 employees and nearly 200 newspapers. There was an exemplar, another father, a paragon who couldn't be touched by questioning:

> I just want to say that I was brought up by a father who was not rich, but who was a great journalist, and he, just before he died, bought a small paper, specifically in his will saying that he was giving me the chance to do good.

But that father, Keith Arthur Murdoch, had built his career and accrued his power by navigating ruthlessly a network of connections and exploiting the hidden intersection of press and power. It was a trajectory already set by the time of Rupert's birth, a generation before James Rupert Murdoch came to his father's aid that day in London. The will to power was embedded in the Murdoch DNA.

This is a tale of press ink, radio waves and propaganda; religion, immigrants and race; princes, press barons and generals; girls, guns and golf. Of fathers, fiancés, and mothers. Of nature and nurture, genetics, selection and succession.

Above all it's a story of communication in its most basic form. Of what one father passed to his son.

Those commentators who had predicted the end of Rupert's power in 2011 were to be disappointed. He rode out the storm, and quickly got over the apparent shame of his 'most humble day'. The apotheosis of his power was still to come.

On 4 May 2017 Rupert stood shoulder to shoulder with the 45th President of the United States on *USS Intrepid* in New York Harbour. With the Australian burr that three decades as an American citizen had failed to shake, Rupert introduced the newly inaugurated commander-in-chief as 'my friend Donald J. Trump.' An awkward hug later and the unlikeliest of Presidents was telling the audience of his gratitude to 'my very good friend Rupert Murdoch. There's only one Rupert, that we know!'

Sponsored by The American Australian Association, an organisation Rupert's father was instrumental in founding, the event was ostensibly to celebrate the bonds between the countries' forces on the 75th anniversary of the Battle of the Coral Sea. Trump, returning to the autocue feed, pointed to how 'Those ties were sealed with the blood of our fathers and grandfathers'. But for many observers, the event served more to illustrate the ties between the populist politician and his enabler. Suitably enough, FOX – the network that had provided a platform for Trump as he built his political persona and carried relentless coverage of his campaign rallies into homes across America – ran a live broadcast of proceedings.

Trump praised Rupert for helping to keep history alive 'for the next generation.' But the Murdochs were well practised in helping keep their own history not just alive but shaped and protected – a point I was to discover when I set out to answer the seemingly simple question:

How had Rupert risen to his position of influence over public debate and the political landscape – and from what?

INTRODUCTION

MOULDING A MYTH

Books on Rupert constitute whole shelves in libraries but his father Keith has until now escaped unauthorised scrutiny. Instead, the Murdochs had commissioned and then carefully vetted, two previous biographies. These works, by Ronald Younger in 2003 and Desmond Zwar in 1980, helped frame and set the mythology. In the late 1960s Rupert had previously refused to allow the publication of a full, book-length biography, the result of 5 years' labour by Charles Sayers, despite the fact the family had commissioned the work.

The Murdochs have always been keenly protective of the history of Keith's life – unsurprisingly they know the value of media control and maintaining a good press. And myths can prove useful things, whether in defending yourself before elected representatives or in smoothing multi-billion dollar takeovers, as we shall discover.

The first book-length biography of Keith Murdoch had been published in December 1952, just weeks after his death on 4 October. With quite astonishing speed Keith's former staff at the Melbourne Herald & Weekly Times (HWT) in Australia had managed to write and publish a sixty-page illustrated life, with Keith's favourite and self-deprecating description of himself as its subtitle: *Journalist*. The authors subscribed very firmly to the view that Keith Murdoch was a great man whose deeds should be venerated, setting the pattern that was to follow over the next half-century. That book presented itself 'as an early permanent record for those who worked with him and for him'. Henry James wrote of how death 'smooths the folds' of the person who has died and debate is ironed away. That first biography smoothed a fair few folds. Its dedication declared: 'By world standards he became one of the greatest newspapermen of our time . . . a lay statesman of this country, an internationalist of high standing mourned by all newspaper men and government leaders throughout the democratic world'. Its closing pages recorded obituaries from around the world. That of the *New York Herald Tribune* is typical:

'All who cherish the unity of the English-speaking world are in his debt.' (A more barbed statement on Keith's death would come from Prime Minister R. G. Menzies: 'As a nation, Sir Keith Murdoch left us in his debt.')

In his 1985 unauthorised biography of Rupert, *A Paper Prince*, George Munster pointed to the legacy set in train on Keith's death:

> The obituaries started a legend. Sir Keith's career was presented in stereotype: by dint of hard work and talent, a lowly reporter became the head of the largest media group in the country. He had transplanted modern popular journalism to Australia. The legend omitted some essentials. Sir Keith owed his rise to an intimacy with politicians; and once he was on top another generation of politicians was in debt to him.

In the wake of Keith's death, one leading Australian diplomat wrote a blistering note 'to be used only by genuine historical students' and not to be quoted within his lifetime. He saw Keith's whole career as 'an attempt to imitate Lord Northcliffe', the British press baron, founder of the *Daily Mail* and First World War propagandist. For Keith, 'the journalistic art' had been 'The Art of the Monopolist'. He had possessed 'a will to be rich' and developed 'a rich man's exhibitionism' by surrounding himself with art while pursuing his 'ambition of controlling the formation of cabinets' and installing favoured leaders. The explanation for this aggrandising manipulation and control? The writer of the note felt Keith must have possessed a 'psychopathic strain'.

Once employees were freed from the binds of being beholden, they spoke out. John Hetherington, a journalist who worked for Keith, was another who did not stint when writing about his employer. In his seminal series of character studies *Australians: Nine Profiles* Hetherington asserted that under Keith's guise of a benign newspaper chief there hid 'a calculating, undeviating, insatiable seeker after worldly riches and temporal power'. A recent commentator, while acknowledging Hetherington might have had an axe to grind, saw the profile as comparing favourably with 'some of the subsequent flattery passed off as biography of Murdoch'.

Shortly before Hetherington's profile was published and perhaps in fear of it, Keith's widow Elisabeth began the search for a sympathetic scribe to write a life of Keith that would bear the stamp of definitiveness, drawing from his letters and records. In 1965 Elisabeth and Rupert commissioned Charles E. Sayers, a journalist who had recently published a biography of the crusading editor of the Melbourne *Age*, David Syme. Sayers was enthusiastic, hopeful, as he wrote privately to a colleague, that his study would 'be wide ranging and far reaching: a warm human document'.

But Sayers's papers, now safely held in the State Library of Victoria, reveal a tragic tale. The process seems to have been a difficult one from the start. In 1966

Rupert writes to Sayers admitting you 'must be getting impatient with me'. But for five years Sayers doggedly went through a huge amount of family papers and persisted with what he termed in his diary 'the Murdoch chore'. By 1969 he felt he had managed to build his dossier of research into a 'formidable thing' though he conceded that there were still blanks he had to leave. In 1970 Sayers was rewarded with the Victorian government's Captain James Cook Bicentenary Prize for Biography for the unpublished manuscript, an event he described in his diary as the 'most gratifying single event of the year'.

However, despite there being a book contract in place with William Heinemann since 1967, Rupert would not agree to publication. Understandably keen that half a decade of hard work should not be buried, Sayers was still hopeful that Rupert would finally give his approval. But as the letters and Sayers's diary reveal, he was finding it harder and harder to pin Rupert down. His desperate attempts were rebuffed. Finally, in March 1971 Rupert wrote to Sayers in polite but emphatic terms: 'Alas, I am still not prepared to agree to publication of the manuscript'.

The archive was placed in the National Library by Rupert, the finished manuscript itself placed under a not to be accessed or consulted restriction.

In 1978 Desmond Zwar, another author and journalist, was approached by Rupert to write Keith's biography. A self-declared 'warts-and-all biographer' (his last work had been a biography of Rudolph Hess), Zwar did not know whether Rupert would allow such a book about his father to be published. Neither party should have been worried. Zwar produced a lavishly illustrated, photograph-heavy slip of a book that ran to barely 120 pages.

After Zwar finished, the manuscript had been airfreighted to Rupert in New York. A nervous Zwar was later summoned to Cruden Farm, the Murdoch family's country seat outside Melbourne, to meet with Elisabeth and her son. According to Zwar, the only question they raised was on the accuracy of how often Rupert was spanked by the nanny. Publication in 1980 and blanket promotion of the book in the Murdoch press rapidly followed.

Zwar's biography may have been titled *In Search of Keith Murdoch* but it was not greeted as a probing or revelatory account. One review bore the headline 'The search for Keith Murdoch continues'.

A decade later, as the half-century anniversary of Keith Murdoch's death approached, the Murdoch family commissioned another, trusted biographer: Ronald Younger. The book was to be published by News Corporation's HarperCollins and it appeared designed to reinforce the received history of Keith as war hero and benevolent media boss.

One critic reviewing Younger's authorised biography (for Rupert's national daily, The *Australian*, no less), wrote of how it was a pity that 'for all its solid detail and considerable merit' the book was 'so often uncritical of Murdoch and marred by lapses into hagiography ... containing "paeans of adulatory prose"'. Less surprisingly Bruce Page, a long-term critic of Rupert Murdoch, was struck by the book's omissions and troubled by its overriding sense of reverence. The prose, Page thought, was more suited to North Korean tributes to its leaders, being 'resolutely sycophantic'.

The family have served and stoked the memory of Keith – scholarships, galleries, prizes all bear his name. In December 2012, Rupert's eldest son Lachlan Keith Murdoch spoke at the Melbourne Press Club's inaugural Hall of Fame as it inducted Keith. Dame Elisabeth Murdoch, the family matriarch, had died the day before, aged 103, and an emotional Lachlan broke from his address to reveal that on his last visit to his grandmother he had presented his words about Keith's life and career for her approval. His speech touched on all the popular myths, and underlining the family's attachment to its patriarch, Lachlan described his grandfather as 'a man I feel I know intimately but whom I never met'.

Conjured memories and myths as well as genes, it would seem, have been fed and nurtured before being passed down through the family. This is a family that maintains Keith's legacy not only in its sense of duty to act through the power of the media, but to possess and wield that influence as completely as possible.

The present book introduces a founding father very different from the man hitherto known. By debunking the mythology and bringing to light events that until now have remained hidden, readers may reach a new understanding not only of Keith Arthur Murdoch but of his son, Keith Rupert – the man who, within the bounds of his empire, signs himself 'KRM'.

1 ROSEHEARTY

The north-east coast of Scotland, 25 June 2016. A golf buggy lurches along fresh tarmac through the coastal dunes. On its rear-facing bench seat sits an 83 year-old billionaire in a sports jacket. Up front, a blonde former supermodel sits next to the driver whose own improbable golden locks are secured under a white baseball cap. Donald J. Trump, fellow billionaire with dynastic ambitions and newly minted Republican Party presidential nominee, is driving Rupert Murdoch and the media titan's wife number four, Jerry Hall. Trump's own model wife number three, Melania, is absent. It is three months since Murdoch and Hall married, and Rupert foreswore using Twitter with a final message: 'No more tweets for ten days or ever! I feel the luckiest AND happiest man in the world!' His penultimate tweet that day focused on the likelihood of Trump winning the Republican nomination. Rupert had already nailed his colours to the mast, claiming the Republican Party 'would be mad not to unify' if Trump won out. Trump eagerly retweeted this endorsement.

Now it was time to seal the deal of support with a publicity-friendly jaunt in Scotland, a location close to both their hearts and key in the origins of their families. Trump's mother Mary Ann MacLeod had emigrated to America from the Isle of Lewis, while the Murdochs had reluctantly left Scotland's shores for Australia.

The white golf cap Trump wore as he drove the buggy bore the populist slogan that would help sweep him to power that November: 'MAKE AMERICA GREAT AGAIN'. Five years earlier, in the summer sun of London to the south, as the hacking scandal unfolded, Rupert Murdoch had sported a cap of his own. A week before he delivered his stumbling testimony to the committee of MPs and told them of his father's legacy, he was photographed power-walking the paths of Hyde Park in a blue crew cap. It bore the name 'ROSEHEARTY'.

Rosehearty was the simple fishing village on the barren Aberdeenshire coast where in 1844 Keith's grandfather James had founded a Free Church of Scotland ministry. Brought up in the manse there, James's son Patrick went on to become Free Church minister of Cruden Bay, just a 20-minute drive up the coast from Trump's Scottish golf course.

In 1884 God, it seems, intervened, delivering a mission call to Patrick to emigrate to Australia. More prosaically, it offered a chance for the family to escape the convulsions in the Free Church and the scourge of tuberculosis that was picking off its numbers.

The Murdochs were a family of solid Presbyterian stock with a Calvinistic dedication, propriety and diligence. But Rupert's blue crew cap came from another *Rosehearty* – his multimillion-dollar superyacht. World leaders had been guests on that yacht and had seen the dining room – with its wall-wide map of the world showing America at the centre – the scene of secret unrecorded meetings. It was the stateless zone of the super-rich where deals could be struck and the media and political world carved up beyond the range of telephoto lenses.

In 2008 it was to this *Rosehearty* that British Prime Minister David Cameron, when still Leader of the Opposition, had been flown by Murdoch family Gulfstream jet and granted an audience in his successful effort to gain the support of the Murdoch press in the forthcoming general election that would bring him and his Conservative Party to power.

A century earlier, in 1908, Keith Arthur Murdoch had been in London, far away from his Australian home. A handsome and physically imposing young man with intense brown eyes under a heavy brow, a casual glance would not have revealed him as the homesick, painfully shy man he then was. He also suffered from a cruelly debilitating condition: under stress his breaths became shorter and his throat muscles constricted, strangling his voice and shutting down his ability to communicate.

At just twenty-two, Keith had left Australia and the security of his father's manse in suburban Melbourne for the first time. He had arrived in London hoping to find immediate success in Fleet Street as well as the best expert on speech available. But he found himself in a strange and hostile city, torn between a passion to pursue a career in journalism and the pressure to continue in the line of family preachers. His plan to gain the valuable experience he craved in this centre of the world's press had so far come to nothing.

During one lonely, doubt-racked midsummer evening, Keith stopped to rest on a bench in Hyde Park. He was suddenly gripped by what he described in a letter to his father as a 'religious experience'. But even so he simply could not reconcile himself to devoting his whole life and career to the Church, as his stern clergyman father had always hoped. Journalism was a calling as much as the ministry, and Keith imbued his choice with a missionary zeal: 'Tonight I fancy that my path lies clearly along journalism, where undoubtedly great work can be accomplished.' He assured his father that however his future developed, he would pray 'for strength throughout the years to work for Christ'.

The break was made, the decision set. After all, as he pointed out, with his speech impediment he would not be a suitable preacher. Henceforth, Keith Murdoch and his descendants would find other platforms and a bigger congregation.

He was determined to make his name in the city and wouldn't leave whatever the cost, until he was a good journalist. With Fleet Street as his training ground he was sure he would learn an enormous amount, and, all going well, he 'should become a power in Australia'. As he told his father:

I know that you have never been keen on my profession and would have preferred a more stable walk of life nor do you trust press work for any good end. I assure you I would be happy and relieved to give it up but I see the opportunities and necessities and I shall go ahead to become a power for good. If I consulted my own inclination I would be in a much easier path than journalism but I see enormous possibilities ahead for journalism . . .'

There was a caveat: '[T]hat is of course if I overcome my stammer.' But Keith saw a higher plan even in this. It was surely 'a dispensation of Providence, for to him that overcometh shall be given not a crown – I don't want that – but enlarged opportunities for useful service'.

Keith's letters reveal the bubbling cauldron of his mind – ambition clashing with a sense of inadequacy mixed with a Calvinistic streak of denial and Darwinian principles of self-improvement. He foresaw 'a pretty bad time' over the next eighteen months but faced it 'confidently because I want a struggle'. 'The "survival of the fittest" principle is good because the fittest become very fit indeed. I've sacrificed a nice easy position, comforts, friends and hundreds of pounds by coming here but I hope to get very fit.' His life, he felt, had 'been altogether too easy' so far.

But Keith's childhood in Melbourne had not been easy in some ways. Determined and vocal, Reverend Patrick Murdoch held a series of prominent positions in the Presbyterian Church of Australia, including a time at its head as moderator-general. A 'cleric who valued social connexions', his standing in society was high, but his clergyman's stipend remained low. And so, though Keith grew up playing with the sons of the wealthy and influential, he did so, as he would painfully recall, in patched pants. The importance of capital – or at least access to and friendship with those who had it – was a lesson Keith absorbed early in life. He also felt the weight of family expectation, for he had been named Keith Rupert Murdoch after his father's youngest brother, who had left Scotland to make his career in London and died of tuberculosis, aged twenty, two years before young Keith's birth. Keith was also the eldest son, as his older brother George had died tragically soon after Keith's own birth on 12 August 1885.

School had been an ordeal for a boy who could not read aloud in class, yet Keith had applied himself diligently. He attended various local schools, including the small coaching college set up by his uncle Walter Murdoch, who became a prominent journalist and essayist. There he was drilled in the belief that clear written English is the bedrock to success, and Walter's stint as a parliamentary reporter for the *Argus* helped inspire Keith's interest in journalism as a career. Keith had decided against going to university, fearing the cost and the effect it would have on the upbringing and potential opportunities for his younger brothers (Ivon, Frank, Alan and Alec) and sister Helen, just a year his senior. It was a sacrifice he would come to regret in London, where he felt wholly out of his depth: 'a baby in thought and knowledge'.

In other ways Keith's path had been smoothed for his career as a journalist; before he left he had been given a job at the Melbourne *Age*. The Scots-born proprietor David Syme no doubt accepted him as a favour to the Murdoch family, as he and the Reverend Patrick Murdoch were friends and their wives were on visiting terms.

The going was tough, however. As a lowly suburban reporter Keith had to battle to work up stories and establish contacts. This was made even more difficult because of his stammer, so bad that he often had to resort to drafting notes in order to communicate, even to buy a train ticket. Keith's livelihood depended entirely on the sub-editor's willingness to publish the stories he submitted. He cannily cultivated the 'bearded old terror', marking the start of a pattern he would repeat with increasing utility throughout the first half of his career. After five years of this hard graft, by 1908 he had managed to earn and save more towards his London trip than if he had been a regular staff reporter.

When he set out from Melbourne, Keith had safely stowed in his trunk a light but precious cargo: a sheaf of letters of introduction, including one from his employer praising his 'zeal and industry'. Other letters had been requested from leading figures connected to the Presbyterian Church. But potentially most useful and certainly most impressive, with its embossed Commonwealth of Australia letterhead, was the letter from his father's friend, the Australian Prime Minister Alfred Deakin, introducing 'a well known and much respected young journalist'.

The letters of introduction might have been impressive but the list of contacts Keith had to pursue after his arrival in Britain was hardly at the dynamic edge of Fleet Street. Trusting that God's support was already in the bag, his more mundane hopes of gaining the entrée to experience rested on the church journalist and publisher William Robertson Nicoll. However, Nicoll delivered a rebuff and the 'cold stern slaughter of some hopes', saying he was only prepared to help Keith indirectly. Nevertheless, writing up pieces from the Pan-Anglican Congress for the *Church Family* newspaper gave Keith three days' work. A few freelance pieces in the *British Weekly* and *Daily News* on church politics followed. But Keith was soon worn out with worry that his writing was going nowhere. Still, his resolve and ambition reasserted themselves and he told his father, 'I'm going to become a moving force yet.'

On the other side of the world, Reverend Murdoch could only worry at his son's state of mind. Keith admitted to having had a breakdown, which in London had manifested itself as 'repeated headaches, a constant feeling of weakness, clouded depression over the brain, condition of speechlessness with strangers, fear now and then of doing mad things – in fact, pure nervous depression through over work'. He had tried to do too much too quickly. It was time to put the piecemeal, desperate attempts at press work to one side and instead confront the underlying block to his prospects of success.

In the British autumn of 1908 Keith 'decided to run for health and speech' back to Scotland and the safe, comforting haunts of Rosehearty and Cruden. Travelling between relatives and enjoying golf in Dumfries, he regained his spirit and concentrated on eliminating his stammer. While still in London, he had sought out the best elocutionist and voice expert he could. Madame Behnke claimed that having practised her method for forty years, she had identified the main cause of the problem for those afflicted: blockages in the nasal and respiratory passages. Contributory factors included 'public-school life' and less convincingly 'worms'. After assessing Keith, Madame delivered her expert opinion: he was suffering from 'rheumatism of the throat', a condition not helped by the damp, foggy conditions of the approaching London winter. Strict adherence to the Behnke Method's programme of rigorous muscle exercise was deemed necessary not just for the sufferer, but 'for the sake of his ... possible descendants'. While he laboriously repeated 'rhythmic speaking' Keith planned to purchase the latest travelling typewriter with which he could bash out words as fast and fluently as the keys could strike.

Though this whole British adventure would leave him 'poorer in pocket', Keith took comfort in the hope that by its end he would be 'richer in justified and settled ambitions and ideals, and richer in knowledge and friends'. But so far, with his travel between London and Scotland, boarding with family members, and finding conversation difficult, friends had eluded him. Trusting that his contacts would still secure him openings in London, Keith settled on a new path, enrolling at the newly founded London School of Economics (LSE). Fearing that his father might think that he had not taken on responsible work, Keith explained his aim: he was going 'to study men and politics'.

The search for student digs had been an eye-opening experience. Following a day spent 'hunting in queer holes about the north and west', he suddenly came across the Caledonian Christian Club. Although it was badly run, adjoined a singing school, the bathroom was next door, there were 'fleas in the bed' and a drunkard lived above, Keith declared it 'OK'. Character-affirming self-denial aside, he had a positive reason to overlook its negatives: its address. The lodgings were centrally located in Bloomsbury. The centres of press and political power were now in reach. He could walk to Fleet Street and Westminster.

Keith's Scots-linked press connections in London were still fresh. Aided by his Scots heritage and a passion for golf he scored a lunch with Sir Robert Donald, editor of the *Daily Chronicle* – 'a very "big" man in London ... I was never so anxious in my life'. Donald told him that his 'colonial experience' was useless and that training him up would be pointless in view of his plans to return to Australia. Nevertheless, Keith managed to secure Donald's informal support and a new sheaf of letters of introduction.

The connections were certainly helping Keith's fortunes. He told his father, 'now the balls are rolling I shall endeavour to get an insight into a London newspaper office'. With this LSE course of study set and with the counsel of his visiting uncle and mentor Walter, Keith's spirits were rising: 'I feel more a part of London now and quite confident that a year of study will be very useful in the future.'

Just before Christmas in 1908, Keith sat down in the room he had tried to make 'cosy' with his growing collection of books and some pictures, to reflect on his routine, fears and hopes:

> I'm spending about 1 hour daily reading aloud and exercising. Two hours writing pieces for the *Daily Chronicle* or *Westminster Gazette* (which usually refuse them) and eight or nine hours attending lectures and reading. I'm learning a great deal and feel much amazed and grieved at my ignorance.

With this letter to his father Keith enclosed the LSE syllabus, although he felt 'a trifle uneasy' about whether the Reverend would approve of the radical views of L. T. Hobhouse and the other lecturers. Stressing that Hobhouse was 'a fine Christian and I fancy will be the leader of Liberal thought in the next decade', Keith conceded that 'the influence of the school is rather anti-Christian. It tends to Rationalism – which of course is not a religion and thus is really a negative.'

The coming months were a testing time for Keith's faith, spurred on not just by his readings in the new social liberalism but by his experience of the gross inequity of Edwardian London. He was stunned by its contradictions, by the 'squalor, cold and hunger and deformity' of the east 'too near [the] luxurious culture' of the west. But while 'London disgusts', with 'immorality stalking the streets', it still held 'a subtle fascination' for Keith. After all, 'Here is the hub of the world and the centre of 20th century life!' It was underlying ambition that anchored him fast as he fretted over his future:

> Journalism certainly is precarious. But I'm young and strong and should not fear. My whole desire I think is to be useful in the world, really useful to the highest causes. And surely if I keep that ambition untarnished I should get my chances.

During the thick fogs of the London winter, Keith bunkered down in his lodgings, away from the corrupting streets, to absorb the texts from the LSE reading list. Keith recommended his father should read Hobhouse's *Mind in Evolution* and *Democracy and Reaction*: 'it will convince you of the need for collectivism'. But he also took the time to devour as many of the city's newspapers and reviews as he could. Keith was 'still very hopeful' that he would get 'the sight I want of a London newspaper office': 'I want 6 months good London experience, and I must have it.'

For the moment, however, loneliness was Keith's main experience. Eight months into his trip, he could count just 'one friend in London'. Keith was racked with 'fits of beastly depression'. Deeply unhappy and unfulfilled in the present, he pined for a future where he could finally do 'great work' and receive 'those gifts of God, bright children, faithful friends, and a comfortable home' that he 'so earnestly' desired.

The time scarred him. Years later he inadvertently revealed the pathetic low point he had reached. In an article on international politics and defence, he recalled:

> In the heart of London, Bedford Square, W.C., there stands a quiet home, and in its front room there sit around the table each evening a pleased father, and a satisfied mother, and a bevy of small, laughing children. And the table is pleasantly laden, and the children are pleasantly clothed and the scene is the pleasantest on earth. I know it, because I saw it. I peeped beneath the lowered window-blind, and my loneliness became a great and despairing loneliness.

Four decades later, Keith's son would also rail against his first experience of a British winter, writing home to Australia: 'Oh for the bloody sun! . . . If it weren't for good friends, I'd have shot myself in this bloody place long ago. Rain, wind, sleet, slush, shit, snow, and starch!"

Back in the sapping, damp winter of 1909, Keith was also thinking of the return home. He asked his father once more to network on his behalf and call on Geoffrey Syme at the *Age* (Syme's father David had died). In the meantime, he was starting to feel 'very unsettled' in his beliefs. One night his roaming took him to the Embankment of the Thames. A parading ground for the fashionable in the daytime, after nightfall it took on an entirely different character. Keith witnessed dozens of starving men and women sleeping rough. The sight affected him deeply, stirring him to political thoughts: 'London is a Socialistic influence.' Predicting his father might be shocked by the turn his thoughts had taken, he explained: 'The trouble is to reconcile Socialism with (1) self-help, (2) justice, (3) liberty.'

Inspired by his LSE readings, he resolved to direct himself in the model of Plato's philosopher-kings – 'Marcus Aurelius has it: We ought to check in the series of our thoughts everything that is without a purpose and useless, but most of all the over-curious and the malignant.' Though he was dejected and alone, at least the hours of studying were paying off – 'My mind is certainly broadening and gaining in stature: but what is ahead?'

As winter started to lift, so did Keith's spirits and his enthusiasm for what London could offer culturally. His mother Annie – a shy, gentle woman who combined an 'artistic temperament and love of beautiful things' with ambition for her sons – had come for a visit, and he was happy to show her the sights. Here was Keith's excuse to neglect his studies for dinner parties and trips to the theatre and picture galleries.

Keith's parents gave him an interesting dual inheritance that helps explain the apparent contradictions in his character: a strict Calvinistic work ethic and moral conservatism clashing with a sensual streak and an appreciation of the finer things in life. In later years this tension propelled Keith to accumulate the material markers of success, his devotion to hard work enabling him to fund his increasingly conspicuous consumption.

Later in 1909 Keith crossed the English Channel for a cultural and sensory adventure, taking in Switzerland, Venice and Rouen before finally exploring Paris. The city proved a revelation and Keith felt an instant affinity and ease with its people. The young man so racked with doubts and questioning of his religious faith recognised that 'devotion to art has taken the place of the priesthood of France'. Matisse's startling, huge canvas *Dance I* with its joyfully vivid pink figures springing from a green and blue abstract landscape had recently been exhibited, marking a new dawn in modern art. Keith decried this new 'barbaric modernism' as 'art without moral laws', but nevertheless felt 'much broadened in view'. The passion that was to develop into a lifetime's devotion to fine art and collecting had been stirred.

By widening his horizons, socialising and engaging more with people in the know on the spot in London rather than relying on connections made from afar, Keith was reorientating his view on the press figures he had assumed would be his ticket to Fleet Street opportunity. He wrote bluntly, 'I find Robertson Nicoll is very generally detested in London ... the unanimous opinion that he is a vitriolic, selfish, slave-driving conceited old bear.' In his growing confidence he decided to have nothing to do with the old British establishment either. Witnessing the pomp and pageantry of the official opening of Parliament, the ranks of Royal Horse Guards and the gilt coaches Keith declared it 'all beastly humbug'. To him the king was simply 'a most useful public servant'.

By March of 1909 Keith was feeling optimistic. Spring, which had 'made a wonderful difference to the appearance of London', had finally come. He was following in the path of history-shaping figures as diverse as Marx, Lenin, Kipling and Twain by now studying in the British Museum reading room, his favourite place for work that 'contains the best brains of all generations. So there may be something in telepathy after all (!)'.

Keith was studying with such intensity ('this week – history and scope of journalism') that he was suffering terrible headaches. As well as books on journalism Keith was absorbing G. H. Lewes's 'excellent' *Success in Literature*. The Victorian philosopher and evolutionary psychologist argued that literature was at once the cause and effect of social progress. Its successful application had become not only the ambition of the highest minds but the ambition of minds intensely occupied with other means of influencing their fellows. Statesmen and rulers dissatisfied with the reach of their usual power could discover 'the nobler privilege of exercising a generous sway over the minds and hearts of readers'. For Lewes, simplicity of expression was the key principle. After all, it was 'idle to write in hieroglyphics for the mass when only priests can read the sacred symbols'.

Marking a distinct shift away from the previous introversion and self-absorption of his correspondence, Keith was now holding forth at length on international and political matters of the day such as the Naval Race, testing out his journalistic style in letters to his father and pieces for journals and using these as the impetus for musings on political philosophy. Keith wrote:

> It seems to be impossible to get efficiency with class rule. I have no faith in rampant democracy – in fact I have no faith in government of men by themselves. They seem to be quite incapable of the task. I don't think they are better fit now than they were 1800 years ago – in fact they would welcome a tyrant now who would give them security and not charge them too much for it.

He had formed this view after attending a Naval League meeting where he had witnessed a fascinating phenomenon. Keith had discovered how 'It is as easy to play upon the feelings and emotions of the British public as it is to whip up highly strung horses.'

Increasingly preoccupied with attending political meetings and gatherings, Keith bravely told his father about the loss of his Christian faith, seeing 'no evidence of soul in man'. While he claimed to have 'not settled on any new beliefs – that all is clouded and confused', he nevertheless held tight to one core belief, 'the one undying law – morality'. This he argued was indispensable if men were to live together. 'Without it, the family life, on which rests the State and all civilisations, becomes impossible.' Though he conceded that it was impossible to know what 'the complete evolution of human nature' could be, he foresaw an evolutionary golden age that would 'carry humanity to a higher plane'.

Keith was shocked by the widespread 'blind unmoral surrender to passion' among modern people and by the 'advanced biological thought' that proposed 'that love is a physical product'. Keith's father could trust that his son would continue to follow the teachings of the Church and home, even in the absence of faith. Keith would also continue to 'love morally': 'Perhaps I am not tempted as other men appear to be.' There was a strict utility to sex: 'For that passion must be groomed to produce good fruit. It is man's servant and must not be his master.' He found consolation in thoughts of a lineage to come: 'the only everlasting things I produce are my deeds, and my loves . . . I mean of course . . . my life that I live in my children and in theirs'.

Keith's next letter to his father marked a remarkable shift in tone and topic. He announced, 'I am going to get rid of my stammer: and prepare myself for great work.' He claimed to have already read every single book the British Library held on what he called 'voice moderation'. As a result he now fancied himself as quite an expert, telling his mother he would make short work of his younger brother Ivon's own stammer when he got home. He had joined the Colonial Institute and the Press Club; watched a match between Australia and the MCC at Lords; and 'had a most interesting night' in the viewing gallery of the House of Commons where he was impressed by the Liberal speakers. His spirits had been raised further by Reverend Murdoch's positive report of meeting with Geoffrey Syme. Keith's zeal for and belief in his career was back:

> Syme will evidently give me a good chance. Well, I think *The Age* can be made an even greater power for good than it is, and I think if I have strength and ability I should serve my generation well through it – to commence with.

A month later, in June 1909, representatives of the press from all around the Empire came to London to attend the First Imperial Press Conference. Keith was surprised that so few working journalists were among them and incredulous that the Syme who represented the *Age* was a Melbourne surgeon who had nothing to do with the day-to-day running of the paper. In the same spirit, he railed against the land-boom solicitor Theodore Fink, declaring that he was interested in the *Herald* simply because he 'has a few shares in it'. (Fink, who was actually much more hands-on than Keith thought, was to become a future employer, business partner and ultimately bitter rival.)

The seat of Empire was putting on the pomp to impress delegates with extravagant banquets and whistle-stop sightseeing tours in ranks of shining new motor cars, all topped off with an orchestrated display of naval might in the Solent. Keith was struck by the message of strengthening Empire ties and communication in the face of the growing threats in Europe. But one editorial declared bluntly that the conference had been 'turned into a kind of amateur "war council", largely organised by the directors of the "Daily Mail"'.

Keith managed to attend all the meetings and a number of the 'great social functions', but he bitterly regretted not having invested in a frock coat to further penetrate these elevated circles. The Australian prime minister's letter of introduction had proved invaluable, he found, for it took him anywhere. Keith admitted that he had probably appeared rather pushy, but reminded his father that 'you cannot disapprove for your last words were, "Don't lack cheek"'.

Dizzy with admiration, Keith revelled in detailing his impressions of 'all the great men here'. All the speakers, he noted approvingly, attached enormous importance to the influence of newspapers. But as a lifelong stammerer his greatest revelation came from observing someone who conveyed his importance without having to deliver a speech:

> A prominent figure has been Lord Northcliffe (Harmsworth). He never speaks, but his management can be detected in all the splendid arrangements for this

conference. He is tall, fair with a large head and a very kindly face. He does not give an impression of great strength (though certainly strength is there) but rather of clear sighted, deep general capability. He seems to have a great knowledge, and to be simple and direct in his purposes. That I think is the secret of his success. He knows what he wants and goes straight for it.

As well as this focus, direction and drive, Northcliffe, the founder and proprietor of the *Daily Mail*, also appeared to fit the mould of Calvinistic material denial. 'I expected to find him a bounding, unscrupulous, showy man of the world, but he seems to be simple and kind (he wears steel framed spectacles) and I must say I liked his appearance.' But it was the reach of Northcliffe's growing press empire that impressed Keith most: 'He now owns *The Times* . . . and a great many London and provincial papers and one Paris newspaper.' This man would later become the greatest single influence on Keith Murdoch's life and success.

Two West End plays of the time gave another view of press proprietors and their machinations, one probably not lost on the theatre-loving Keith. Arnold Bennett's *What the Public Wants* was a satirical comedy portraying a 'Napoleon of the Press'. More serious was *The Earth: A Modern Play* by James Bernard Fagan, described as 'a furious attack on the halfpenny daily newspaper, made strongly personal by presenting, as the villain of the piece, the owner of several such newspapers'. For theatre critic and playwright George Bernard Shaw it was the most significant play of early 1909. For G. K. Chesterton, this 'fantastic picture of the Press, put before the footlights for the frivolous' nevertheless 'spoke of some real things that were never mentioned in the whole of the [Imperial] Press Conference'; an example of how it was often only in 'amusing entertainments' that 'the serious truth is told'. The *London Illustrated News* reviewer found the themes explored in *The Earth* – 'the sins of the "Yellow" Press, its moneygrubbing, sensation-mongering, advertisement-seeking policy, its readiness to pander to the worst tastes of its public and to encourage prejudices and vulgarities of the more ignorant classes' – all recognisably persuasive.

For most theatregoers, the inspiration behind the villainous character at the heart of the play was patently clear. The depiction of the circulation-obsessed main character, his predilection for stirring up controversy and exercising dubious justice, as well as his megalomaniacal mission to expand his empire until the circulation of all his papers was the same as the population of the world, closely mirrored the career and ambitions of Northcliffe himself. The script was peppered with bons mots and satirical swipes at the self- importance and claims of press proprietors, with statements such as, 'My circulation is the proof that I represent public opinion.'

Tales of the most powerful figures in press and politics might have been drawing audiences to the theatres, but Keith was now in touching distance of real press power. A special lunch at the House of Commons proved simply 'glorious' as he mixed with the famous and influential. London life was suddenly busy and fulfilling. Previously, Keith had jumped at any opportunity to escape the city and run to Scotland on the invitation of relatives. Now he wrote of declining an invitation to head north again because 'I must remain here to pick up all the crumbs [of experience] I can get'.

He might be short of money still, but he had developed a taste for London life. Keith was making new connections that straddled the worlds of politics, business and international relations rather than relying on Church networks. As he told his father, he was 'having a very good time now in club land!'

The associations were helping raise his profile and self-esteem. Submitting a letter for publication to the *Nation* weekly Keith signed off with a flourish by adding the impressive-sounding address of the 'Grosvenor Club, Piccadilly, W'. Keith found the Grosvenor 'tremendously swell' if 'rather stiff'. It had started life as the Clergy Club, but had changed its name, dropped the religious ties and expanded its membership so that it now declared itself 'almost cosmopolitan in character': This was a shift reflecting Keith's own.

There was now energy for a trip to the Open Golf Championship at Deal and a £10 investment in a frock coat and tall hat. It was not long before Keith was 'getting very fat' as his girth expanded along with his socialising in club land. But he was keen to keep in touch with both sides of the city, heading to the East End's music halls to see 'how the people there spend their nights', gaining that insight into the popular imagination he desired. He found it a mixed blessing.

> I was very favourably impressed with the shows and their onlookers, but the crowds in the filthy parts were horrible. The music hall people love to roar out choruses led by some fat songstresses past their prime, but they spend jolly, pleasant and clean nights. The people would be A1 here if given good wages. With low wages they can't live decently and their self-respect is injured.

For Keith, this was 'the great mistake' in the English system. The rich prided themselves on their superiority, holding up their wealth as the test of worth: 'The common people greatly believe this, and they are as conservative as the wealthy.' He implored his father to read *The Condition of England* by the journalist and Liberal MP Charles Masterman. The book was a blistering attack on what lay beneath the imperial splendour – echoing Keith's own identifications – of a society 'fissured into unnatural plenitude on the one hand and . . . an unnatural privation on the other'.

Masterman's analysis now reads as a prescient account of the decline of Empire and the rise of popular culture and a consumerist mindset. He feared where 'the grasp of money power more and more concentrated in the hands of enormous corporations', together with the 'edifice of credit', would lead. Masterman particularly targeted the 'yellow' or popular press because of its dumbing down of culture and its hypocrisy:

The young men of the suburban society, especially, are being accused of a mere childish absorption in vicarious sport and trivial amusements. It is curious to find this accusation driven home by just that variety of newspapers which has most completely exploited the nascent hunger of the sedentary boyhood of these classes for the excitements of gambling and adventure. The cheap and sensational Press found here a field ripe for its energies. It attained an immense commercial success from the provision of the stuff which this population demanded.

Defined by 'vacuous vulgarity', the yellow press was 'mean, tawdry and debased'. While the world was living through a time of enormous technological advances, a time of 'telegraphs, telephones, electricity, bombs and aeroplanes', moral progress had been left languishing. Religious faith had become 'irrelevant to the business of the day', the whole edifice collapsing 'slowly and in silence'.

Masterman might have viewed the popular press as both symptom and cause of the moral collapse, but Keith retained his faith in the form. For Keith, the press offered a solution to the modern condition: a way to lead the masses as religion lost its grip. As a journalist and – dare he hope – perhaps one day, a press tycoon in the mould of Northcliffe, he could become the 'power for good' he felt driven to be.

Keith was now torn between remaining in London and going home to Melbourne; he was 'burning' with 'a hundred separate strong desires' for his career and it was difficult to know which to follow. The reason for this was that Keith had wasted his chance of getting work with the *Pall Mall Gazette*. As a result of Deakin's letter and his roll call of introductions, he had been interviewed for the job of managing a new branch office. He had passed all the tests with the managers and sub-editors, but when he came to the final one – the few minutes' talk with the editor – his 'speaking collapsed'. As Keith sat in front of the editor mute, 'we both realised that I would not do'. After all his months of effort, the hours of daily exercises and practice, his stammer had let him down.

On 20 November 1909, Keith boarded the Cunard liner RMS *Mauretania*. As it steamed out of Liverpool, he let the failure of the *Pall Mall Gazette* recede in its wake. It was time to regroup and rebuild his ambition. There was resolve in Keith's regret: 'I was a coward in not ignoring my stammer more,' he told his father. He had felt too afraid to 'interview men and visit people', to play on the links, but would be held back no longer. Now the largest, fastest liner afloat was taking him westward to a new adventure: his first experience of America.

2 AMERICAN IMMIGRANT

Away from his disappointment in Fleet Street, crossing the wide horizon of the Atlantic, Keith's thoughts were already energised with the global possibilities for journalism. The lack of a frock coat might have barred him from the choicest gatherings of the Imperial Press Conference, but he had been able to attend all the meetings he wished of the alternative International Press Conference that had recently met in London to discuss 'journalistic subjects and the reading of papers', with delegates from twenty-two countries, including European nations, the USA, Japan and Russia.

The official proceedings had lasted for eight days. Keith heard the UK Postmaster General assure attendees that 'public opinion was the best censor in regard to the question of what should or should not appear in the public press', while adding that journalists, with their rising status, had responsibility to be 'useful leaders' of that public opinion.

Events concluded with a grand dinner for 500 addressed by Sir Edward Grey, the Liberal foreign secretary. Having first toasted 'The Associations of the Press', Grey mapped out the present and increasing power of newspapers in terms that were to have particular relevance for Keith's subsequent career. It was not always easy 'to reconcile and smooth the path of international relations with the expression of the patriotism which rightly belongs to every newspaper', but the press was now 'a great department of public life, and between all journalists and public men there must be something of a fellow feeling'. While public men had to face being well known, the press had to a great extent 'the privilege of anonymity'.

A subtle shift in power relations was evident beneath the bonhomie. The politician conceded that newspapers were 'essential to public men, for without newspapers public men would not be public'; while laughter greeted his quip 'How far public men are essential to newspapers I must leave it to you to answer'. Both had the same object, that of giving information to the public, and the same positive intentions, in encouraging good opinion while correcting 'bad opinion'. Grey concluded with a rousing call: 'The power of the Press is acknowledged on all hands – the growing power, greater and greater every year, spreading its influence wider and wider.'

Keith could take something else away from the conference: *The Evolution of Journalism Etcetera*, a booklet by Henry Wellcome, a maverick pharmaceutical entrepreneur, marketing genius and collector of anthropological and medical curiosities. This illustrated story of communication and its centrality to all human achievement was traced on the broadest canvas possible: from Australian Aboriginal rock art via the clay tablets of the 'Ancient Babylonian News Chronicle' (as Wellcome termed it), to the Gutenberg press and on to the current London periodicals, culminating in the recent launch of the *Daily Sketch*. Wellcome's history was accompanied by a shameless account of the invention of the 'Tabloid' pill, his revolutionary 'compressed drug'. Since it had been trademarked in 1884, the term 'tabloid' had become shorthand for anything in reduced form. But at the turn of the century it began its journey to a whole new meaning.

The US newspaper publisher Joseph Pulitzer had been intrigued by the meteoric rise and success of Alfred Harmsworth, later Lord Northcliffe, and invited the British proprietor to guest edit his prized New York *World* for the first edition of the twentieth century. Northcliffe had seized the opportunity with relish, reducing the size of the page, redesigning the layout to appear more like a weekly magazine cover and presenting the news with such brevity that it could be read 'in sixty seconds'. In an unabashed editorial Northcliffe had declared that through his 'system of condensed or tabloid journalism hundreds of working hours can be saved each year'. It was a new media product, tooled for modern life: one that could be carried in a pocket or read on a streetcar. But Northcliffe's vision did not stop at newspapers. To help the 'busy man' keep up with new books and publications of every kind worth reading, he said these too should be submitted to 'careful condensation'.

Northcliffe had featured heavily in Wellcome's history of the press but the towering figures of American 'yellow journalism', Pulitzer and his younger archrival William Randolph Hearst, had not been mentioned. Not that they needed to be, such was their worldwide fame.

For Pulitzer, now in his sixties, glory days were fast receding. Suffering ill health, he had reluctantly stepped down from the day-to-day running of the *World* but still tried to control his editorial staff from his sickbed aboard his huge private steam yacht *Liberty*.

Hearst had suffered his own setback, one that would end his hopes of political office. He was already thoroughly disliked by President Theodore Roosevelt, who had described him as 'the most potent single influence for evil we have in our life'. Hearst had attempted to gain the Democratic presidential nomination in 1904 with the backing of his newspapers, but failed. Two years later he waged an unprecedented modern media campaign, including moving pictures and use of the new 'talking machine', in support of his run for governor of New York. He lost that contest and – just days before Keith set off from Liverpool – he had experienced his worst ever result: coming third in the New York mayoral election. In defeat Hearst unleashed his vindictive streak. His *Journal* had obtained and printed some confidential letters that embarrassed the victor. One target claimed that a 'Hearst spy' had bribed a maid to hand over the contents of his wastepaper basket.

His political ambitions rebuffed, Hearst never again campaigned directly for public office. From this point on, he would concentrate his energies and genius into wielding influence solely – and perhaps more effectively – through the media under his control. Earlier in 1909 he had founded the American News Service, followed by the International News Service, to syndicate and coordinate his newspapers' content, its wires radiating out across the country from the New York headquarters. He would go on to build the Hearst Corporation, a sprawling empire of interlinked interests that at its height boasted twenty-eight newspapers in seventeen cities. The events in New York that year marked a break with the past and heralded the new age and expanding power of the media corporation.

And so it was that in 1909 the USA, particularly New York, was where the press appeared most vital. Keith Murdoch was about to experience American newspapers for the first time.

Back in 1909, Rupert's father might have crossed the Atlantic on the most luxurious and well-equipped vessel in the world, but the speed of the ship was the only benefit he could appreciate from his third-class bunk. Following an expensive and disappointing year, economies had to be made in the service of self-denial and punishment. Nevertheless, Keith's choice of steerage also opened up opportunities for writing about the immigrant experience. Travel to the USA had been a long-held dream; the now dog-eared letter of introduction from Alfred Deakin, written more than eighteen months before, had stated that Keith wished to visit the United States as well as Europe.

The *Mauretania*'s passengers had been due to disembark on Thursday 25 November: suitably enough, Thanksgiving Day for 1909. But as a violent storm raged around the ship, they were forced to brave another night off-shore. Liberty's welcoming torch remained shrouded in a blizzard. As Keith later told his father, the journey had been turbulent enough. But even with a calm sea and clear skies, the day he disembarked would prove 'the roughest I have spent'.

Being evaluated at the immigration station on Ellis Island was the worst part of the experience. 'We were treated like cattle: big-mouthed filthy officials and heartless bullying doctors bullied us for 5 hours.' Keith acknowledged he could have easily escaped the ordeal, being a bona fide 'non-immigrant alien', recorded as 5 feet 11 inches tall, dark-complexioned, black-haired, brown-eyed – not a polygamist, anarchist, deformed or crippled – with no identifying scars, just a 'baby mole on right cheek'. But he had wanted to 'experience the emotions of a new arrival – without money, without friends, without strength'. And an experience it certainly proved to be.

Keith was stirred to passions he had never known. He told his father that the experience 'made my blood boil and my senses reel ... a great deal of the misery inflicted here is unnecessary and I mean to tell them so'. He and his fellow travellers were eventually 'chucked ashore at New York, starving, weak, and oh! so angry'.

Newspapers offered some compensation. Here were the *New-York Tribune*, the *Sun*, Pulitzer's *World*, Hearst's *Journal*, all fresh off the presses. Keith noted the novelty of their make-up and devoured their content. There was spicy gossip: a sexagenarian millionaire marrying his youthful nurse. There were lurid tales of tragedy: a baby's grave robbed and the body ransomed, a 'Boy Spitted' through the jaw by a runaway truck, 'Impaled at Play in Snow'. And there were outlandish curiosities: 'Telepathy Gives Clue to Snug Harbour Thieves'. But there were other, more staid newspapers to serve as models too. Aptly enough the current edition of the *Wall Street Journal*, which became the jewel in the crown of Keith's son's empire a century later, carried its monthly report on immigrant arrivals.

Keith's first night in the USA proved a rough one. Worried that his hosts would not appreciate a visitor 'direct from the steerage pens', he had stayed at the YMCA. The organisation first suffocated him with details of its 'deadly dull work' before turning loose on him 'an army of fleas'. Nevertheless, though he hadn't slept, Keith set about finding the first edition of the *New York Times*. One of the first Americans he had met on arrival the day before was a *Times* reporter scouring the Ellis Island queues for interesting characters and stories. Keith had happily given a short interview and now looked forward to becoming part of 'All the News That's Fit to Print'. Grabbing a copy, he eagerly scanned its pages before spotting the headline 'Studies Steerage Travellers: Australian Reporter Trying to Determine Best Class of Immigrants'. The story asserted that he was 'making a study for the Melbourne *Age* of what class of immigrant is desirable for Australia and the best way of turning the tide in that direction'. Going 'around the world in steerage' was the 'mission of Keith Murdock [*sic*]'.

As he read on, Keith realised he had been quoted at length by 'the biggest liar of a pressman I have met'. Keith insisted to his father that though he had tried to be civil during the interview he had kept his main impressions to himself, intending to make use of them in his own reports. However, the *New York Times* quoted him as observing that 'the northern countries produce the best class' of immigrants, particularly Scandinavian couples, 'a strong, sturdy lot' possessing 'determination and willingness which go far toward success'.

Regardless of exactly who put forward a preference for Scandinavian stock a century ago, the preference appears to persist at the highest level in America. On 11 January 2018, the *New York Times* reported President Trump's query: 'Why do we want these people from all these shithole countries here? We should have more people from places like Norway. For once, Trump was slow to label this 'FAKE NEWS'.

Thirty-three years before, on 4 September 1985, at the US District Court in Manhattan, Rupert Murdoch pledged his allegiance to the United States. As his then wife Anna and their teenage children Lachlan, James and Elisabeth watched on, Rupert swore to 'renounce and abjure all allegiance and fidelity to any foreign prince, potentate, state or sovereignty, to whom or which I have heretofore been a subject or citizen'. The 185 others who had become American citizens that day alongside him lingered but the Murdochs made a notably swift exit in a limousine. Rupert had pressing business to attend to now that he was free of the Federal rule that limited a foreigner's ability to expand into US television.

Back in 1909, Keith found a comfortable base in the suburb of Orange, New Jersey, and hospitable hosts in family friends who had attended his father's church in Melbourne before emigrating. He threw himself into American life, eager to 'observe much and learn much'. Keith was shocked that boots were not cleaned in the house, instead being 'worn dirty or cleaned in the streets', and added, 'Picture me perched on a high stall chair magnificently pulling at a cigar (5 cents) while a nigger blacks my boots (10 cents) and expectorates. Everybody expectorates – goodness knows why, it does him no good and it doesn't interest his neighbour.'

Though New York was 'a remarkable city', Keith felt it was 'given over to rank materialism, and industrialism and from many aspects is exceedingly ugly'. He was not alone in his views: during Keith's first week in the city even the *New York Times* featured eye-catching reports on 'The Feverish Spending' and 'Fad of Spending Money'. The metropolis's 'Ultra-Fashionables' were embracing the latest 'Extravagant Manias', such as 'decking cats with gems'. However, the newspaper couldn't help but take pride: after all, 'New York is the city of supreme extravagance, of boundless display, of greatest expenditure'.

Faced with this supercharged commerce and rampant capitalism, Keith saw lessons for Australia on what to avoid. Paramount, he stressed, were 'graft and trusts'. The newspapers were full of the latest developments in the Roosevelt administration's 'trust-busting' campaign against the Standard Oil Company of New Jersey – the Rockefeller megacorporation that controlled most of the American oil industry. After years of evidence-gathering and argument, a federal court had found that Standard Oil acted as 'a combination and conspiracy in restraint of trade' and had through 'illegal means . . . secured an unlawful monopoly' in violation of antitrust law. (In 1911 the Supreme Court upheld the decision and the trust was broken up.) In time, Keith's own embrace of a media chain business model would lead to accusations of monopolistic behaviour.

Whether jostling for space in trolley cars, riding the elevated railway lines or joining in step with the commuting throngs on the sidewalks, Keith was struck by one overriding and invigorating observation. Everyone seemed young: 'a man over

40 years old is a rarity'. But for Keith, only just twenty-four, Americans were not only youthful in body, but 'all babyish in ideas' – all except his new enthusiasm, William James.

The brother of the novelist Henry James, William was a pioneering psychologist and philosopher. His interests had grown to encompass the fields of mysticism, religious experience, psychology and the prospect of telepathy as a pure unmediated form of communication – all topics that Keith, given his recent crises and thoughts, found fascinating.

During Keith's visit a remarkable advance was demonstrated in the concert hall above the Madison Square Garden arena. Over a thousand moviemakers, representatives of the press, and society's select jostled for the prime viewing spots. What they saw on the stroke of 9.00 pm on 11 December stunned them. For the first time in America, onto the screen sprang moving film images bursting with natural, lifelike colours. Movie pioneer Charles Urban was demonstrating his patented 'Kinemacolor' projector and films. As one witness commented, 'It seemed like a glimpse of fairyland, with life and color and beauty appearing at the touch of some magic wand.' The witness was stirred by the world-shrinking possibilities of a technology that could bring the experience of any climate or scenery to those 'comfortable at home'.

The day after the Madison Square demonstration, news reached New York that two Frenchmen claimed to have invented a system 'enabling people talking over a telephone to see as well as hear each other'. One commentator, having just witnessed the Kinemacolor display, worked out what this might mean: 'Just imagine a plant similar to that now used by the telephone companies furnishing all the theatres and nickelodeons in a city with talking pictures – and in natural colors!'

Broadcasting would soon become a reality. Experiments with television were already underway and within a couple of decades another son of a Scottish clergyman, John Logie Baird, would make his mark by demonstrating the first colour transmissions.

More immediately successful, however, and more important for Keith's own career were advances in radio broadcasting. In Stockholm, hours before Urban's New York Kinemacolor demonstration, the 1909 Nobel Prize for Physics had been awarded jointly to Guglielmo Marconi and Karl Ferdinand Braun 'in recognition of their contributions to the development of wireless telegraphy' heralding the freeing of mass communication from physical constraints.

Keith spent Christmas in New York but after that it was time to head home to Melbourne, then the seat of the federal government, in time for the 'Parliamentary work' of the coming months. As Australia prepared to go to the polls in April for only its fourth federal election, Keith was told he had secured the position of federal reporter for the *Age*. With assiduous cajoling he had finally changed his luck. And this new sense of confidence would help him control, though never eliminate, his stammer and prosper.

3 FINDING HIS VOICE

Los Angeles, 27 February 2011. In Britain the hacking scandal might have been threatening to break but in America it was time to celebrate. Rupert's third wife, Wendi Murdoch, guided her husband down the red carpet of the 83rd Academy Awards ceremony at which *The King's Speech* was hot favourite to win the Oscar for Best Picture. Stopping for a rare and apparently off-the-cuff interview, Rupert began to explain that his father Keith had been treated by the Australian speech therapist Lionel Logue, the man at the heart of the film. A starry-eyed Wendi launched in excitedly, finishing Rupert's sentence and compressing a life and legacy into an impressively efficient but questionably reductive soundbite: 'Because Lionel helped his father to overcome speech problems, he became confident, and then he founded News Corp.'

Rupert had previously explained to Joe Morgenstern, the Pulitzer Prize-winning film critic of his newly acquired paper, the *Wall Street Journal*, how Logue had treated his father. When Morgenstern wrote up the story he had to hedge on the dates of exactly when the therapist had 'cured' Keith 'in less than a year and set him on his way as a journalist'. Rupert had told Morgenstern that he understood Logue had treated Keith in Australia during 1910. If Keith received treatment around this time, when Logue was giving private voice coaching to Australian politicians and other prominent figures, it would help explain something that has puzzled Keith Murdoch's previous biographers: the shift from the previously 'shy, almost speechless' Keith to the 'confident, brash, forceful, thrusting' man who soon emerged.

When the Ellis Island immigration bullies asked Keith Murdoch to name his country he had hedged with, 'Australia, Great Britain'. But when asked to choose his 'Race or People', he had answered without equivocation: 'Scotch'.

The Murdoch family's Scottish links had provided a support network in Britain. But now, welcomed back to the *Age* by its Scots owners, Keith found this heritage gave him an easy affinity with the movers and shakers of the increasingly powerful Melbourne Scottish diaspora.

During Keith's absence the role of prime minister had toggled between Alfred Deakin and Andrew Fisher – another Presbyterian Scots emigrant who, like Deakin, also handily happened to be a friend of Patrick Murdoch. Deakin led the new Commonwealth Liberal Party but by April 1910 Fisher had regained office for Labor, wielding a healthy majority in both Houses of the fledgling Commonwealth parliament.

The Scots connection not only opened doors but also emboldened Keith to quite literally barge through them. On one occasion, Keith turned up unannounced at the home of a Scots artist, a refuge to which he knew the Australian prime minister retreated to escape his noisy household and busy office in order to nap. Keen to secure a scoop, Keith had pushed his way into the hall, declaring, 'I want to see Mr Fisher.' Fobbed off with protestations that the prime minister wasn't there, Keith retreated – but only as far as the wall outside, on which he sat conspicuously to wait things out. The artist's daughter recalled: 'He wanted some information for the press, so father came in and woke Andrew and he said, "Keith Murdoch's out there." "I don't want to see him," came Fisher's reply. But [father] said, "Oh come on, Keith's a Scot like ourselves," and Andrew said, "Oh, all right."' Keith was learning fast that pushy persistence could pay off, particularly if genes and heritage were shared.

Scots were experiencing enormous success and prominence. In the first few years of the twentieth century, thirty-nine new Scottish societies were established in the state of Victoria alone, leaving the president of Melbourne's St George Society to wonder just 'why it was that societies of Englishmen were afflicted by apathy while Scottish societies were springing up like mushrooms after rain!' The newly prosperous and influential Scots contingent in Melbourne was passionate about their national game of golf, which provided great opportunities for networking as well as socialising.

Golf now had enthusiastic adherents in politics everywhere. A 1904 report in the Melbourne *Argus* related that the British leader Arthur Balfour's 'out of harness' moments 'are spent with almost unwavering fidelity on the golf links'. The Hobart *Mercury* observed that between golf and politics there seemed to be some subtle affinity, which made both flourish together. The sport's growing importance and utility were demonstrated by its most famous US advocate, Standard Oil's billionaire owner John D. Rockefeller who, according to his biographer, 'had two consuming passions in life: God and Golf'. The golf course 'was a highly structured setting, where he could socialise without worrying. He was in a social situation he could completely control.' For Keith Murdoch too, still troubled by the prospect of his stammer reappearing, a structured situation in which he was a confident master proved a godsend.

Golf was in the Murdoch blood. Keith's father Patrick had gained renown as one of the 'golfing parsons' of Melbourne, playing a game whose popularity had exploded in any part of the Empire where Scots congregated. According to the

West Australian, in 1909 golf sticks were 'plentiful as tabby-cats'. The men of the Murdoch family found themselves in the happy position of being old hands at this most useful game.

Keith's own prowess on the course had prompted glowing press reports as early as 1902 when he was still only sixteen. He used his club membership and experiences to write a golf column under the pseudonym of 'Niblick' before kick-starting his career proper as a reporter by striking a deal to teach golf skills to the co-principal of his school in exchange for receiving instruction in Pitman's advanced shorthand.

In the National Library of Australia in an archive file that holds Andrew Fisher's treasured collection of richly embossed royal invitations and black-bordered mourning cards can be found a smaller memento only a few centimetres across. It is titled 'Riversdale Golf Club, Scoring Card', dated 16 March 1912 and signed by the two players – 'A. Fisher' and one 'K. A. Murdoch'. The fact that the prime minister was playing the game for the first time and the novelty of this pairing made news columns across the country. Fisher's biographer contends that taking up golf allowed the new working-class prime minister from rural Queensland 'to hobnob with people of influence in Melbourne'. Perhaps even more pertinently, keeping the scorecard acknowledged the closeness of his relationship with Murdoch and also confirmed to Fisher that he and the Labor Party he represented were socially accepted.

Away from the competition of the links, relaxed socialising could also offer benefits to both guest and host. Keith learnt quickly that stressed politicians appreciated the offer of a space to rest and unwind. Instead of being the person who barged in and demanded information, Keith was soon acting the role of protective host, organising getaways for Fisher and his colleagues to the newly opened guesthouse run by his aunts Grace and Elizabeth. Set high in the refreshing air of the Dandenong Ranges just east of Melbourne, the Misses Murdoch had named their house 'Braco Park' after a Rosehearty farming estate back in the old country. Here amid the lush fern gullies ties were formed, opinions shared and a subtle sense of obligation built. Information flowed convivially in relaxed surroundings. Keith would perfect this pattern of operation, developing the fine art of hosting over the years to come.

Keith's career and rise continued apace. On 23 May 1912, representing the Age for one of his last times, Keith joined his fellow political correspondents as they filed into the Melbourne office of the minister for home affairs. Gathered around the table were the board of judges whose job was to assess the international competition to design a new national capital city at Canberra. Minister O'Malley, on opening the envelope containing the result, was 'surprised to find that an American had been successful'. (It would be years before Walter Burley Griffin's plan for 'my ideal of the city of the future', as he described it to the New York Times, would be carried out, and then only partially.) A camera captured the scene, to be titled for posterity as 'The Birth of A Continent's Capitol [*sic*]'. In the photograph Keith stands confident, completely secure in his stature. His appearance speaks for him. Dapperly dressed, thick-haired and clean-shaven, his youth and winning air of success are marked, given that the bewhiskered old gents who sit beneath him are like relics from a fading era.

Around this time the tobacco manufacturer and bold businessman Hugh Denison offered Keith £9 a week to leave the *Age* and join his new Sydney daily the *Sun*.

Compared to the modern newspapers Keith had devoured in London and New York, the *Age* had remained defiantly old-fashioned. Readers were forced to wade through pages of classified advertisements and announcements before reaching the news and leaders, which were staidly presented, with photographs a rarity. Denison's *Sun* was far more vibrant and dynamic. Its masthead showed a horse-drawn chariot leaping from a sunburst above the legend 'Above All for Australia'. The *Sun* claimed to be the only daily paper in Australasia that provided world news, thanks to its independent cable service. A typical front page of 1912 led with a sensational report in arresting block capitals – 'CRIME CARNIVAL ... A DEGENERATE ENCOUNTER – VICTIM MUFFLED AND ROBBED' – spiced with some gossipy titbits – a famous jockey with a wandering eye – all framed by eye-catchingly illustrated advertisements for the latest 'fashionable fancies' in hats and shoes. The classifieds were very firmly confined to the inside pages.

If he joined the *Sun* as political correspondent Keith would not even have to move from Melbourne, as the city remained the seat of the federal government until Canberra was ready.

While the 1910 federal election had been a landslide win for Labor, that of May 1913 proved nail-bitingly close. Keith did his best to put a good spin on his friend Andrew Fisher's prospects but it was to no avail. Fisher and his Labor Party lost to the Commonwealth Liberal Party by a single seat and Joseph Cook became the sixth prime minister of Australia. As Labor retained control of the Senate, Cook's ability to govern was severely compromised. For Keith, however, activity in work, socialising and the fusion of the two was unbridled.

Prime Minister Joseph Cook soon experienced the savage nature of party politics. In mid-1914, hoping to be re-elected with a workable majority, he engineered a double dissolution of parliament. The election was set for 5 September but events overtook his plans: on 4 August the British Empire declared war on Germany.

Marshalling the opposition in the run-up to the poll, Andrew Fisher reminded voters that Labor had long promised an Australian defence force. Labor seized the public mood with a populist campaign, orchestrated by Billy Hughes – an ambitious Welsh firebrand who had partaken of Keith's hospitality in the Dandenongs – to support the mother country 'to the last man and the last shilling'. (Keith was fully in line with Hughes's belligerent 'race evangelism'. To mark the ceremonial arrival of Australia's new Navy to its shores the previous year, Keith had written of how the booming guns marked only 'the beginning of security' against 'the ever-present sense of racial hatred and racial danger.' For Keith, Australia's task was nothing less than to become 'the guardian of white civilisation in the Pacific', for which the Empire should be grateful.)

Labor won the election but Fisher, prime minister for the third time, now had to start planning exactly how he would deliver the expeditionary force of 20,000 men he had promised towards the Empire's war effort.

From the tone and content of Keith's journalism it was clear that he had managed to position himself at the heart of the new government, with easy access to those in power. But it was not only Cook's plans that had been upset by the outbreak of war.

A few weeks before war broke out Keith received a secret offer from Labor Papers Ltd. The company, sponsored by the Australian Workers' Union, had been trying for nearly a decade to establish a daily newspaper in each of the capital cities that would be union owned and controlled. It wanted Keith to join its projected Sydney *World* as news editor on a salary of £800 per annum, a sum quadruple what he had received on his return to Australia in 1910.

However, only a few days after Keith received his letter of appointment, the country found itself at war and the scheme unravelled. (Years later, Keith would confide to his wife that he had been 'very young' and, if the plan had gone ahead, 'might have made a sorry mess of my life'.) One hope may have been dashed, but another, far more exciting opportunity soon presented itself.

In Wellcome's *Evolution of Journalism* lavish advertorials had extolled the virtues of first-aid kits, specially designed for 'Journalists, War Correspondents, Automobilists, Aeronauts ... etc', as well as a special leather case of 'War Correspondent's Equipment', which Wellcome stressed had been tested under 'trying circumstances'. For Keith in 1914 this was an item that he could only desperately hope he would need. The role of war correspondent was suffused with glamour and importance, widely considered the crown of journalistic ambition and the heart of its adventure and romance.

Following the outbreak of war in August 1914, the British government invited Australia to appoint an official war correspondent to accompany the troops it was soon to send north. Keith had put himself up for the coveted role but lost out to the Oxford-educated Dr Charles E. W. Bean, a leader writer for the *Sydney Morning Herald*. Frustrated and disappointed, Keith could still rely on support from his politician friends. He might be stuck in Australia for the moment, but he would soon put his own brand of war service into action.

In early 1915 Keith was offered the plum position of managing editor of the United Cable Service (UCS) in London, the newsfeed run by the Sydney *Sun* and Melbourne *Herald* for much of Australia's press. This was Keith's great chance. He was keenly aware of the power in the position. Six years previously, back in London at the Imperial Press Conference, he had witnessed the fierce debate over the importance of international cable news services and the monopoly exerted by some companies. He would have agreed with the *Nation* newspaper that 'the cablegram, with its terse, bare, dogmatic statements imposed simultaneously upon millions of minds has become the central source of power in the modern newspaper'. This was a power that Keith now had within his grasp, as he told Fisher.

Keith moved to Sydney to learn the ropes of the cable business, while continuing as a political correspondent for the *Sun*. In the corridors of power he had already become known as the unofficial publicity agent for the defence minister. One insider later recalled how much Keith had 'boosted George Pearce ... no doubt getting much in return'.

Keith cranked up a production line of puff pieces and glowing profiles of the Australian minister for defence, George Pearce and his 'War Machine'. He also contributed publicity strategies for the department of defence, aiding its drive to secure the recruits Australia had promised to contribute to the Imperial Force. In an unofficial letter Pearce thanked Keith for rallying the public to the cause while stressing not all members of the press had been so helpful in encouraging enlistment. The editorials in the *Sun*, to which Keith probably contributed, were unequivocal in their support for conscription, both back in the mother country and in Australia if the call came. The blurring of the line between reporter and government operative had begun.

In his unpublished biography, Charles Sayers asserts that Keith was already in the habit of carrying out a little 'gentle espionage' for Fisher. It is in this light, perhaps, that Keith's letter seeking the prime minister's informal blessing for his new job is best viewed. He wrote it just before his departure for London: 'Of course I feel that I can do excellent service in London and that it is my own special job but I cannot overlook the fact that all the cabling and writing in the world is not going to win this war.' He reassured his friend that he was open to the idea of serving in the military: 'I could joyfully perform any task you set me in the service of my country.'

Fisher had always thought Keith would make 'an indifferent soldier' and his reply was pithy and clear: 'Advise London.' (In fact, Keith's speech impediment might have prevented him from signing up to fight if he had actually tried.)

Early in April 1915 an article asserted that 'a stimulus should be given to recruiting' by the new 'patriotic drama *Will They Never Come?*' The *Sun*'s readers were informed of the film's upcoming premiere and presented with a stirring advertisement for it. Knowing the powerful influence of films and their potential attraction, Pearce had officially sanctioned the production. (Films were indeed the coming attraction. Just a couple of months before in America, the scramble to invest had resulted in the birth of a new company: The Fox Film Corporation.)

Three weeks later those recruits who had signed up early were landing in the dead of night on the Gallipoli peninsula, in what is now Turkey, with Charles Bean alongside them. The Australian public would be kept in the dark about the landing and the plan to gain control of the Dardanelles Strait for another two weeks. Only on 8 May were Australian newspapers able to present the first glowing account of their soldiers' action, written by the English war correspondent Ellis Ashmead-Bartlett, whose vivid report trumped Bean's more considered despatch. Ashmead-Bartlett's account of the landing, full of evocative detail, was all the more remarkable given the fact he was over a mile away offshore, in the black of night, when he 'witnessed' the action. Indeed it was England's war correspondent, not Australia's, who was responsible for planting the seed of the Anzac myth.

As Keith prepared to leave for London in early July 1915, the finishing edit was being applied to a sequel to *Will They Never Come?* Billed as 'The Official Recruiting Film', *A Hero of the Dardanelles* told 'The Story of the man that *did* come', and it proved sensationally popular. Again, Pearce had supported the production, with the department of defence providing hundreds of soldiers for the re-enactment of the landing and charge up the barren cliffs of Gallipoli, all filmed at Sydney's Tamarama beach with its clearly visible steps. The *Sun's* pre-release tie-in article said the scenes had been 'recorded by the camera with a realism that is stirring and inspiring . . . exactly as reported by Ashmead-Bartlett'. The same edition reported 'exclusively' that Pearce was 'exceedingly pleased' with the way recruiting had progressed. The day after its premiere the *Sun* trumpeted the results of a 'Great Recruiting Week' – the intake including 'three actors' – with the highest figures since records began the previous September. The lavish advertisement for the film carried by the *Sun* emphasised Pearce's promise to its producers: 'I'll give you all the soldiers you want.' It was a promise set to bring pain to thousands of Australian homes.

4 'MURDER, HISTORY, WAR'

Sydney, 7 August 1981. Flashguns strobed as Rupert Murdoch led his mother up the red and purple carpet for the black-tie premiere of his first feature film as producer: the First World War drama *Gallipoli*. Although Rupert's father did not feature in the film, the front page of Murdoch's national newspaper the following morning showed Keith staring out, serious but dashing in officer's uniform as a war correspondent, above the beaming smiles of the film's star: a young Mel Gibson. The legend next to the photograph of Keith pointed to his censor-dodging letter about the doomed Gallipoli campaign. The letter 'that stunned Australia' was reprinted in its 8,000-word entirety in that day's magazine section.

This was the first, and – as it transpired – the only production from Associated R & R Films. Rupert had been sure of success from the first moment he read the script: 'It's going to be great. It's murder, history, war ... We can't lose.'

The film's plot delivered a three-act tragedy. In outback Australia two young athletes answer the recruitment call drilled into them by the press. Training in Egypt, they bond over anti-English japes and the sowing of their wild oats. Finally at the hellish warzone, they are sacrificed by incompetent colonial commanders in a diversionary action while the British are 'just sitting on the beach drinking cups of tea'.

One otherwise glowing review from outside the Murdoch stable conceded that those 'who resent emotional manipulation will be affronted by this film'. The charge of propaganda was not only levelled at the film; it has been levelled against Keith's famous 'Gallipoli letter' of a generation before. It is the letter that made his career, and has been woven into an untouchable myth. It's a myth that Rupert and his sons have deployed to deflect criticism of the sharper edges of their own careers – a myth that has overshadowed Keith's darker legacy.

In 2007, facing a critical backlash on journalistic standards when mounting his takeover for the *Wall Street Journal*, Rupert wrote a personal letter to its owners, the Bancroft family, in an attempt to persuade them to accept the deal. He emphasised that 'the credit for building' their respective media giants 'goes to the members of the family . . . My father, Sir Keith Murdoch, was himself a celebrated journalist, best known for uncovering the British debacle at Gallipoli in 1915'. On the centenary of the campaign in 2015 Rupert would stress again how 'Gallipoli has been important to our family . . . I have always felt this and I know my own sons feel it.'

Back in 1915, colonial lines of communication and control, centred in London, meant that even Australia's prime minister and its minister for defence had been kept in the dark about the movements of Australia's forces; they were not informed of the plan to land at Gallipoli until after the event. However, as the weeks went by they feared the worst. The blunt facts of high casualty rates for little or no apparent gain flew in the face of the upbeat official and heavily censored press reports. Fisher and Pearce wanted an inside account of the campaign's management and a realistic assessment of its prospects. Keith saw his chance to oblige and suggested that he could do so under the guise of investigating mail arrangements and provisions for the wounded in Egypt.

Pearce agreed. Following the announcement of the unusual commission he told questioning senators that despite the rumours Murdoch had not accepted a role in London 'with the Defence Department'. He was undertaking his inquiries in Egypt while remaining a civilian. After all, a reporter was 'just about the best man' who could be assigned such a task. Senators joshed in response: 'Sometimes they ferret out things you do not want them to know' and 'frequently they ferret out things which never happened at all!' Pearce good-humouredly agreed before observing that reporters also 'sometimes exercise a very lively imagination'.

The letters of introduction Keith took with him this time were not scratchy and perfunctory, favours pulled in from family connections. Rather they were acknowledgements of his now firmly established position and indicators of the possibilities their authors saw for his ability to act for them. Most crucially Pearce gave Keith a letter that introduced him to Sir Ian Hamilton, the British commander of the Dardanelles campaign. Fisher also wrote to David Lloyd George, the ambitious, recently appointed minister for munitions, stressing that Keith was now the representative of 'a very influential cable service for several important newspapers in Australia'. Lloyd George was vocal in his support for a greater push to war organisation in Britain. Although he had originally supported the strategy of opening up a Second Front against the Ottoman Empire – championed by Winston Churchill as First Lord of the Admiralty – he was now one of the coterie already plotting its abandonment.

Arriving in Cairo in mid-August, Keith investigated the mail arrangements and hospital conditions for the Australian wounded recuperating there. A copy of the *Sunday Sun*, which contained the launch publicity for *A Hero of the Dardanelles*, was put to good use as the centrepiece of an inspiring photograph of the men on their ward, sent back to Sydney on the next ship south. However, Keith soon wrote to Hamilton, enclosing Pearce's letter and requesting permission to visit the Anzac force on the Gallipoli peninsula. He stressed he would be going across 'in only a semi-official capacity, so that [he] may record censored impressions in the London and Australian newspapers' he represented.

Keith also emphasised (in a line that would become infamous given his subsequent actions) that 'any conditions you impose I should of course, faithfully observe'. To this he added a few more obsequious lines of praise and the passionate plea: 'May I say that my anxiety as an Australian to visit the sacred shores of Gallipoli while our army is there is intense.' General Hamilton hesitated to let him go but was persuaded by his insistence that he would accept military censorship. In his diary a month after their meeting, when the first rumblings of Murdoch's actions reached him, Hamilton wrote: 'All I remember of his visit to me here is a sensible, well-spoken man with dark eyes, who said his mind was a blank about soldiers and soldiering'; he had entered into 'an elaborate explanation of why his duty to Australia could be better done with a pen than a rifle'.

Keith landed at Gallipoli on 3 September 1915. Morale was desperately low following the disastrous August offensive that included the battle of the Nek. Keith spent the next three and a half days walking 'many miles through the trenches', speaking with soldiers and whatever senior and junior officers he could find. Hamilton would later snipe that Keith had spent one week at the press correspondents' camp on the Island of Imbros and only a few days at Anzac Cove and Suvla.

Whatever were the actual days or hours spent with the soldiers, it was Keith's meeting with Ashmead-Bartlett at the press camp on Imbros that most informed the terms of his subsequent actions. The British correspondent was a flamboyant and volatile personality. He had initially supported the British strategy but had recently been hauled over the coals by the War Office for spreading disillusion and boasting of his machinations to remove Hamilton from command. (Ashmead-Bartlett, as a perennial bankrupt always in need of a moneymaking opportunity, had a £5 bet riding on this happening before the end of September.) In the version of events agreed by the pair, Ashmead-Bartlett said that Keith, feeling his own word would not 'carry sufficient weight with the authorities', had begged him to write a letter 'telling the plain truth' about the campaign. ('I have coached him on all essential points, but he says he wants something definite under my own signature.') Keith would then carry the letter secretly back to London, so evading the censorship restrictions. Ashmead-Bartlett went straight to the top, addressing his letter to the British Prime Minister Herbert Asquith. It detailed the 'true state of affairs out here', the incompetence of the command, the collapse in the morale of the troops and the dire prospect of the winter conditions to come.

Following Keith's departure, Hamilton, having got wind of the plot, managed to cable ahead so that at Marseilles the sealed envelope was seized from him by military police. Even though Ashmead-Bartlett's letter did not make it to Downing Street, Keith had absorbed the pessimistic outlook and bitter criticisms of this 'most ghastly and costly fiasco': of the appalling waste of life, of 'muddles and mismanagement', 'the absolute lack of confidence in all ranks in the Headquarters staff', and how the 'splendid Colonial Corps' had been 'almost wiped out'.

Combining Ashmead-Bartlett's views with his own brief observations, Keith began composing his own letter, to his own prime minister.

Having arrived in London from Gallipoli with information about what was happening there, Keith was in demand. With barely a chance to settle in at the United Cable Service office housed in the *Times* building, he was whisked off for lunch with the newspaper's powerful editor Geoffrey Dawson. It was later claimed that Northcliffe, hearing that an Australian journalist was on his way to London from the Dardanelles, said, 'He may prove to be the lever we want.' In line with the anti-Second Front strategy views of its proprietor, *The Times* sought to expose the true course of the campaign and refocus energies on fighting the Western Front. Dawson was 'moved by the sincerity and vividness' of the 'word pictures' Keith painted of organisational debacles and dire conditions. In a flurry of letters and meetings, the cogs started to bite. Keith retold his story to Sir Edward Carson, chairman of the British Cabinet's Dardanelles committee.

Recording the details of a secret meeting that took place on the following day, Baron Murray of Elibank tried to disguise the names of those who had been there. The report's recipient, 'Mr H', it has been speculated, was the Conservative Leader and Secretary of State for the Colonies in Asquith's coalition government, Andrew Bonar Law:

Today, Lord —, Mr A, and Mr B, lunched with me. Mr B is an Australian of high standing and influence who has been despatched by the Australian Government to report to them on the condition of affairs in the Dardanelles. . . . Mr B who is rather inarticulate owing to a stammer in his speech, apparently did not convey to Sir — the gravity of the situation, and therefore Lord — was very anxious that Mr A, whom he regards as a man of action, should hear the full story. Mr B is making a confidential report to his government, but we persuaded him to see Lord Kitchener and likewise to give a copy of his report in advance to the Prime Minister and Mr A in order that it might be communicated to the Cabinet.

Substituting *The Times*'s proprietor Lord Northcliffe for 'Lord —', the Dardanelles committee chairman Sir Edward Carson for 'Sir —' and the then minister for munitions David Lloyd George for 'Mr A' offers the most likely reading. Lloyd George was certainly keen to bring Bonar Law on board, writing to him the following day. Keith later said that the 'most pregnant interviews' he had at this time 'were with Mr Lloyd George and Mr Bonar Law'. So, as he dictated his letter to Fisher, Keith was able to incorporate the reactions and confidential views of ambitious Cabinet ministers.

Keith was embarking on a fine balancing act. He wanted to account for a complete military failure while upholding the reputation of the Australian troops in their first engagement as a force, apportioning the blame solely to the British commanders. By extolling the virtues of the Australian soldiers in a letter that, though nominally to the Australian prime minister, would be read by the most influential and powerful figures in the British government, he sought to promote the standing of his countrymen (and by association, his own standing).

He began his letter with the words: 'I shall talk as if you were by my side' and over the twenty- five typed pages that followed, his language became increasingly emotional. Complicated issues were dramatically over-simplified by the 'very lively imagination' Pearce had feared. 'Australians now loathe and detest any Englishman wearing red,' he wrote; the 'countless high officers and conceited young cubs' were 'plainly only playing at War'; and sedition was 'talked round every tin of bully beef on the peninsula'. Although Keith disclaimed any military knowledge, General Hamilton was described as having completely failed as a strategist. The prescription, devised by Ashmead-Bartlett, was straightforward: 'undoubtedly the essential and first step to restore the morale of the shaken forces' was to recall the general and his chief of staff. Keith recommended that Hamilton be replaced with a 'young leader . . . around whom the officers can rally'.

However, Keith did not suggest abandoning the campaign and evacuating the peninsula. Since the Australian divisions would 'strongly resent' the confession of failure that a withdrawal would entail, he hoped the Cabinet would decide to hang on through the winter for another offensive, or for peace. 'The new offensive must be made with a huge army of new troops. Can we get them?'

Keith's overriding priority, he insisted, was the protection of the Australian forces both in strength and reputation. He assured the prime minister that although they were 'dispirited', having 'been through such warfare as no army has seen in any part of the world', they were 'game to the end'.

Keith was placing the Australians on the highest of pedestals. Bean would later observe that during the war 'Murdoch's admiration of the Australian soldiery rose almost to worship'.

To convey immediacy and paint the scene for his readers back home Keith dwelt on the men's bodies in evocative articles about his time at Gallipoli, experimenting with writing in the first person present tense. Praise was wrapped in self-deprecatory rhetoric. Though he did not 'wish to idealise the Australian soldier', the contrast 'between him and other fighters' was so great 'that the tendency everywhere in the Eastern Mediterranean' was 'to worship him as a super-type'.

By contrast, in Keith's letter to Fisher the lowly Tommies were 'toy soldiers' showing 'an atrophy of mind and body that is appalling . . . childlike youths without strength to endure or brains to improve their conditions'. Their cowardice, anathema to the Australian troops it would seem, had led to an order 'to shoot without mercy any soldiers who lagged behind or loitered in advance'. (This was a claim that Keith would regret the following year when pressed to substantiate it before the Commission held to probe the Dardanelles campaign.) The Australian stock was eulogised as 'all of good parentage':

> But I could pour into your ears so much truth about the grandeur of our Australian army, and the wonderful affection of these fine young soldiers for each other and their homeland, that your Australianism would become a more powerful sentiment than before. It is stirring to see them, magnificent manhood, swinging their fine limbs as they walk about Anzac. They have the noble faces of men who have endured. Oh, if you could picture Anzac as I have seen it, you would find that to be an Australian is the greatest privilege the world has to offer.

To protect reputations and morale Keith advised Fisher to take up the case of Sir John Maxwell, the English commander overseeing Australian recruits in Egypt. Keith had been incensed at Maxwell's reaction to the Australians who had been rioting in the Whasa brothel district of Cairo: Maxwell had described their actions as 'wilful murder'. Keith insisted that 'only a very few of our men' had 'burnt some houses in which they had been drugged and diseased', and he accused Maxwell of attacking the good name of our 'clean and vigorous army'. The men's reputation was 'too sacred to leave in the hands of' those who would undermine it with unpalatable truths.

Keith's actions were naïve – he had been shocked by his first experience of the reality of warfare – but also cynical. The letter was a tool of persuasion.

Keith would state in 1920: 'I have a perfectly clear conscience as to what I did. I went to London and I hit Sir Ian Hamilton as hard as I could. I thought the vital thing was to get a fresh mind on the spot.'

Two days after sending his letter to Fisher, Keith sent a copy to British Prime Minister Herbert Asquith at the suggestion of Lloyd George. Asquith could see the close relationship between the newly arrived cable manager and the Australian prime minister. Keith clearly had a position of trust at the heart of the Australian government, and he could be candid in discussing issues about which others might have been more reticent. As the former war correspondent and military historian Sir Max Hastings said, 'Boy, Keith Murdoch understood how to promote Keith Murdoch.'

Asquith circulated copies of the letter to the War Cabinet, using the duck-egg-blue foolscap writing paper of the Committee of Imperial Defence, 'the stamp of the ministerial Holy of Holies'. Keith's letter was being read by those at the highest level in the world of the press as well as politics. (A handwritten note at the top of one remaining copy reads: 'Please return to Lord Northcliffe, *The Times*'.)

Within a week the British prime minister was backing away from the letter that he described as being 'largely composed of gossip and second-hand statements'. Winston Churchill believed that Hamilton should not be troubled with 'defending himself from the malicious charges of an irresponsible newspaper man'. Churchill had forwarded Asquith a note from the editor of the *Daily Chronicle* who had met with Keith and 'was not much impressed':

> When I questioned him on details of his report he gave me rather evasive replies. It is quite obvious that he had not seen the things which he described, nor has any personal knowledge of the men he condemned. His information was largely second-hand. I do not say that much of it is not correct, or that some of his criticisms are not justified, but my personal feeling about him is that his statements must be accepted with caution.

Writing a few days later to Lord Murray with a copy of his report to Fisher, Keith was almost apologetic – not for dissembling but for putting his case with 'perhaps excessive frankness'. However, he had 'lived long enough in the world to know that reforms are secured only after heavy jottings'.

In contrast to his first sojourn in London, Keith had wasted no time in making his mark. He joined with the Australian business and political elite in the city: in Bean's view he would come to be 'much the most influential figure' among them. It would be half a century before the contents of Keith's letter were read by the public at large, but through its select circulation he was becoming a central player in the upper echelons of the British Empire. The Canadian prime minister cabled Sir Maxwell Aitken, the powerful press and political operative soon to be ennobled as Lord Beaverbrook, to obtain a copy of it.

Keith's goal now was to influence political and military strategy more generally. Following Ashmead-Bartlett's dismissal from Gallipoli by Hamilton, Keith wrote suggesting that they meet up as soon as he arrived in London. A subsequent edition of the *Sunday Times* had a damning account of the Gallipoli situation by Ashmead-Bartlett; presented as an interview, it sidestepped the censor. Northcliffe asked to reproduce it in *The Times* and *Daily Mail* while Keith cabled the account to his Australian newspapers.

Keith claimed that the English correspondent's despatches had been 'more valuable to Australia than probably any other writings of any other man since Australia was discovered'. Ashmead-Bartlett's actions following his return to London had 'dragged out into the open, past the censorship, facts about the bungling at the Dardanelles expedition'. Keith gave a heavy hint of his own involvement in this tale, alluding to as yet unpublished circumstances, as well as 'an important letter'.

Though the cogs were already in motion, Keith believed his letter had sealed Hamilton's fate. On 16 October the general received a telegram from Lord Kitchener recalling him from Gallipoli. Once on the ground, his replacement Sir Charles Monro confirmed the appalling conditions and dire prospects for success, and recommended the full of evacuation of the peninsula.

The heat of intrigue over the Dardanelles debacles would forge a lasting relationship between Keith, Bonar Law and Lloyd George, and an even closer, life-changing bond with another figure: the supreme moulder and destroyer of reputations Lord Northcliffe.

Keith had initially expressed concern about how widely the owner of *The Times* was circulating his letter. The letter 'was of so intimate a character' that its circulation would expose a friendship with Fisher that he held 'sacred'. Nonetheless, Keith placed himself in Northcliffe's hands, and the young cable manager was soon signing his notes 'Yours very truly'. Northcliffe in turn started addressing notes to 'My Dear Murdoch', displaying a paternal interest in Keith's professional advancement and his personal wellbeing. He advised him to join the Automobile Club – most useful for interacting with Cabinet ministers – provided him with stopgap funds, and invited him to Sutton Place, his palatial Tudor home. (The mansion found later infamy as home to the reclusive oil baron John Paul Getty III and is now owned by a Russian billionaire friend of President Putin.)

Being based in the same building as 'the greatest newspaper in the world' gave Keith workaday proximity to Northcliffe. Keith had failed utterly in 1909; now he was secure at the very heart of Fleet Street and crucially, he was his own boss. Keith told his Australian readers that he had been 'privileged these days to get far behind the scenes – to meet and talk frankly with the men in London whose decisions mean life and death to thousands', and Cabinet ministers were asking him 'anxiously what Australia would think of this or that projected move'.

In one of his first newspaper despatches back to the 'saddened Australian homes' who were only now learning of the crushing toll of the August offensive at Gallipoli, Keith tried to rescue a sense of achievement. His countrymen could take pride in how Charles Bean's 'stirring account' of 'that painful and yet heroic air in which Australians went face forward to certain death' was being given 'great prominence' in not only the main London newspapers but also the provincial ones. He assured his readers that their sons' sacrifice had not been in vain: they had enabled Australia's reputation to be placed 'as high as any national reputation can be'. And he invoked another emotional image, the scene conveying Keith's new standing as well as the high regard in which the Anzacs were held:

> Yesterday I was with a London newspaper proprietor, who is sometimes called Emperor, so powerful is his influence. We discussed a picture of the men of an Australian field battery feeding the guns. Stripped to the waist, straining at their work, with faces like classical statues of ancient gladiators, these magnificent Australians gave an impression of noble young manhood. The Londoner turned away his head. 'I cannot look at it,' he said, 'or I shall weep at the sight of such splendid life.'

On the copy of the photograph Northcliffe gave Keith as a personal memento the 'Emperor' wrote 'Splendid Men'.

The image would soon gain massive public circulation when printed as an illustration in *The Times History and Encyclopaedia of the War*. Writing up the chapter on Gallipoli provided Keith with an early chance to fix the history and mythology of the tale. In a promotional despatch for the volume Keith told his Australian readers that it would be 'devoted to the spirit of Anzac'. Sandwiched between the other chapters of propaganda to be printed, bound and distributed around the world, he held aloft the banner of a new religion: Australianism. For Keith Murdoch 'Anzac was sacred soil; the Australian army was a sacred institution'. Though beset by problems of communication and – he implied – command strategy, the Dardanelles campaign had stiffened the backs of the Australians, leading to a 'renewed determination to see the war through' as its leaders 'moved Londonward . . . to take a greater part in Empire control'. Australia had received a boost, but the commission to write this new history would be used by Keith to help his own cause too.

In his bestselling book *Gallipoli*, Australian journalist and author Les Carlyon suggests that Keith at the time 'might just have been walking around with "pawn" written on his back'. Keith was cannier than that. He might not have been the official war correspondent but he was determined to get to the Western Front, and he could see a way to do it. Keith's keenest ambition, as Bean noted, was '[t]o wield great power', his diplomacy to this end 'heavy and obvious, but masterful and usually successful'. Keith's letter to Pearce, the Australian minister for defence, seems a perfect example:

I have been asked today to write the Anzac number of *The Times* History of the War, and you can bet that I mean to do justice to my country, its leaders, and my countrymen. But I am wandering, the purpose of this letter is to beg you to send me to the front here.

Invoking his actions and the Gallipoli letter Keith suggested that the British government would have no objections to this request, saying that several ministers he had seen 'at their own request' had told him that the ministry 'is under an obligation to me for what I was able to tell them about the Dardanelles'. His request was granted.

In 2011 a contrite Rupert Murdoch told the family of Milly Dowler, the murdered British schoolgirl whose voicemails had been hacked by the *News of the World*, that his newspaper had failed to live up to the standard set by his father: an honourable and respected man, though the British 'never forgave him for what he exposed about Gallipoli'. Four days later, Rupert trotted out the anti-establishment line of victimhood, mirror to the retooled Gallipoli myth, before the committee of MPs. But in 1915, Keith's gamble had paid off. His actions had gained him favour not only with the Australian government, but had also acted as an entrée to the most influential in British politics and, most crucially, the most powerful powers in the press. A pattern of politicians, whether Australian or British, finding themselves under 'obligation' to a Murdoch had been set.

Keith might have claimed that tales 'of hardship' from Gallipoli 'act more as a magnet than as a repeller', but the realisation of how pointless the campaign had been, and how terrible its conditions, would set many Australians against sending their men into further, potentially forlorn actions on the Western Front. The story of how Keith would nevertheless seek to persuade his fellow countrymen to the cause over the remaining years of the war has been almost entirely ignored. It simply doesn't fit with the mythology. And so, for a century and more Keith's role in pushing for conscription and beating the drum for the Western Front action has been hidden.

A typical example of this selective presentation of history came in 2010 with the publication of a book reproducing the full text of the Gallipoli letter in transcript form as well as facsimile. A long, glowing introduction detailed Keith's early life and career but stopped abruptly with the successful evacuation of the peninsula. As we shall see however, Keith's efforts to drive and shape Australia's deeper involvement in the war was already well underway by the autumn of 1915.

When Keith arrived at the correspondents' camp on Imbros in early September, Ashmead-Bartlett had just returned from filming a staged charge from the trenches on the peninsula itself. The conspiratorial chat between Keith and the English correspondent that led them to write their respective letters almost failed to take place. Ashmead-Bartlett's plan to film more action that day had been stymied as the weather was so bad. His revolutionary handheld 'Aeroscope' cinematograph, supplied by his commercial agent with a promise of significant profits to come, sat idle in a corner of the tent. Alongside the dramatic footage of artillery bursts that he already had, Ashmead-Bartlett was most excited by the sensational appeal that images of the 'magnificent' soldiers bathing would create. Keith, too, realised the stirring power of the bathing imagery, invoking in his reports comparisons with antiquity and classic epics under the headline 'Men love the beaches'.

Keith was just one among many at this time who saw the war as a regenerative process for the Anglo-Saxon race. Bean would describe Keith's admiration for the Australian soldiers as 'almost idolatrous'. Keith's fascination with development towards physical perfection, at times verging on the homoerotic, would last for the rest of his life, a passion finding outlet in his shearing sheds, at sportsgrounds and in the pages of his newspapers.

Soon after Keith departed from Gallipoli, Ashmead-Bartlett replied to a theatrical promoter back in England that he would now only lecture in big centres for 'big money'. His head had been turned by the prospect of a more lucrative market for his slides and talks; 'I could make a very great deal in Australia.' Wasting no time after leaving Imbros, in Cairo Keith cabled a Melbourne promoter to line up a deal. On his return to England Ashmead-Bartlett began a series of twenty-five lectures at £100 apiece. The first was a disaster.

Mindful of the Australian tour he was encouraging, Keith put the best spin he could on the muted reception to the first lecture. He expressed disgust that 'never during the two hours in which that brilliant talker told of the splendid heroism and endurance of this ill-fated venture did the audience rise from its own temperate level'. The only time they cheered was 'when on the screen were thrown pictures they had learnt to admire . . . of the Australians preparing for the landing . . . and of the heroes of Anzac in their daily life'. Ashmead-Bartlett's diary reveals that, already ill, he had sought solace in getting drunk before being 'pushed on to the stage, really not knowing exactly what was happening'. (Little wonder perhaps that the projected slides were the only thing in focus that evening.) Still he managed to revive for the celebrations that followed, heading off 'to see the wonderful film' *The Birth of a Nation* at the Scala Theatre. A charity performance had been organised with the proceeds going to a special Dardanelles fund.

W. G. Griffith's epic of the American Civil War, originally titled *The Clansman*, was billed as the cinema event of the year and was destined to remain the highest grossing film in the world for a quarter of a century. As the historian of the Fox Film Corporation noted, it was that film which showed bankers and investors 'the potential of the movie industry'. It also sparked discussion in London on the 'great progress of the art of the cinematograph' with the success of this 'ambitious attempt' in presenting a 'historical drama'. According to *The Times* the pre-war 'anxiety in some quarters about the effect upon public morals and taste wrought by' the new medium, where the 'clergy foresaw the corruption of youth and the hardening of mature wickedness' and 'school teachers had good cause to complain that their pupils' faculty of keeping awake and attending was being impaired', had been blasted away by such an instructive and rousing tale. Another article described how the battle scenes were so 'beautiful' the author could 'believe hundreds of young men have been stirred to enlist by them, longing for the joy and rush of battle, willing to endure all the miseries of trench warfare for the one culminating rapture of a glorious old-fashioned charge'.

Keith railed against the War Office's failure to use this new, cheap form of visual 'amusements' in the Dardanelles as a wasted opportunity. He had criticised the powers that be in his Gallipoli letter for not providing 'cinemas, or entertainments' to raise the spirits of those diggers in the trenches. He expanded the point in his *Times History*, stressing that communication was valued by the men above all.

Keith continued to smooth the way for the international leg of Ashmead-Bartlett's lecture tour. The Australian government raised its fears with Bonar Law in his role as colonial secretary that 'a great deal of harm' could be done to morale if the criticism of the Dardanelles campaign was too severe. When summoned to meet Bonar Law, Ashmead-Bartlett promised he would do his 'best to put the best construction on a bad case'.

Concerns allayed, official approval for the tour was granted. A couple of days later, Keith organised a final meeting, bringing together Ashmead-Bartlett, his agent, the Australian theatrical promoter and the London correspondent of the *New York Times*. America would be a crucial first stop in the itinerary, providing a chance to spread the fame of the Anzacs and to inspire public support for the war in a country that was still neutral.

The day before setting off, Ashmead-Bartlett joined Keith and Northcliffe for a farewell round of golf. The trio finessed the publicity strategy to come. Northcliffe had arranged an introduction to 'the sinister Mr William Randolph Hearst' (as Ashmead-Bartlett would later describe him) in New York. Keith handed over a bundle of tailored letters of introduction for use in Australia. Key figures in politics and the press were told that Ashmead-Bartlett 'should get the best of treatment': 'He and I have stood under fire together.' Whether this fire was the heat of criticism or battle, or perhaps both, was left for the recipient to ponder.

With 1915 drawing to an end, Keith could reflect on his own extraordinarily rapid elevation. He had secured the scoop of an interview with Bonar Law, whose own power, as a committed critic of the Second Front strategy, was in the ascendant following the change in policy and order to evacuate Gallipoli. Even in withdrawal triumph was spun. On the day *The Times* announced the successful evacuation of the peninsula, 'A Special Correspondent' (described as having visited after August, so fitting Keith's timings) detailed how 'The Anzac Corps fought like lions and accomplished a feat of arms in climbing these heights almost without parallel.' They had been close to 'a great success' had they not been handicapped by others failing to secure positions. 'It was a combat of giants in a giant country', which had proved 'the marvellous hardihood, tenacity, and reckless courage' of the Anzacs.

With the imminent visit to London of Billy Hughes as the new Australian prime minister to be planned and press managed, and the building issue of conscription on the horizon, Keith's war service was about to reach another level. He would seize new roles as publicist, unofficial press secretary to the prime minister and propagandist. Far from railing against the futility and the waste of life in the war, he would soon be actively campaigning for more Australians to be compelled to take part in the far deadlier Western Front action. His involvement with those in the ultimate seats of power, and Downing Street in particular, would also take a highly personal and romantic turn.

5 HEARTS AND MINDS . . . AND BODIES

Los Angeles, 19 March 2003. As the prime-time-friendly invasion of Iraq began with a 'shock and awe' blast, a relieved Rupert Murdoch monitored the panel of seven television screens in his office. After all the months of global debate and protest, the American-, British- and Australian-led coalition forces were finally free to follow the path that had been prepared among their publics. For once, Rupert had even allowed his own voice to broadcast his views, telling an Australian news magazine the month before: 'We can't back down now'. He had assured its readers that President George W. Bush was 'acting very morally, very correctly', while Rupert dangled an upside to the pending war: "The greatest thing to come of this for the world economy, if you could put it that way, would be $20 a barrel for oil. That's bigger than any tax cut in any country."

Over the months of inspections and debate, the Murdoch media around the world – from its quality dailies to red-topped tabloids – had spoken with astonishing unanimity in bolstering the claim, later to be discredited, that Saddam Hussein was hiding weapons of mass destruction. Critics and cautious voices had simultaneously been undermined. Fox News's star performer, Bill O'Reilly, had primed his audience with the message: "Everywhere else in the world lies. If you see the foreign coverage, it's just a bunch of propaganda."

The invasion not only meshed with Rupert's worldview but would also aid his business interests. With its breathless coverage from specially embedded reporters in the field, and politically charged commentary back in the studio, Fox News saw a 300 per cent increase in the number of its regular viewers, its ratings leaping ahead of its rival CNN for the first time. Ted Turner, CNN's owner, duly lashed out at Rupert as 'a warmonger': 'he promoted' the war. But despite the criticism that was to come as Iraq unravelled, Rupert, in backing the hawks so vehemently, had bound conservative and neoliberal-minded politicians even closer to his outlets while cementing a patriotic, military-minded base of voters. As we shall see, it was a technique mastered a generation before in another war, by another Murdoch.

On his first visit to Britain, Keith Murdoch had been deeply affected by Charles Masterman's bleak assessment of the condition of society and press standards in a country at peace. Now in 1915, as Keith returned, Masterman had a new and secret role: directing opinion in a country at war. From the central London base of Wellington House, Masterman led the War Propaganda Bureau (WPB). The high-minded aim was to stir the intelligentsia, those thought to be the leading framers of public opinion, to the cause. First directed at neutral countries, the WPB's output had expanded to cover Allied nations and the home front itself.

Masterman was keen that his department should avoid sensationalism and baser appeals to the popular imagination. Typical of the WPB's clandestinely commissioned publications, the novelist John Masefield wrote a pseudo-medieval romance version of the Gallipoli campaign, directed particularly at American readers. As 1915 ended Keith and some fellow journalists attended a dinner given to welcome the visiting Dutch artist Louis Raemaekers, the man Masterman had been advised was the best cartoonist to employ for a more emotive campaign.

Keith was learning the power of visual imagery. As he told Theodore Fink (the Melbourne *Herald* owner and now his co-employer with Hugh Denison), he had personally commissioned a cartoon from Raemaekers to express 'the soldierly spirit of the Australians here. It is, I think, of historic value.' Raemaekers's sketch showed two dashing officers with a pretty English girl between them, arm in arm in Trafalgar Square, adding a further rakish virility to the Anzacs' standing. It made its way to Australia with a more typically ghoulish Raemaekers cartoon. 'Victims of German Gas' showed bedridden soldiers clasping their throats while a nurse wept over them. The startling image dominated the *Herald* front page, and was framed by a lengthy despatch by Keith about 'Why Conscription Is Needed'.

Raemaekers's cartoons were exhibited in fine art galleries, paired with watercolours of Gallipoli scenes and made into a series of cigarette cards. They were also published by the WPB in book form with explanatory descriptions by leading writers intended to shock the neutral American population. But one particular cartoon among the collection was a harbinger of a shift to come: it showed the trussed-up bodies of German soldiers with a text declaring how 'an eminent chemist' had informed the writer that 'six pounds of glycerine can be extracted from the corpse of a fairly well nourished Hun'. As we shall see, Keith Murdoch would play a leading role in spreading the claim that the Germans had developed a 'corpse factory' to render the bodies of their dead – the 'master hoax' of the Great War.

In short, from 1916 to the end of the conflict, Keith would continue to rouse his countrymen in the cause of an increasingly mindless war. Through the tests of conscription referenda and a controversial election, the promotion and protection of Australia's reputation would be bound with his own standing. Keith would go on to act 'far outside the line of his duty as a journalist', as Sayers wrote in the biography Rupert refused to publish.

Keith embraced an aggressive shift in propaganda that broke with Masterman's softer approach, and aligned himself with the new masters of the art of persuasion and influence. Two press barons now rivalling the politicians in the exercise of power set a pattern for Keith's future development and success. One, as is well known, was Lord Northcliffe. The other, also a model of self-made power and a fellow son of the manse from the Dominions, would be Lord Beaverbrook.

On 8 March 1916, in a piece very likely written by Keith himself, *The Times* announced the arrival of the new Australian prime minister to London. The major press campaign mounted by Keith helps explain how a 'small, wizened, colonial Welshman, very deaf, often unwell and with a rasping voice' came to have such an impressive effect. Within two days of his arrival Billy Hughes had been made a privy councillor by the King and was breakfasting with Lloyd George in Number 11 Downing Street. Covered extensively and billed as 'A New Crusade' by the Northcliffe press, Hughes's heavy rhetoric called for Empire defence under the banner of pure Anglo-Saxonism against a degenerate Germany.

However, it was behind closed doors that much of the real action was taking place. Keith had organised a discreet dinner at his flat to welcome Hughes to London, attended by Sir William Robertson, chief of the imperial general staff; Lloyd George; Bonar Law; Lord Milner; Northcliffe and Dawson. In the upper echelons of power there was increasing dissatisfaction with Asquith's prime ministership and his handling of the war. This jostling for control meant that most of the key players in British politics, not least Lord Northcliffe, had their own reasons for supporting Hughes. Their support attracted comment from the USA and Germany; Hughes was simply happy to ride the wave that Keith was manufacturing.

Keith's own devotion to Hughes was neither total nor blind. The battle between two strong characters, under the stress of a fulltime media campaign, would sometimes lead Keith to declare that he 'wouldn't work for the little bugger any more'. However, his belief that he was working for 'that great country Australia' – and knowing on what side his bread was buttered – kept him where he was.

Writing to George Pearce, now acting prime minister back in Australia, Keith declared that the first month of Hughes's visit had been a 'phenomenal' success. 'We ... introduced Hughes properly to the proprietors and editors, to the leader writers, got out some books on him, and so forth, and Hughes himself did the rest.' A collection of Hughes's speeches titled 'The Day' – And After with an editor's note by Keith proved a bestseller. Reviewed as 'flamboyant but forcible', the book's text had been broken up by Keith with pithy sub-headers such as 'Stripped for the Fray', 'John Bull Aroused', 'On National Regeneration' and 'Survival of the Fittest'. Keith presented Hughes's lines on how the war was 'purging' the race of its 'dross' under the title 'The Silver Lining'. Bereaved families may have wondered at this meaning.

Keith also helped in the rapid production of another book, this time a Hughes hagiography bearing the portentous title *From Boundary-Rider to Prime Minister: Hughes of Australia – The Man of the Hour*. The book was centred on 'Mr Murdoch's fine study of Mr Hughes' from the *British Australasian*, and bulked the text with further speeches and Hughes's 'Great Sayings', under such restrained chapter headings as 'An Australian Abraham Lincoln'.

Keith was excited by the fervour he had helped to create, telling Pearce that a great effort was being made to keep Hughes in Britain: 'Better than anybody else he can rally the fighting spirit of the country.' Indeed, if it were not for Hughes's physical exhaustion, Keith said the Australian prime minister could be pushed on to the very highest office in the Empire. With Keith keeping 'the bulk of the press' as well as the Northcliffe papers on side, 'he should have a good solid party'.

In contrast, the former Prime Minister Andrew Fisher, now living in London as Australian high commissioner, was sidelined and grappling for any contact he could gain with the new prime minister. He could only write in pathetic terms asking Keith as gatekeeper to 'please persuade' Mr and Mrs Hughes to come to lunch.

But Hughes was being showered with far more pressing invitations. Two months into his trip he was the honoured guest at the Newspaper Press Fund anniversary dinner. The speeches of that evening throw a spotlight on the press's sense of its own importance and its role at what would prove to be the midpoint of the war. The host Lord Derby, the director general for recruitment, declared that in the absence of a formal political Opposition, 'it has fallen upon the Press to put forward the views and aspirations of the country as a whole'. To knowing laughter, Derby said a public man was no longer looked upon with 'the most terrible suspicion' if he was thought to be 'in with the Press'. Hughes declared that the Australian press had thrown themselves into this great campaign 'with an earnestness and vigour which had done great things in helping to rally men to the flag'. He was keen to stress that during elections the Australian press had been 'excellent' and they gave 'equal space to the spokesmen of each party'. The hollowness of this assertion was soon to be demonstrated.

On 23 June 1916, as Hughes's trip came to an end, the powerbrokers who had welcomed him privately at Keith's discreet dinner now attended a grand public feast in his honour at the Ritz, hosted by the leading 'Australians in London'. But the tour touting 'total war' had been a strain for Hughes as well as a triumph. On his homeward journey he made clear how much he relied on his public relations chief. Keith had had to endure both books and insults hurled by the fiery Welshman, but now he received a letter addressed to 'my dear old chap' declaring that he missed him dreadfully and valued his friendship, and was confident that Keith, at the very centre of things, would keep him 'posted on matters of great moment'. There was to be a trade-off for all this help and devotion. Keith asked the prime minister to 'give me a boost' the next time he saw his employers, Fink and Denison.

With Hughes safely at sea, Keith obliquely publicised the role he had played in stoking the enthusiasm for Australia's prime minister and at the same time gave an insight into his views on influencing opinion and then wielding it for political ends. In an article for the Sydney *Sun*, Keith noted how the platform of the press had made Hughes 'a man of power'. Having 'the people of Great Britain massed behind him' meant '[n]o democratic Government – much less the Asquith Government – could refuse him anything', a power legitimised in Keith's mind through a rather neat, though questionable, logic: 'The popular newspapers throughout the Kingdom expressed the popular will.' 'Having been privileged to occupy an inside seat in the circle', Keith stressed that Hughes 'has not promised conscription . . .'. But the suppressed issue of how to honour the commitment to the Allied cause was about to rear its head. And tackling it would require a far more covert form of press management and direct propaganda from Keith.

Hughes returned to Australia to find that recruitment numbers were plunging and a political storm brewing. He wished Keith were 'by my side' as there were 'hot times ahead': Hughes's own Labor Party had passed 'strong resolutions against compulsion'. For the rabble-rousing leader and his publicist who had just triumphed in Britain by typifying their countrymen's dedicated pluck, the omens were not good. Hughes deputed Keith to persuade the Australian soldiers in Europe to vote an emphatic 'Yes' in the coming referendum on conscription, hoping this would encourage civilians back in Australia to follow suit when they voted a few days later.

Keith had already taken the initiative, with a drive to garner support from leading British figures for the anticipated campaign. Key among these was General Birdwood, the English head of the 1st Anzac Corps.

At the beginning of October, under the heading 'SECRET AND CONFI-DENTIAL', Keith cabled Hughes to assure him that the pro-conscription manifesto had had a 'good effect' on the men. It included such temperate lines of argument as to fight for one's country was 'the sacred duty of every free man', while those who failed to do their bit would 'cover Australia with the mantle of eternal shame'. Keith had 'reached' the soldiers in 'every way possible' through literature and newspapers. But for the moment he was finding it impossible to arrange speeches to the men and so gain the resolutions to publicise back in Australia. Keith had used 'all the influence of the War Office' in order to secure the permits to cross the Channel. However, Sir Douglas Haig, the British commander-in-chief, had held out on allowing any meetings of soldiers to be addressed by soldiers. As Keith later complained, 'That would be subversive of discipline, because it would introduce politics in a virulent form.' It was only after 'fighting' Haig's 'whole staff' that Keith gained permission. Keith detailed all his efforts and expenses. He required not only monetary compensation, but crucially a more valuable reward: privileged access to the Front for the benefit of his own journalism.

Three days later, Keith was able to assure Hughes he had 'enlisted' the sympathy of Lloyd George and Bonar Law. Conscious of the strong Irish constituency in Australia, Keith was trying to 'induce them' to give the Australian prime minister the 'credit' for the expected removal of martial law from Ireland. Keith was off to France with 'every expectation' of getting interviews and messages from Sir Douglas Haig and his French counterpart Joseph Joffre, the French Prime Minister Aristide Briand and Sir William Robertson, chief of the imperial general staff. He would then try to send these to 'every Australian newspaper'. He was already able to relay supportive quotes from the 'Labour Adviser to [the] Government' and secretary of the British Labour movement. Acknowledging the diplomatic risks of how far he was pushing things, Keith warned the Australian censor that these 'messages must not be cabled back' to England. And as the day of the vote approached, Keith's attempt to pressure Robertson for a more explicit statement led to a stern warning from the military chief that he did not want to seem to be interfering 'with political matters in Australia'.

On the day of Robertson's rebuff, Keith was making a last, desperate appeal to Lloyd George for 'a statement or interview ... to be published ONLY in Australia, concerning the gravity of the war situation'. On the same day, conscious of imminent defeat, and mindful to manage a PR disaster, Keith wrote to Birdwood relaying a further suggestion he had made to Lloyd George. He had 'asked the Army Council to insist upon the merging of the soldiers' votes in the general totals so that the results will never be published or known to anyone'. As journalist turned renowned historian Les Carlyon put it, 'Here was something unusual: a journalist telling a politician to suppress a news story, and, better still, a story that would have been of real interest to the journalist's constituents.'

For Keith, the supposed dedication of the Anzac force was inextricably linked to the political standing and influence of Australia itself. He signed off to Birdwood: 'You have only to tell us what we can do for our army, and it will be done. Certainly command me, General, to the death.'

A convenient postponing of the vote by Birdwood gave Keith the extra time needed for the addresses to the troops. He 'instructed' his three 'resolutionists' ('my birds') before they spoke, but they 'failed utterly'. When Keith cabled that he had secured a 'message from representative soldiers as follows: Anzacs demand to be reinforced', he already knew the game was up. He also knew just how *un*representative those purported views were. His birds had come away with the 'impression that 95% of the men were opposed to conscription'. The men in France, experiencing the horror and pointlessness of trench warfare, would vote three to one against conscripting their countrymen to share their fate.

In line with Keith's plan, back in Australia a special regulation was enacted to make disclosing these figures illegal. The full, official result, rolling the military totals together with the general population's, made for a close call: rejection of conscription by 49 per cent to 51 per cent. Hughes managed to cling on to power, despite having been expelled from the Labor Party, declaring to Keith that 'Caesar still lives!' Looking to the future, Keith was 'confident' that Hughes would form a coalition 'and proceed with another test of the people's wishes, and next time you will carry conscription'.

Keith was candid and steely in his letter to Hughes exploring the defeat. Demonstrating his growing interest in the mechanics of public opinion, it was 'very important that the exact causes leading the men to vote No should be ascertained so that after diagnosis the sickness may be removed'. In a detailed post-mortem he listed seven reasons for the result, from left-wing agitation to mismanagement. But read today, number three holds the most resonance. The 'wonderfully generous' men simply 'did not like compelling others to enter the hell they are in'.

Keith took it upon himself to spin the result in the British press, and explain its ramifications privately to Lloyd George and Bonar Law in meetings (as 'I always do quite informally and unofficially'). He also saw the episode as instructive in terms of how political communication and persuasion worked, with lessons for future British and Australian political campaigns. In the next Australian campaign, money and business contacts would be added to the arsenal and swung into action.

The war might have been going dreadfully but 1917 started well for Keith. He could now walk into and out of the rooms of Cabinet ministers 'as a close friend' to the amazement of English reporters. After all the plotting, pressure and intrigue, Britain finally had a new prime minister who afforded Keith the scoop of an interview to tie in with Australia Day. Keith enthused, 'Never have I found Lloyd George more confident, more alert, more master of the situation.' One of the things Lloyd George was attempting to bring into line, right from the first meeting of the new War Cabinet, was the management of disparate, uncoordinated government propaganda. Even as Keith scribbled his shorthand notes during the interview, a new department of information led by John Buchan, author of *The Thirty-Nine Steps* and a *Times* war correspondent, was being set up with Masterman sidelined. The move towards a more aggressive, proactive campaign of propaganda and disinformation had commenced, and 'newspapermen' would become increasingly central players.

There was a risk that Australia herself could soon have a new prime minister. On 5 March 1917 Hughes's coalition government announced an immediate election. Just a couple of weeks later Keith told Hughes he had formed an organisation of sympathisers that he proposed calling 'Hugheses [sic] win-the-war party'. He had already collected £2,000. The first gathering of the twelve 'Australians resident in London' took place in a discreet location in the commercial heart of the city. The meeting's minutes detail how the assembled businessmen were there 'to assist the present National Political Party in Australia by influencing as many of the soldiers' votes in that direction as possible'. Their overarching aim was to 'win the war' and to 'make absolutely plain that we are ANTI-GERMAN'. But second was the more nuanced task to '[p]ut information before the Australian soldiers (and showing them how to vote) in such a manner as not to appear inspired'. It noted 'care must be exercised' not only with 'its propaganda' but its terminology, avoiding 'words likely to create suspicion'. The 'Literature' produced was 'to be brief and to the point'. A strategy of coverage was set out. They would 'enlist' the support of Lord Northcliffe 'to obtain a column in the Daily Mail'. Horatio Bottomley, the bankrupt former MP and fraudster with his hugely selling sensational weekly magazine *John Bull*, was also to be approached. Bottomley's reputation in Australia was already notorious. An article titled 'Secret Diplomacy: Influence of the "Press"' had described him as the 'Jingo, Patriot, Imperialist, Tory, Anti-Socialist, Anti-Democrat . . . and one of the biggest swindlers in Britain'. Keith's committee could rest assured that Bottomley's 'Anti-German' credentials were impeccable. He had called for the extermination of Germans living in Britain.

Keith also kept tabs on rivals, asking Hughes to cable the 'worst speeches' of the Opposition back in Australia, and to be told when 'and by whom' the first message was sent from London 'warning them of publication of your manifesto'. (Hughes had drafted this 'manifesto on the lines' suggested by Keith.) Another potential problem was tackled with brutal force. A war-supporting Labor MP currently serving in the army, Alfred Ozanne, was an inconvenient rejoinder to the picture Hughes was seeking to paint of the Opposition.

Rather than leaving Ozanne's crucial swing constituency to remain uncontested as a 'khaki seat', Keith helped coordinate a smear campaign, bringing Birdwood and Major-General John Monash into the collusion. It culminated in the false charge of desertion being applied retrospectively to Ozanne's military record. As one researcher who has brought light to a tale that is otherwise completely absent from the approved biographies states: 'The propriety of an informal political agent obtaining military information from serving officers for party political purposes in the midst of an election campaign seemed not to occur to either Hughes or Murdoch.' The pursuit was 'ruthless and unscrupulous', the tactics of the 'political character assassination' displaying 'little moral compunction'. Ozanne lost his seat, while the key cable against the MP from Monash, obtained and clandestinely sent by Keith, 'destroyed him as a public man'.

Still, safe under the cover of the 'win-the-war' committee, Keith continued with the black arts. He impressed the strength of his position to Birdwood: 'I can get all the money here for a strong campaign'. Keith revealed his plan 'to distribute literature' under various cloaks including 'the YMCA, Comforts Fund and Red Cross organisation'. Birdwood agreed that Keith could 'do a great deal by way of' the forces' paper, the *Anzac Bulletin*, suggesting it be 'sent over' from London to France 'in largely increased numbers'. But Birdwood warned that as this newspaper was paid for by the Australian government, their 'enemies out there [in the Opposition] would of course make capital' if it were seen to be 'urging the claims of any particular political party'. He added: 'But of course this would not apply to the liberal publication of Australian telegrams.' For the General, caution and discretion were key:

> You will I know thoroughly agree how inadvisable it would be to give any opening of this sort. Also, there cannot of course be any question of any particular party being officially favoured at the expense of any other, for it will be quite open to anyone to send newspapers as they think fit through the post.

This was a neat, if wholly disingenuous, manoeuvre. After all, what other party had at that moment the resources of a business cabal to fund a mass mailing, and a press operative to tilt the newspaper coverage of the very newspapers being sent in the first place? Even more, a new newspaper would be created just for the purpose. One that could be regarded as the Murdochs' first.

The leader of the 'Official Labor Party' would describe this mysterious new publication, *All for Australia*, as telling 'more lies to the square inch than any other newspaper I have ever seen'. One of Keith's own employer newspapers railed against an 'electioneering campaign among the Commonwealth troops by means of a small newspaper'. The Sydney *Sun* insisted that it was 'essential that the troops in England and France should receive a fair statement of the political disputes in Australia, and not a wholly ex-parte account of them'. It thought it 'would be interesting to know by whom this is being done, and whether the Government has any degree of cognisance of it'.

It is perhaps unsurprising that Keith's first newspaper was a publication since quietly forgotten. Within a few days of the first issue would come the most notorious piece of disinformation yet manufactured by the Allied press.

With little more than a fortnight to go before the election, voters in Sydney on 16 April 1917 could be forgiven for having trouble swallowing their buttered toast as they read the *Sun* headline 'Human Fats – The German Method'. Melbourne *Herald* readers had to digest the news of 'Margarine from Corpses'. Keith's cables revealing the apparent depravity of 'The German Beast' continued a drip-drip feed of horror for a week: 'Oil from Corpses', 'Prussian Cannibals', 'Dead Desecrated – Facts Undeniable'. All he needed to do for the moment was relay the supposed eyewitness accounts that spoke for themselves:

> Trainloads of naked corpses from the west front daily arrive at the factory. Employees, wearing oilskins and masks, and armed with long hooked poles, push the corpses on to an endless chain, which picks them up with a big hook. The chain carries the bodies to a long, narrow compartment, where they are disinfected, steamed, dried and finally automatically detached from the chain and dropped into a great cauldron ... slowly stirred by machinery for eight

hours . . . The refined oil, which is of a yellowish brown color, is packed in small casks.

Although Hughes immediately recognised the value of the sensational revelations to his campaign, he sensibly sought from Keith 'very urgent' proof of their veracity. Keith responded straightaway, assuring the prime minister his reports provided 'authenticated details', while giving further evocative descriptions of bodies being stripped for oil and pig food. Hughes brandished this cable during at least one campaign address, declaring that he had received a 'message from London amplifying earlier reports with regard to the utilization of dead bodies by Germany in boiling-down factories'; the nation was barbaric and had lost the right to exist 'in a civilized world'.

Meanwhile, New Zealand's prime minister, then in Britain, was also receiving covert press management and introductions from Keith. W. F. Massey delivered a speech condemning 'the German madness', which 'had culminated in boiling down the slain soldiers for commercial requirements'. He trusted that, given such horrors, 'the German evil power would be broken for generations'.

Keith's cables continued to inflame Australia as the poll approached. He claimed that a 'wave of intense disgust and loathing' at the news in Europe had 'produced a greater moral affect [sic] than all the previous German brutalities and crimes', and hinted that the Germans may be 'using the Allies' dead for the same abominable purpose'. Keith even helped spread the rumour of germ warfare against civilians.

In a detailed follow-up despatch on the corpse factory published in July, Keith explained his case why a claim that was so 'loathsome' that 'most people prefer not to believe it' was in the 'balance of evidence' true. Employing the wily art of discrediting one source in order to make the supporting of others more credible, Keith told his readers that Belgians couldn't be trusted when speaking of the 'Huns' practices, for Hunnish cruelty and oppression have coloured their minds'. Instead it was the evidence in the 'diplomatic circles' to which he was privy, of the Americans who had lived in Germany and the 'official statements of the Huns themselves' that proved incontrovertible. These killed the lie of mistranslation claimed by the German authorities.

Keith also conjured a motive. The enemy was 'desperately hard up for fats and oils . . . Imagine their temptation'. The practice 'would not be out of keeping with the Huns' view of life' and 'methods of warfare'. Keith compounded the list of atrocities: 'their sinking of hospital ships, murder of infants, and cruel use of gas'. After hinting at the curious absence of German dead on ground taken by Australian troops, he turned again to a tried, though hardly trusted, source. The 'best commentary' on this point was to be found in 'a cartoon by Raemaekers'. The public need only absorb this one conclusion: 'The Huns had long been in such depths of depravity that these signs of animalism – it is almost cannibalism – need not be surprising.'

Conspicuously, Keith appears never to have written or commented on the claims again in the years that followed. However, Bean would later write of how he had 'never believed the myth, knowing that the Germans treated their military dead with particular respect'.

The journalist Charles Montague recalled the bitter reaction of an Australian sergeant surveying the site of a supposed corpse factory: 'Can't believe a word you read, sir, can you?' For Montague 'another good man had been duly confirmed in that faith, ordained as a minister of the faith, that whatever your pastors and masters tell you had best be assumed to be just a bellyful of east wind'.

On the same day that Keith first relayed the depressing claims of the corpse factory, he told Birdwood of his plans to lift Australian spirits by reporting on their troops' latest action. He would be heading over to France, having communicated with John Charteris, the head of army intelligence, (long Northcliffe's sympathetic 'propaganda liaison with the army' and another figure central to the corpse factory tale). As a pay-off for all his work, Keith instructed Hughes to cable the Colonial Office and make 'the trip semiofficial'. The visit, he told Hughes, would help gel the final stages of the election campaign. Keith might have added that his own privileged access to Hughes would steal a march on his cable competitors and aid his own career.

Keith assured Birdwood he would be zealous in working for the Australian Imperial force (AIF) and the Empire once at the Front. He thanked the general for his letters that 'help me to give my newspapers the enthusiastic point of view'. On 16 April Keith sent a report while still in London on the battle of Lagnicourt. It appeared under the headline 'Entirely Australian Affair'. The Official Press Bureau had allowed him 'to pin the whole battle on to Australian troops' and he was sure, as a result, 'that the Commonwealth is to-day ringing with the great news'. (The proprietor of the *News of the World*, Lord Riddell, confided to his diary how the press were 'booming' the colonial forces so loudly that the achievements of the British troops were being drowned out.) Complaining about inter-governmental communication, Keith would later tell Hughes that even he as prime minister had been kept 'in the dark about Australian disasters – Fromelles and the first Bullecourt battle, for instance'. (The latter bloodbath has been described as 'the nadir of Australian military competence' during World War I.)

But Keith's despatches were giving a very different view to the electorate back home. A week before the vote he told Birdwood:

Very full cables have gone out to all our newspapers about the heroic fighting at Bullecourt and Lagnicourt, and I am confident that Australia is much more proud than sad over the affairs. Of course it has not been wise to say much about our heavy losses on the Wednesday, but in any case the gallantry of the men is our first consideration.

Hughes triumphed in the May election. As we shall see, the gratitude he felt to Keith and his methods in this fight would be demonstrated by the arrival of yet another coded cable request marked 'MOST SECRET' a few months later. In the meantime, Keith would not relent in his mission to keep his readers inspired by tales of heroism and success.

Keith's exaltation showed no signs of waning. During his trip to the Front, he produced lengthy despatches on the second battle of Bullecourt that helped to cloak the disaster of the first. Back in Australia they were presented as a numbered serial, complete with 'To be Continued' at the end of each instalment. Jauntily written, using 'we' for victories and captures, they told of the youthful 'mateship' between 'fine-featured, eager-eyed' boys and the 'extraordinarily numerous' escapes of the battlefield. Keith felt it 'wonderful how these boys face wounds and death, thinking nothing of either, even courting them, and going cheerfully half-way to meet them across open shell-strewn zones ...'. His account of how Scot and Australian 'joined hands at Bullecourt' was printed up as a lavishly illustrated broadside, the narrative interspersed with lines of death-defying, patriotic doggerel taken from his poem 'Who Said Retire?'

The Anzacs' bodies were again employed as stirring exemplars of a superior race. Under the sub-headline 'Australians "The Perfect Soldiers"', Keith relayed that General Castelnau had told him, 'They are ... *les soldats complets.*' In contrast, poking around in an abandoned German encampment, Keith found signs of 'moral degeneration' and vice to add to the physical weakness of the Huns. A photo-feature from the Paris *Le Miroir* was sent back to Australia for publication ironically depicting the gormless 'Supermen developed by Kultur'. Meanwhile, Birdwood excitedly updated Keith on how he had diverted two hulking Anzacs from the Front 'to be placed on special duty at Australia House' as 'a real good advertisement'.

Keith marketed the Anzacs with increasing fervour. While Bean felt unable to rise to the 'wretched cant' of 'over-written' reports and 'write about bayonet charges like some of the correspondents do', Keith had no qualms in sending back vivid tales of hand-to-hand combat. One typical report depicted a German and Australian locked in a struggle to the death, the victor predictable. 'Most of the fighting in this sector was Homeric', he concluded. In 'Samson and the Philistines', Keith described how one 'man of Herculean type ... astonished the Germans ... by breaking an officer's neck with his fingers'.

Despite his own heavy eulogising, Bean confided to his diary how the 'truth is soldiers are not the fictions which war correspondents have made of them, but ordinary human men...'. Writing to Keith about their respective approaches, Bean stressed: 'I believe in telling the simple facts, neither more nor less, and letting the truth do its work', even if it did 'not seem to serve for the moment'. Nevertheless, he signed off acknowledging their shared patriotism: 'We are all in it for the same object anyway ... though we have different ways of expressing it.'

Central to Keith's inspirational, if increasingly sensational, tales was an attempt to stir recruitment and convince Australia to accept conscription. One despatch caused a rebuke in Europe and a ruckus back in Australia. Keith had described the 'moving sight' of 'our attacking troops, very weak, through reinforcements not arriving' during an action at Daisy Wood. One Australian minister, encouraged by General Legge, complained to Birdwood that he could not 'understand such statements in view of 50,000 men being in depots in England. Please prevent such misleading statements being cabled in future.' Legge also raised the matter at a conference of editors in Melbourne. He told the meeting, 'Mr Murdoch is a very fine writer, an extremely picturesque writer but I do not agree with the accuracy of all the stuff he sends. I know that myself from my own observation.' More important than whether it was correct, Keith told Birdwood the statement had been 'intended to rouse Australia, to end forever the recruiting difficulties, to force either another conscription campaign ... or to straighten out the recruiting difficulties by an appeal to public feelings'.

As well as encouraging men to enlist, Keith sought to inspire the wider community to sympathise and empathise with the army. His letter directed to 'mothers, wives, sisters and girlfriends' at home attempted to reassure them that, away from the Front, their boys were 'kicking a football on a patch of green' and 'bathing in the canals'. They were, Keith relayed their 'Padre' as saying, filled with the 'true spirit of religion – self-sacrifice'. This self-sacrifice was portrayed as no less than martyrdom, as when one machine-gunner stayed at his post to be 'licked' by the flames of a German 'fire sprayer'.

Back in Melbourne, one local paper was moved to praise Keith as the son of a clergyman 'who has made such a name for himself as a war correspondent by his graphic and real heart-interest writings of our boys'. On the other side of the country in Perth, the *Daily News* asked its readers:

Are you an eligible and hesitating whether you should offer for military service? If so, read what Mr Keith Murdoch has to say about your hero-brothers in France: ... 'We are a dwindling band, our life-blood ebbs away.' ... That thought pulses like a heart-beat in men's minds.

Fink proclaimed how 'your stuff has sunk into the public mind' and is 'greatly appreciated by all classes'. Though Fink was content for the moment with runaway sales, he confided to Keith that 'the great newspaper problem after the war will be how to continue to interest the public with ordinary fare, after the highly spiced dishes we have been used to'.

Haig's Western Front offensive at the end of July 1917 proved to be a disaster. Nevertheless, a few weeks later, attempting to gain an exclusive interview with Haig, Keith assured Charteris that he would 'emphasise the merits of the high command' in his write-up. As lives were thrown into the hopeless battles, the call for their replacement once again went out. But in September and October monthly enlistments in Australia were half that deemed necessary by the Army Council. On 6 November Hughes sent Keith a 'MOST SECRET' cable advising that another referendum was imminent. The Anzac vote would again be 'vital to success'. Hughes asked Keith to reassemble the committee that had done 'such splendid work' during the election, and to discreetly start to take steps for a 'very vigorous campaign'.

Keith swung into action. He wrote to the agents-general: 'Another conscription campaign is on us at once. It is to be a lightning stroke, and we require all the efforts of all stalwarts over here.' He arranged for a meeting of supporters, 'confidential and select', with the 'hope to arrange for a campaign amongst the soldiers'. Updating Hughes, Keith outlined a two-part strategy. Firstly, a month of rest for the weakened and tired soldiers should be announced to coincide with the official announcement of polling day; secondly, a jolting announcement 'should be made immediately' for the 'breaking up of a division', so demonstrating the need for men. This would have a 'striking effect' on both the 'public opinion of [the] Force and in Australia'.

Keith drew Birdwood into his scheme, advising the head of the force to announce and then commence the break-up of a division, but 'always with the proviso that conscription will enable you to reform it some day'. They should then 'strike hard with a referendum campaign before the military situation finds a level' and the public get 'dull and hopeful again'. Birdwood agreed to proceed with the plan. Nothing would be left to chance. Keith disclosed to Birdwood, 'very frankly, knowing that you will regard this as confidential', how he was going to sweeten the Corps' rest in the run-up to the vote by spending 'plenty of Red Cross and Australian Comforts money on their winter comforts during this time'.

On the 'literature' side, Keith told Hughes the campaign was 'proceeding splendidly' though with care. He had made sure the committee had 'not advertised' itself to the cable manager of the rival Australian Press Association (APA) in order to 'remain camouflaged against opposition'. Apart from the APA, Keith claimed to be in command of a virtual monopoly of the news services with 'all the Reuter, Times and United Service cables ... under my direct control'. However, he had plans for 'collaring' the APA service 'and running it with mine'.

On 20 November Keith cabled the Australian prime minister with a list of his achievements. The Paris *Daily Mail* was publishing a 'daily half column' of 'special propaganda'; the British press was publishing the 'principal parts' of Hughes's proclamation speech; and the 'Full use' of the London press had been arranged. Finally, the new issue of *All for Australia* had been distributed to all the men – 180,000 throughout the fields of action – that day. Text boxes either side of its masthead advocated 'Yes' votes. Keith explained that he was denying the word 'conscription' and referring to 'reinforcements by ballot' and so 'differentiating clearly between the two [conscription] campaigns'.

In a post-war debate on censorship, one Australian senator who served at the Front commented: 'I often heard the fellows at the Front say that the name of it should have been *All for Hughes*, because that was really its policy.' He highlighted how the men overseas 'could only form an opinion on the basis of such literature as was supplied, and as the Government only allowed them to read *All for Australia* naturally they only heard one side of the case'.

In a further discussion of the censorship of the time which allowed *All for Australia* but not other literature to be distributed, the Leader of the Opposition recalled how when they tried to place advertisements 'in the English papers, our money was refused. They would not publish anything in favour of the Labour party'.

However, there were rumblings of disquiet in Keith's own firm. He had already 'smelt trouble from my Australian directors', and a week into the campaign he had received 'a cable from Campbell Jones', the former United Cable Service manager and Denison's ambitious right-hand man, 'which practically made further open work impossible'.

Keith had to be cautious for the sake of his career. This was not the first time the probity of his activities had been questioned. Following the election in May, Fink told Keith that back in Sydney he stood accused of 'trying to run the Empire too much, and in fact dissipating his forces, wasting energy in personal interviews with leading statesmen and so forth'. Fink had defended Keith, stressing that his 'qualities have enabled him to establish very excellent relations with leading public men', which was surely 'a great asset for a newspaper – the greatest'. Campbell Jones would later report to Fink and Denison his concern that Keith's role should be more clearly defined. After all, it was not 'the personal views of Keith Murdoch which our clients are buying' but the news which should be 'confined to the absolute facts'.

Though he at least officially withdrew from the campaign committee, Keith continued to handle what he termed 'the press side' and 'propaganda'. As well as the special columns and editions of the *Daily Mail*, the weekly issues of *All for Australia* remained subject to Keith's 'pass'. However, they were 'not exactly' how he would have liked, being printed 'too heavily' and not treating the 'men quite frankly'. Ironically, this was a view echoed by Theodore Fink's son Thorold serving in France. He wrote to his parents: 'The powers that be have circulated a miserable screed called "All for Australia". The object appears to be to influence votes in favor of Conscription.'

The content was indeed miserably poor. As well as supposed interviews relayed in painfully contrived Aussie lingo ('I voted NO last Referendum, but fair Dinkum! I don't do it this time ... Struth, there's not a mother's son who'll vote NO'), an additional, rather suspect, example of 'The German Brute' was given. 'A new Hymn of Hate' had apparently been taught to the enemy troops. *All for Australia* reproduced its last verse as a red rag to wavering voters:

Sons of Germany! The great hour has come! Neither women nor children must be spared, . . . Forward! Shatter, destroy, thrust, burn, Kill, kill, kill, kill, kill!

As 'nothing' was 'being left to chance', Keith was confident of scoring 'a good win here' in Europe and expected a 'rich haul' of votes. He even enlisted covert family support, asking his brother Alan to write 'two bright half-columns each to the following papers: *Evening News*, *Daily Mail* and *Express*', pointing to 'what the Canadians have been putting through the Continental papers.'

The highlighting of the *Express* and attention to the Canadians' own propaganda effort, recognised as one of the most successful of the war, was telling. Keith was keenly tracking its proprietor Sir Max Aitken's own career path and strategies. Aitken was at this time encouraging the Canadian Expeditionary Force to vote for Sir Robert Borden's government in the Canadian federal election of December, with the campaign framed around the need for conscription. Canada's subsequent introduction of conscription in January 1918 following Borden's victory has been described as 'as much a political as military necessity'. One historian claims the 'same could be said of Australia and the five AIF divisions on the Western Front'. Hughes and Keith hoped to carve a new, elevated status for Australia, mirroring the strategy Canada was also pursuing during the war. And the very last line of the *All for Australia* issue that had irked Thorold Fink seemed to typify the point: given its allies' lead, 'Australia's honour demands a unanimous YES'.

Writing on 11 December 1917, Keith assured his Australian readers that they should not be concerned at the conditions they were sending their sons to. There were 'wonderful supplies of food, wire, timber, clothes, iron, weapons and rainproof. I saw a reserve company actually feeding on fried fish and chips.'

As the poll neared, Keith was pushing his content to the limit of acceptability, and in some cases beyond. Responding to a confidential warning from the officer in charge of the press and censorship operation at GHQ about 'political references' in his despatches, Keith claimed that his output was 'enormously appreciated in Australia'. Seemingly still bitter at having lost out to Bean in the vote among their fellows to the coveted role, he added that the 'official correspondents have never been able to get a hold on Australian public opinion, and newspapers make a great deal of the unofficial despatches'.

Despite all the efforts the December referendum was lost, and by a far greater margin than before. Writing to Birdwood, Keith conceded the vote had 'indeed been a disaster'. One of the great 'mistakes' had been neglecting the relationship between the force and the Australian public: 'We have failed to keep the large mass of Australians personally interested in the Australian Army, and now our punishment has been visited upon us.' In future, he suggested rallying missions should be sent home with populist figures such as Albert Jacka, first Australian winner of the Victoria Cross, who 'would be worth a thousand recruits if he visited Australia for one month'.

As before, Keith produced a detailed post-mortem for select circulation. He was bitterly disappointed that his plan 'to rouse martial feeling in Australia' by going to the Western Front three weeks previously had been thwarted by a GHQ ruling forbidding any despatches that might have a 'political bearing'. And he was amazed to learn that this 'was done at [Hughes's] express request'. (Hughes had greatly increased the censorship provisions back in Australia.) But putting the clash to one side, Keith again set himself the task of spinning the result 'to soften the blow here'.

At the start of 1918, after concentrated lobbying, Keith finally secured a pay increase from Theodore Fink and Hugh Denison. They believed it reflected 'the real value' of his 'services', as well as the cost of entertaining that Keith was incurring 'in keeping in personal touch with people who counted in the World's affairs'. (Keith had become accustomed to a certain style and throwing dinners at the Savoy for guests such as Winston Churchill wasn't cheap.) Though his byline was used in Victoria, Keith asked for it to be applied more widely, Denison understanding that what he really wanted was "'publicity" in a personal sense, so as to get the "kudos" attached to the authorship'.

Keith's own machinations in the shadows between political and military control caused a breakdown in his relationship with Birdwood. In early April the general had refused accommodation in his headquarters, and not made a car available as usual for the visiting correspondent. Keith was hurt by the decision 'as we naturally think the Australian Press has a proper place in the Australian Corps'. Birdwood responded firmly that two official representatives already filled that role. But the 'proper place' of the pressmen in the war had already blurred. And those at the top were getting heady with the power seeming to come their way. Sir Max Aitken had been ennobled to become Lord Beaverbrook, and in February was given an important, newly created post in government.

In stirring both the British and Australians into action, there 'were few limits to Murdoch's machinations'. Keith had become emboldened. In early 1918 he and Bean began a campaign to install Major-General Brudenell White as Australian commander. But their campaign came up against the decision by the Australian Cabinet to appoint Major-General John Monash to the position. Keith told Hughes that White was 'immensely superior' to Monash and was 'more likely to inspire the men'; this despite the fact that White had no experience of commanding in the field and had himself declared Monash the 'abler man' for the role. Hughes, in the US on his way to Europe, was suitably spooked, cabling Pearce back in Australia to postpone the decision.

The deputy adjutant-general also cabled Pearce but to tell him of the 'organized attempt being made by a small outside clique in London to bring about a change in command of the A.I.F.': 'There is a great feeling of resentment throughout the force here at this apparent attempt of MURDOCH to interfere with our administration.' Les Carlyon would title his coruscating chapter on this reckless attempt to undermine Monash 'The Press Gang'. For Carlyon, Keith 'was playing courtier and journalist at the same time. Elected by no-one, apparently accountable to no-one, he was as powerful as anyone in the cabinet in Melbourne.' What had been farcical to begin with 'became muddled and nasty'.

In his personal files Monash labelled the correspondence relating to the affair 'Keith Murdoch's Intrigue'. Writing to Hughes, Monash challenged Keith's self-appointed 'right to be the spokesman of the A.I.F.'. Though Keith had assured Hughes his proposals had the 'unanimous, support' of the force, Monash stressed 'that this is wholly misleading and absolutely incorrect'. Keith, in turn, wrote to Monash seeking to flatter him into accepting a lead position in London instead, in a letter described by the general's biographer as an 'explicit bribe'. In it Keith combined a clunking appeal to trust and 'use me in any humble capacity you can', with a barely veiled flexing of his power to influence and frame opinion through the '250 newspapers' that took his cables. Keith invited Monash to 'drop me a line' from the Front every now and then: 'I hope to be able to familiarise the Australian public with all your good work.' Monash was not to be swayed. As he told his wife, 'I profoundly distrust this man.'

White, Birdwood and Monash closed ranks against Murdoch and Bean; Hughes, now in Europe and thus able to investigate the true allegiance of officers and troops on the spot, realised how grossly he had been misled. Defending himself against Birdwood's exasperation at his meddling, Keith tried to strike a humble note; he was 'only a youngster trying' to do his best for his country and countrymen with 'no right to force my views upon anyone'. Birdwood also brought Keith to heel for cabling his newspapers that there was 'a strong unanimous view' that Monash should be made the 'supreme administrator' in London while White led the Corps. Keith admitted that 'the word "unanimous" was ... too strong'. He explained evasively that it should not have been taken as meaning the view of the soldiers but 'the opinions of Australians in London'. In fact, the original source of the opinion was a single Australian – its official war artist Will Dyson, who had made his name with the *Kultur Cartoons* collection. Dyson, Bean and Murdoch were central to the close-knit group described charitably as the 'AIF's unofficial brains trust'.

Monash felt that the move against him was motivated, at least in part, because he was Jewish. He wrote to his wife, nine days before the crucial battle of Hamel: 'It is a great nuisance to have to fight a pogrom of this nature in the midst of all one's other anxieties.' The success of that battle, as well as the progress of the August offensive under Monash's invigorating command, closed the matter. Bean would later describe the plot against the 'pushy Jew' as a 'high-intentioned but ill-judged intervention'.

One of Monash's biographers has described the action of Bean and Murdoch as an 'outstanding case of sheer irresponsibility by pressmen in Australian history'; another claimed 'Murdoch's case would have made Machiavelli proud'. But the story is absent from the two previously published biographies of Murdoch. Zwar remains completely mute; Younger simply states: 'In May General Monash became Corps Commander.'

The wool pulled from his eyes, Birdwood wrote to the governor-general, Sir Ronald Munro Ferguson. It was difficult to pin down 'exactly what' Murdoch's position was: 'He should, I presume, be a journalist pure and simple, but I gather he is more of a private agent and interviews the Prime Minister and others.' Publicising this relationship gave Keith 'an opportunity of putting in his oar undesirably'. Though Birdwood was glad that the 'strong unanimous view' cable – an 'effrontery' – had been stopped by the censor, Keith was still pulling 'all sorts of other wires' in this direction:

> . . . he is one of these busybodies, who in his desire to have his fingers in every pie, would like to have a man [in London] to whom he could, to a certain extent, dictate – who would come to him with all news regarding the force and be influenced by Murdoch's ideas.

Munro Ferguson concluded Keith was 'obviously one of the most ambitious of the pressmen who set themselves up to rule over us'.

In a reflective piece written in July 1918, Keith looked back over the sweep of the war to assess the new 'Leaders Behind The Fronts'. Chief of these was Beaverbrook who, in Keith's words, had become 'Minister of Propaganda, or Information, as it is called'. While he didn't stress the parallels to his own emigrant and Presbyterian upbringing, Keith related that the former Max Aitken, born in a Canadian manse, was now so successful 'he can buy newspapers, control banks, finance political movements'. Drawing from their interaction 'in various settings', Keith acknowledged the plotting and intrigues of the man with 'penetrating' brown eyes and 'eloquent' tongue who 'pulled many strings'. Aitken had 'a great hand' in the making of 'the Lloyd George–Bonar Law Cabinet' and remained Bonar Law's 'closest confidant and trusting friend'. Keith was confident that Beaverbrook's role now was 'one of infinite opportunity . . . His job is to spread the gospel of Anglo-Saxonism, and convert even the German. He has raised a mighty department and his trumpets sound in every land.' With the help of the manager of Reuters, Fleet Street editors and the young Canadians in his ministry, Beaverbrook was 'carrying his propaganda from audacity to audacity, and from success to success'.

In a telling phrase that has echoed down the generations since, Beaverbrook explained his methods:

> 'No propaganda reaches the hearts and minds of the people unless it is so convincing and attractive that the public mind is ready and anxious to pay a price to see or read it.'

Beaverbrook's biographer A. J. P. Taylor described a man whose actions provided striking parallels with Keith's. Beaverbrook was a government–military go-between 'who could write his own instructions' as well as 'a publicist, diplomatist, and organizer rolled into one'. Taylor stressed that Beaverbrook's first key invention in capturing popular influence had been to make himself Canada's 'eyewitness' at the Front; back in Australia in 1917 Keith was being presented to his readers as '"THE SUN'S" SPECIAL EYEWITNESS AT THE FRONT'.

In Lloyd George's progressive drive to improve and coordinate propaganda, Beaverbook had been appointed Britain's minister for information on 10 February 1918. Learning from his success in influencing Canadian public opinion, Beaverbrook had deliberately concentrated his propaganda on journalism and the press. (In 1916, Northcliffe had told Beaverbrook how press was the 'best propaganda', citing how the 'Australians use the newspaper and use it very well'.) But Beaverbrook also used photography and film and pioneered the use of war artists as a means to connect and inspire. He had commissioned Augustus John to paint a huge canvas for his Canadian war memorials fund, although by 1918 John had managed only a half-scale charcoal cartoon. However, a small, delicate oil study, *Head of a Canadian Soldier*, was later bought by Keith. Until the end of Keith's life it would provide comfort and inspiration, being hung in the private sanctuary of his dressing room.

In a series of memoranda Beaverbrook set out his views on the differences between informal public opinion and formal or diplomatic opinion. The object of his ministry was not to get in touch with the official line but with the powers that 'sway and mould the thoughts of their fellow countrymen'. Masterman had aimed at the intelligentsia. But Beaverbrook's target was the man in the street and the newspaper was the key tool in reaching him. Beaverbrook went further, declaring that newspapers were a necessity 'without which the modern state cannot properly govern itself or direct its full energies to the war. The mind misses news and comment quite as much as the body misses food.'

By the midpoint of 1918, rumblings of discontent at the power of the 'Press Lords' were increasing. Beaverbrook in particular was locked in battle with the Foreign Office over the extent of his reach. In an extremely hostile House of Commons debate in August 1918 about the Ministry of Information, the radical MP Leif Jones pointed to the potentially sinister aims behind Beaverbrook's use of films, and Stanley Baldwin admitted that '[p]ropaganda is not a word that has a pleasant sound in English ears'. Concerns were also raised about the ministry's plans to establish an imperial news service based on a chain of imperial wireless stations. 'The spectre raised was of a ruthless press tycoon bent on acquiring the implements for mass brainwashing of the public', in the words of Beaverbrook's biographers. Beaverbrook used the excuse of ill-health to withdraw from the fray, eventually resigning in October.

Keith now knew that trusted newspapers and stirring images could be far more powerful in shaping minds and hearts than government-funded publications and clunky censorship. He had also learnt that the strictly factual account wasn't always the most effective. In the words of Charles Montague, the jaded critic of 'the great fat-boiling yarn':

When a man feels that his tampering with truth has saved civilization, why should he deny himself, in his private business, the benefit of such moral reflections as this feeling may suggest?

6 A ROMANCE INTO AIR

In the late 1950s Rupert had begun the expansion of his media holdings in a whirr of propellers as dust-caked DC-3s flew him around Australia. He even made an air hostess, Patricia Booker, his (often forgotten) first wife. By the time he married his second wife Anna Torv in the 1980s, he owned Ansett Airlines, enabling him to secure control of the TV station within the same group. It was an unplanned addition, but one soon groomed into a profitable member of the corporate family.

However, it also led to Rupert's first appearance before a US Senate committee. He successfully defended himself against the accusation that he had traded his newspapers' support to US President Jimmy Carter, then seeking re-election, in return for a cheap government loan to purchase a fleet of new Boeings for Ansett. But the Murdoch association with the political, business and romantic entanglements of aviation had actually begun with Keith sixty years earlier.

Keith Murdoch was perfectly placed to witness the rapid technological developments in aviation that took place during World War I. He had privileged access to the factories, training aerodromes and field bases at the Front and close contact with the star flyers, innovators and politicians shaping the new age of flight beyond the peace. It was a link that would last into the final decade of his life. He would confide to a close ally in his business chain: 'I am sure we ought to have a plane ourselves as soon as these things become possible. Why should we not be very free in our movements?' Uncovering the early development of this passion reveals his excitement at the possibilities of aviation for communication as well as a devotion to its fearless pioneers. It also helps to give substance to a doomed personal romance: Keith's first engagement has otherwise vanished into thin air.

As early as 1916 Keith had started to inspire his Australian readers with the romance of machines that were enabling 'our intrepid young aviators to reconquer the air'. But after the disappointment of the failed conscription referendum and the harsh reality of entrenched warfare on the Western Front, a new breed of inspirational Australian hero was needed.

By 1917 Keith was detailing the lofty exploits of the 'Anzac Birdmen', building up a new and exciting narrative that transcended the horrific war of mud and stagnation below. This was 'work for boys without nerves ... the most intense form of an intense war'. Keith assured his patriotic readers that no airmen were more capable or keener than the Australians. He spent time in France with the newly formed Australian Flying Corps, whose 'splendid deeds ... should make the country ring'. These were men to be admired and emulated, men who had 'chosen to enjoy, and would not leave their hazardous, ever-thrilling occupation'. Always with an eye to recruitment, Keith cabled back calls for volunteers to run alongside these exciting tales, confident that thousands of applications were assured.

Back in London Keith cut a handsome figure. He was seen as eligible and prosperous, with a dash of Antipodean exoticism. Resplendent in his officer's uniform he enjoyed the profile of being a war correspondent, socialising at the officers' Australasian Club on fashionable Piccadilly and hosting dinners on Saturday evenings at the Piccadilly Grill. In the view of his employer Theodore Fink, Keith was 'a rising eagle of the newest journalism (and I hope best)'. Attention from women was unavoidable. 'Khaki Fever' was everywhere, with one commentator claiming to have seen 'some young Colonials running for their very lives to escape a little company of girls ... [as if] ... they had tigresses at their heels'.

The gift of a cigarette case from Billy Hughes had been accepted by Keith 'as another token of that friendship which is one of my main inspirations'. Keith wrote in his letter of thanks how the case was 'the admiration of the Town' before wryly adding it was costing him a small fortune in cigarettes, 'for only the best are worthy of it, and all must see it and partake of its contents'. Emphasising the elevation in his social standing, Keith remarked that his clothes came from Bond Street and now he had a valet. His previous attacks on those who kept servants while able-bodied men were needed for war duty had apparently been forgotten in his rush up the social ladder.

But things had not seemed so hopeful earlier that year. Keith had told Billy Hughes that his journalistic and public work was his passion and that the social side of his life was still 'undeveloped – I won't say fallow or barren but waiting its chance'. He feared that at the early age of thirty-one he was doomed to remain an uncle and godfather. He had challenged Hughes to use his 'irresistible' Welsh charm in wooing a 'matronly Australian mate' for him.

Hughes teased Murdoch that if he could only restrain his matrimonial ambitions for a little while he would fall victim to the manifold charms of Hughes's daughter Helen. She was only two years old at the time, but the jest was not too far from the mark, as time would prove. (Keith's future wife Elisabeth was then aged seven.)

Keith was visiting the aerodromes of France at around the time Hughes's letter arrived. While his articles to date had been rabble-rousing paeans of praise to soldiers fighting with masculine fortitude, this trip in September 1917 appears to have affected him deeply. The shift in tone and focus – and even the decision to visit aerodromes at this particular time – might have had a deeper and more personal cause. The Australian army chaplain he interviewed said that the men wrote home 'in most loving terms' and 'always put plenty of "wire entanglements" [kisses] at the bottom' of their letters to mothers, sisters and sweethearts. Such loving bonds would help them return home to be better men and citizens of their country, more able 'to protect the women to whom they are devoted'.

Keith might have had three particular women in mind when he wired these emotive lines. As well as his own mother and sister 12,000 miles away, he had a sweetheart in the very heart of London, a young woman who was undergoing the agony of her younger brother being missing in action. She had also just learnt that another brother was transferring to a Royal Flying Corp (RFC) fighter squadron in France. The life expectancy of a RFC pilot was less than three weeks during heavy fighting and the move was effectively 'a form of ritualized suicide'.

Within a week of his trip to the aerodromes Keith wrote his first article that focused on women at war. He indicated the type of woman for whom he held respect, and those for whom he did not:

All the old ideas about the New Woman have been shed. She is in short skirts, as du Maurier [the *Punch* cartoonist] depicted her; but she does not wear a man's coat and hat, nor has she a love for tobacco. Those who love tobacco are the useless women of the West End, who put on gorgeous raiment though it is war time, and carry puppies, and crane their necks for looking glasses while they smoke cigarettes in the great hotels.

The 'true new woman' did not wish to imitate man, though she was quite equal to 'heavy responsibility' and willing to work for long, tiring hours. Of particular note were the volunteer hospital workers at the Front and in Britain. Although he did not mention her by name, Keith's impassioned description described the dedication of one such volunteer nurse: his secret fiancée Isabel Law.

The first mention of their engagement comes in a letter from Billy Hughes to Keith at the end of January 1918. Hughes found delight in some 'most "awfully interesting" news . . .!' disclosing that one of Keith's aunts had told him 'her nephew Keith is engaged to be married to a young leddy named Law, dochter of Bonar Law Chancellor of the Exchequer no less! What do you think of such goings on ye graceless young devil? Why did ye no tell it me? Eh but you're the sly one!' Hughes ended with a flourish, wishing that Keith and his 'line live 10,000 years . . .!!'

It is easy to imagine why Hughes's hard-to-decipher scrawl hid the importance of the information this letter contained when the Murdoch Papers were selected and donated to the National Library of Australia. Following this date there is a gap in the retained correspondence between the pair; the next surviving letter to be found is in the Hughes Papers. Written by Keith on 3 May 1918 it is marked

'Confidential' with a handwritten postscript 'Tear this Up', perhaps indicating similar previous instructions that had been carried out.

A single reference has possibly been viewed as too weak a source for previous biographers: all have drawn mainly on the papers supplied by the family and do not mention the engagement. But in a diary entry for 3 March 1918, George Ernest ('Peking') Morrison, the Australian journalist and political adviser to the Chinese government, recorded a meeting with his friend Theodore Fink in Melbourne. Fink had recommended that Morrison contact Keith Murdoch, who was 'the correspondent of the *Herald*, intimate with Northcliffe and Lloyd George and to marry the daughter of Bonar Law'.

One undated letter to Keith from Theodore Fink in about August 1919 and marked 'Very Confidential' also referred to Keith's 'intimate statement about an attachment you have formed' in a handwritten note that Keith had appended to his letter of 9 July:

> I am touched by your confidence which of course will be respected scrupulously. But I hope all ~~developments~~ [*sic*] will go as you wish – and as wisely and fortunately for both – as possible. Your choice of your wife and with your experience and testing of life should be such as to make your friends glad.

Fink also referred to the spectre of international distance and the concern with family reactions, but counselled Keith to follow his heart. It seems at least one heart was broken back in Australia. Keith's sister Helen could only add a forlorn postscript to a letter: 'Has Flora still a chance?'

Time and the vagaries of personal correspondence have frustrated the search to establish the course of the relationship between Keith Murdoch and Isabel Law. However, while the details are perhaps lost forever, the reason for Keith's choice of fiancée is easier to discover.

'Charm she had in abundance, but she had something more' was one contemporary verdict of Isabel Law. She was the eldest daughter of the Chancellor of the Exchequer and future British Prime Minister Andrew Bonar Law: Keith had known him since his arrival in London two years previously. By 1917 Isabel was living in Number 11 Downing Street. Only just entering her twenties, she acted as her widowed father's political hostess, even representing him on occasion. In the male-dominated world of Whitehall during the war hers was a rare and privileged spot: a young woman present at formal state events and also privy to the unofficial meetings and dinners in which Keith participated. Her interests and passions were varied; as well as her volunteer nursing, she organised charity concerts and plays.

It is not hard to see why Keith would have been attracted to 'Tizzy', as she was known to those closest to her. She was mature beyond her years, but had a sense of fun and vitality. During often bleak and fraught years she cheered and chivvied her elders along. Sharing the Downing Street car with Lloyd George, she would encourage him to sing the music-hall songs of the moment such as 'Pack Up Your Troubles'.

Her father had been born in New Brunswick, Canada, and was, like Keith, the son of a Free Church of Scotland minister. (Until New York native Boris Johnson in 2019, Bonar Law was the only British prime minister born outside of the British Isles.) He had moved to Scotland in childhood and it was there that he became a Conservative MP and started a family. As a self-declared 'Scotch-Australian', Keith was proud to describe how 'Mr Bonar Law' undertook his 'multifarious and onerous duties in Parliament and at the Exchequer . . . with honest Scottish intellect'.

Like Keith, Isabel was the second-eldest child, and had four brothers and a sister. From a young age it was clear she was a spirited girl and fervent supporter of her father. Visitors arriving to console Bonar Law over the loss of his Commons seat in the 1906 Liberal landslide were amused at the sight of ten-year-old Isabel quite literally wearing sackcloth and ashes. Just three years later Bonar Law's wife died and from that point on, the teenage Isabel acted as 'mother' to her siblings. The coming of war would see her again, now a young woman, having to act as the 'pillar of strength and sympathy to her father in his grief'. The timing of these further tragedies may help explain why Isabel might have wished to keep secret the match with Keith and to delay marriage plans.

The year 1917 proved to be one of tragedy for the Law family, a year in which Isabel needed both personal support and comfort but at the same time to maintain a calm front to protect a father already suffering personal grief. In April Bonar Law's favourite son Charlie was reported missing in action; in June there was a false report of his survival, but his body was found in November.

Another brother Jim had joined the RFC against his father's wishes, lying about his age in order to sign up. Isabel made many trips to the training aerodromes to visit him and soak up the atmosphere, and became involved in the excitement of flight. She also brought home and nursed back to health a large black Labrador that had been struck on the head by an aeroplane propeller. The dog, renamed Farman by Isabel after the offending plane's manufacturer, became the much-loved family pet at Number 11.

In September Jim requested a personal transfer to an active fighter squadron. Three days after starting service over the Western Front his plane was shot down and he was killed.

With the loss of two sons Bonar Law sank into a deep depression. Incapable of work, he 'could only sit despondently gazing into vacancy'. Beaverbrook was not only Bonar Law's political cheerleader – he was 'his closest confidant and trusting friend', as Keith described. Through the support of his newspapers, Beaverbrook had helped Bonar Law 'rise to the topmost place in the Unionist Party' and would eventually guide him on to the role of prime minister.

Following the blow of Jim's death, Beaverbrook believed that taking Bonar Law to the aerodrome at the Front and allowing him to speak to his son's brother officers was the best way of breaking this paralysis of melancholy. After talking to some of Jim's fellow flyers, Bonar Law asked to sit in a plane flown by his son. Beaverbrook and the accompanying officer retreated, leaving the chancellor in the bullet-riddled machine, where he remained for three hours 'sunk in a sombre reverie'. Beaverbrook also tried to help the whole family by hosting weekend escapes away from Downing Street at his country house.

Despite the very real risks, in the summer of 1918 Keith was eager to take to the skies himself. In a letter to Fink he gave an excited description of going up in an aeroplane and seeing the German lines, boasting that only one other British correspondent had done such a thing. His cabled report framed the achievements of the scouting squadron and its 'fair-haired, blue-eyed' leader in shining terms. Keith painted a vivid scene of the 'maze of trenches and a desolation of shelled areas' below. His flyers were 'the very epitome of life and daring', 'one in spirit as they carried Australia's message across Hunland', diving and zooming, showing 'their deadly skill which no Hun would dare to defy'.

London air raids had been simply one of the 'minor horrors' of war for Keith. Despite concerns over the German Zeppelins he bravely refused to descend to the *Times*'s shelter. To Keith, airships represented not just the potential for destruction but for progress in peacetime. Two weeks after his first exhilarating trip high above the Front he looked down to the troops training on Salisbury Plain from a huge four-engined Handley Page bomber. His enthusiasm was unbounded and would remain so, despite the fact that one of the same planes crashed the next day, killing six. He believed that warfare taught the lesson that 'life and progress must be bought with blood and sweat'.

Besides, the old constraint of distance was being annihilated. Buffeted in the air, Keith imagined the engines shrieking: 'Fly, Australians – mail service, passenger service, goods service – fly – fly now!' Once back down on land, the rhythmic beating of the engine 10,000 feet above the ground seemed for Keith to 'spell out p-o-w-e-r, emphatically, irresistibly, continuously'.

Britain was abuzz with talk of a potential flight across the Atlantic, and Keith was excited by the possibilities this heralded for international communication. He claimed it was impossible to find a single aviator who did not anticipate a postal aeroplane service between Europe and the US as an immediate effect of the war. The idea that America was six days from London by boat would soon be passé. The world was shrinking: 'New York is now actually nearer London, owing to the aeroplane, than Edinburgh was 100 years ago.'

Lord Northcliffe had offered £10,000 to the first man to fly the Atlantic. As Keith would emphasise, his mentor had been a leading proponent of aviation from its earliest days. Northcliffe's attention-grabbing prizes had proved not only a spur to public enthusiasm but also to technical innovation. Many of the key stages in aviation's early development had been prompted and marked by the challenges he set down. In the same month of 1909 that Keith had steamed across from Dover for his holiday in Europe, Louis Bleriot had claimed the *Daily Mail* prize for the first successful flight over the Channel. The *Mail* called it the 'dawn of a new age of man'. Keith was to learn a dual lesson: the press could both spur advances in flying and benefit in prestige and circulation from the association with heroic tales.

For this Atlantic challenge Keith had interviewed the designer and manufacturer Frederick Handley Page, receiving the insider tip on the likely best route for crossing: a hop from Newfoundland to the Azores and then on to Portugal. A few days later, Handley Page presciently declared that the time would come 'when an Englishman in New York would see his paper the morning after its publication'.

In early 1918, with the course of the war seeming to have turned in the Allies' favour and new issues being raised by the prospect of peace, the Australian Prime Minister Billy Hughes decided to return to Europe.

Keith had advised Hughes to start work on 'proper propaganda – lecture tours, publicity, and a trade revival' to open the Americans up to Australian views. In an effort to make the stop in Washington, DC a success, Keith liaised with key figures in politics and propaganda, including Northcliffe and Beaverbrook. He helped arrange for Hughes to meet President Woodrow Wilson and conveyed to Hughes the line he believed should be taken in the discussions. Keith had warned Hughes previously that without preparing the ground he would have trouble with Wilson over the division of Germany's former territory in the Pacific. For strategic and defensive advantage Hughes wished to gain control of Germany's islands north of the equator, in the face of Japan's own claims, as well as those south of it around New Guinea. During the meeting Hughes's plea for the German territory was stonewalled by Wilson, who sat 'as unresponsive as the Sphinx in the Desert'. Hughes's subsequent barnstorming speeches to American crowds about a predatory Germany would have been better delivered earlier.

Back in Britain the situation that awaited Hughes wasn't much more hopeful. Keith had already rebuked him by saying that he had been labouring a good deal in Hughes's interest behind the scenes. He was fed up. In contrast to the comprehensive publicity system that Canada operated in Britain, whenever something had to be done for Australia Keith had 'to do it, without reward or recognition, simply because no one else would'. However, he acknowledged that official channels would have been less effective, since 'the real work with the Press' was best 'done by a man outside, standing with special relations with Editors and proprietors' – a candid acknowledgement of the niche that Keith had carved for himself and the modus operandi he now excelled in.

In a reflective and keenly analytical piece Keith told his readers why the Australian prime minister would receive a 'Tempered Welcome' this time round. A year earlier he would have been received with great ceremony, but now his prestige had dwindled. The most enthusiastic supporters of the campaign to make Hughes Britain's prime minister had cried off after the failure of the first conscription referendum, or at least had become lukewarm. Keith, while not informing his readers of his own involvement in the campaign, advocated adoption of the same populist strategy that had worked before: to 'appeal by speech and newspaper direct to the British public . . . then drive home the negotiations with the Cabinet with the power of clamorous popularity'. And this time round there would be competition from other Dominion representatives in London. Yet Keith remained confident that Hughes would be successful because 'he knows the British public, and they have been trained to know him'.

Still exasperated over the skewering of his articles and scuppering of his propaganda strategy in the run-up to the second conscription referendum, Keith was drawing back from Hughes, who had become something of a loose cannon. He made clear that he would not directly manage the publicity operation for the prime minister this time, citing pressure of his other work.

Even so, Keith could not resist dabbling in politics. He suggested a 'small dinner' on the day after Hughes's arrival with Milner, Bonar Law, and General Henry Wilson, the newly appointed chief of the imperial general staff, so that Hughes could secure a 'thorough grip' of the situation. Lloyd George also came to Keith's flat for the 'very interesting' party. At the end of August, Bean confided to his diary that Keith was acting as Australia's 'de facto High Commissioner'. Two weeks later a Colonial Office memo commented that 'Mr Murdoch is we have always understood Mr Hughes's alter ego . . . the mouthpiece of the Prime Minister'.

In mid-July Keith told Fink he had been able to avoid doing 'anything material' for Hughes while at the same time preventing 'any breach with him'. He had simply persuaded Northcliffe to pay some attention and this had helped the publicity officials hold their end up. However, they were doing 'nothing like so well as on the last occasion'.

But Keith had seized the opportunity to accompany Hughes to the Front on one publicity trip: this proved to be the occasion when the prime minister heard direct from the officers and troops of their high regard for Monash versus the intrigue cooked up by Murdoch and Bean. In his uplifting report on the mini-tour, Keith described some of the highlights. These included the forest camp in which Americans were grouped with Australians, parades of troops, 'and finally the Australian flying squadron, whose machines circled, dived, and landed at the party's feet'. As one plane chugged to a stop, an official photographer snapped a rare image of Hughes and Murdoch together: the prime minister and his publicist framed by the wire-tensed wings.

At eleven in the morning on 11 November 1918 the Armistice, signed earlier that morning by Germany, came into effect. In celebration, Isabel Law organised a theatre party and her younger sister Kitty rushed home from school in great excitement. However, Bonar Law could muster no joy at the war's end, remaining 'incredibly depressed'.

Despite the fading of hostilities Keith was as busy as ever he had been during the war. There was much for him to do over the coming months, not only to report the peace negotiations in Paris but once more to act as adviser and speechwriter to Hughes. Even before the official start of the Versailles peace conference in January 1919, politicians and journalists from around the globe had been descending on the French capital. Keith, as official correspondent and unofficial adviser to Hughes, was at the forefront of the Australians attending.

Those making the frequent trips back and forth from London to participate or report discovered that air travel was faster than the boat trains over the English Channel. The reams of paperwork, treaty drafts and despatches also found a new, faster means of transport. On the same day that the conference officially opened, a cable was sent to Australian newspapers announcing that the first postal flight between England and France had carried despatches from Hendon aerodrome to Versailles in little more than a couple of hours. By February 1919 the first 'aerobus' to shuttle between Paris and Croydon just south of London was carrying '14 passengers who played cards and lunched during the flight'. However, this new form of transport was not without its dangers. In May Keith's office had to cable back to Australia the ominous news that the country's prime minister had still not arrived in London after leaving Paris seven hours earlier in foggy conditions.

Keith's relationship with Hughes, who arrived safely after all, became increasingly stormy during the intense negotiations in Paris. He found it increasingly difficult to relay Hughes's intransigent and belligerent stances on Wilson's proposals, the future of New Guinea, restraints on Japan and the need for heavy German reparations, without 'some sort of judgement'. Keith revealed his frustration in a private letter to Fink: 'There is no doubt that he has done badly and injured us. Not a good word can be heard for the Australian delegation, and much of the soldiers' fine name has been lost through Hughes' tactlessness and unscrupulousness.' To Northcliffe, now sidelined by Lloyd George and having to observe the conference from its periphery, he added that Hughes was 'pursuing an utterly reckless mischievous line of policy, and will not listen to his colleagues'.

Charles Bean's personal diary gives details of Keith's continuing usefulness to Hughes as a publicist during this period and his gradually dwindling influence on strategic and political decisions. Accompanying Hughes's small party to Paris, Bean detected that 'Murdoch, and not [Alan] Box, is Hughes' chief confidant and adviser'. Hughes was determined to make his voice heard though Keith, attempting to restrain him, and was 'against this appearing to attack or interfere with Wilson'. Keith was again writing 'powerful paragraphs' for Hughes, 'sitting there with his pipe in his mouth, hammering out on his old Empire typewriter'. As Bean discovered, the effort was in vain. 'Billy cut the speech to blazes.'

Another diarist, Fink's indiscreet friend George 'Peking' Morrison who had now arrived in Europe, shed further light on this fracturing relationship and referred to the secret continuation of another.

In the Parisian spring of 1919 Morrison recorded a lunch with Keith. His first impression was of 'a rather common ugly man' who took pains to emphasise the level of his salary, shareholdings and connections – he saw and studied 'all highly confidential documents on British *desiderata*'. But despite what Morrison initially saw as boastfulness, he realised Keith's relationships with Lloyd George and Hughes were even more 'familiar than he has led Theodore Fink to believe'. Morrison also remained under the impression, a year later than he first mentioned it, that Keith intended to marry the daughter of Bonar Law.

Morrison soon warmed to Keith, however, encouraged no doubt by the information he could provide. They would lunch together at the Press Club, the facility set up by the French government in an opulent mansion to cater for the world's assembled media, which provided 'dinners, shows, lectures, and receptions to meet the great and the near-great'. The American press delegation, struck by the rococo décor – a 'forest of obtrusive nudity' – rechristened it 'The House of a Thousand Teats'. Here over some weeks Keith impressed Morrison with his access and reach, including scoops, private interviews with international leaders, and connections among the increasingly self-important correspondents. One such figure was, as Keith described him, 'my friend Mr Charles H. Grasty'.

An American publisher and another son of a Presbyterian minister, Grasty had chosen to come out of retirement and work as a war correspondent in Europe for the *New York Times*. Following the conference, Grasty wrote that journalists now belonged to 'the same general class as statesmen and diplomats' and were in fact 'a greater influence in the world than many diplomats and statesmen'. These sentiments were no doubt shared by Keith.

Keith might have felt his influence over Hughes slipping but his appreciation of his own role as a journalist-cum-political operative was keen. He told Fink that Hughes was in such 'bad odor here' that he was 'scarcely on speaking terms with Lloyd George, and has only one friend – Northcliffe, whom I could remove from him readily enough'. Hughes would not dare to fight Keith: 'One thing is certain – Hughes could never afford to put me in a position in which I would be forced to expose all I know about his doings during the war.'

Information – who possessed, could suppress or obtain it – was becoming the new currency of power. Great care was taken to keep communications during the Paris conference as secure as possible. The letters to and from London were carried by a special service, bypassing the French post. If flown, they were collected from the aerodrome by 'a King's messenger' who took the mailbag by car to Whitehall. The doors to the British Empire delegation headquarters at the Majestic Hotel were guarded by Scotland Yard detectives checking photopasses. The delegates themselves were urged to tear any discarded documents into tiny pieces and warned to 'bear in mind that telephone conversations will be overheard by unauthorised persons!'

The logistical overload of all the various different issues under discussion resulted in the 'Big Five' powers (the United States, France, Britain, Italy and Japan) attempting to decentralise the work to sub-committees. However, Keith observed how these 'broke down so hopelessly that many commissions were scrapped, and four single heads were put together to think out a way through the maze to peace'.

One area that remained under discussion and the subject of attention was the future of military and civil aviation. As Keith saw it, the world in 1919 was 'rushing into the air age': 'You can hear the beat of the engines every day and night in London. Before long the drone will be an accustomed sound wherever men dwell.'

Major-General Frederick Sykes, the air commander during the Dardanelles campaign and the most prominent exponent of aviation in Britain and throughout the Empire, had been given responsibility for the air terms of the peace negotiations. After flying back and forth between London and Paris, he presented Britain's proposals, not just for German aerial disarmament but crucially for the organisation of worldwide air navigation in the future. He helped write and carry out the International Air Code subsequently ratified by the Treaty of Versailles. His career, driven by a desire for a union of the English-speaking world and the necessity for improved imperial communications, would in time include prominent roles in the founding of the BBC, politics and colonial administration. He would also serve on the board of his friend Lord Beaverbrook's press holdings.

Keith's path often crossed with Sykes's during this period. Sykes was the author of the report that had inspired Keith's enthusiasm on the new 'air age' to come, and he was a source of quotes and information.

Eight years older than Keith, Sykes was a restrained and serious figure, physically slight with a prominent domed forehead. But his intensity and aviation achievements, helped perhaps by the dash of a moustache and the RAF uniform, would soon prove attractive to one particular woman: Isabel Law.

Isabel later recalled that, having seen her father off from the aerodrome on his way to Paris in late 1918, she had cheekily asked to have her first flight. Although this was strictly against the rules, her persistence and charm won over the scruples of a pilot. She had just donned an oversized flying suit and helmet and was about to step outside to the open machine when a 'high official' from the Air Ministry suddenly turned up. She was bundled into a cupboard to spend a nervous ten minutes hiding until the coast was clear. The official, Isabel later learnt, was Sykes.

Within six months the excitement felt by Isabel and Keith during their first flights was to be experienced by thousands across the country. The first of May 1919 marked the official, though shaky, start of aviation for the masses. Under the headline 'Civil and Uncivil Flying', the editor of *Aeroplane* magazine had to caution against the risk of public cynicism following the first flurry of joy flights. The antics of some airman nose-diving over crowds had caused panic not only for those in the passenger seats but also below, with 'people running for their lives'. The editor feared this 'ungentlemanly behaviour' would lead to 'a popular outburst in the Press against aviators, similar to that which in the early days of motoring made all motorists unpopular'. However, the experience of an Australian pilot was, with the help of the press, about to confirm the public's passion for the romance of the air.

Harry Hawker, an airman from Victoria, with his Scottish navigator, Kenneth 'Mac' Mackenzie-Grieve, formed one of the teams racing to meet the *Daily Mail's* £10,000 challenge of crossing the Atlantic. For weeks Keith had updated his readers on the frustrations, including bad weather and possible skulduggery, which were delaying their departure from Newfoundland. The news that a rival American team had set out, taking a lower southern route via the Azores, convinced Hawker to launch the attempt regardless of the risks. Keith's reports stressed the betting odds had sunk to 'five to one' against success.

As the cable lines back to Australia were 'in a shocking condition', Keith had to employ the art of concision in relaying the tale. Readers were informed of the key developments with Twitter-worthy brevity as the drama of the Hawker flight unfolded. Single-sentence updates headed with the time of despatch from London were chronicled under each other in boxed sections on the Australian front pages.

At first Keith's rolling account indicated that Hawker and Grieve were well on track to land in Ireland, but when they failed to arrive concerns set in. With no specific news of the flight Keith detailed the growing public attention in Britain as newspaper runners were 'besieged and their papers eagerly snatched'. He relayed the *Daily Mail's* claim that public interest was at an 'unprecedented' level 'not equalled at the greatest moments of the war'. The poet Robert Graves would later recall bitterly that 'nobody cared' when 'the most critical decisions were being taken at Paris' because 'public interest was concentrated entirely on three home-news items'. First among these, Graves stressed, was 'Hawker's Atlantic flight and rescue'.

When after nearly a week of frantic cabling the pair's rescue was confirmed, Keith wrote jubilantly to Northcliffe: 'We are all delighted about Hawker and personally I am very glad of the connection between yourself and our Australian flyers.' There was to be no rest: Northcliffe cabled back immediately, telling Keith to 'get Hawker's story quickly'. Capturing the human interest element was paramount and press photographers were despatched to illustrate the drama. Grieve's parents were photographed reading the edition of the *Daily Mail* announcing the news of their son's rescue from the sea. More remarkably Hawker's wife was shown, hands clasped, with eyes to the ground in trepidation (her toddler held by a nurse at her side) at the very moment she was told by the local vicar that her husband was not dead as feared, but alive.

Keith described the rapturous reception Hawker and Grieve received on arriving back in London, with the streets 'lined by Australian troops, whilst a Royal Aero Squadron flew' overhead. The rewards of celebrity beckoned but Keith cabled that the flyer had 'refused an offer of £600 a week from the music halls'. Hawker told Keith he was simply 'glad to know that an Australian made the first shot for the trans-Atlantic prize'.

The evidence of the unprecedented scenes, of women collapsing and the swell of crowds captured in photographs and stilted newsreels, shows that Keith's reports were no exaggeration. The public's imagination had indeed been captured and whipped up by the media frenzy. One American newspaper wondered why so much had been written about Harry G. Hawker who had failed to cross the Atlantic, while their compatriot Lieutenant Commander Albert C. Read had succeeded in making the crossing, if not in meeting the terms of the competition. It put 'the unprecedented publicity' around the world down to the personal drama and 'the wholly unselfish attitude of the *Daily Mail* concerning the great news of the achievement which it absolutely controlled'.

An instructive case study perhaps for Keith, but the need to heighten the emotional and human elements of news was a lesson he had started learning through his war reporting. He had already impressed its importance on his employer back in Melbourne. Keith told Fink, who was keen to improve his paper, that 'the public appetite' was for popular news stories: 'if the *Herald* tried for too much seriousness and "respectability" it would beget opposition from a sensational paper and even before then lose readers of the uneducated unthinking class'. Keith hoped Fink would 'not neglect what can only be called the human side of the news and reading matter'. He stressed how it was 'done very well by some of the Northcliffe papers' and 'best of all by the Americans'. Human sentiment was 'a large part of life' and the 'rules of privacy' should 'not debar it altogether from a newspaper'. Keith predicted: 'The new form of journalism in Australia will be strong on this side. I am quite sure that some human story should be told in the *Herald* every day that every reader will read eagerly.'

Barely had the airmen returned and been reunited with their families than a grand celebratory luncheon at the Savoy was held and a special consolation prize of £5,000 awarded. Keith was among the leading London military, media, industrial and cultural figures invited to attend. 'Model flying machines' hung above the diners' heads as they feasted on a menu of *Supreme de Sole Atlantique* and *Salade Southern Cross*, followed by *Timbale de Fraises Northcliffe*. The top table was covered in canvas decorated with the familiar red, white and blue roundels to represent the wings of British planes.

Northcliffe, preparing to be operated upon by his trusted Australian surgeon, was absent but sent a message declaring how the partnership of the Australian flyer and British navigator had 'proved what can be achieved by unity of members of our British Commonwealth. Their flight is as great a step forward in the march of science as was the first important but unsuccessful attempt to lay the Atlantic cable, and it will so rank in history.' Ever with his eye on the human interest element as well as the epic, Northcliffe stressed that just as 'remarkable as the exploits of our two heroes' was Muriel Hawker's 'absolute belief that her husband would be restored to her'.

The presence of another honoured guest, General Sykes, was held up as an example of the risks as well as advances involved in aviation. Sykes sat at the table 'fresh from injuries' sustained in a crash landing that had killed his pilot. Keith presumably joined in the cheers to Sykes's health. Was he aware that this man would soon constitute a rival for Isabel's affections?

As 1919 ended, Keith's life and future hopes were shifting. The engagement with Isabel had been broken off. Quite how, when or why remains unclear, but what is certain is that a romance between Sykes and Isabel started during the winter of 1920. It developed through parties held at Beaverbrook's country house, culminating in an official announcement in *The Times* on 1 May.

Bonar Law's reaction to Isabel's second and successful engagement may partially explain why her earlier engagement to Keith had never been officially announced. When Isabel confirmed that she was engaged to Sykes, Bonar Law's reaction was, 'Oh, Isabel ... how could you, when you knew I was so worried about Ireland!' He telephoned Beaverbrook with the opening words: 'Max, a dreadful thing has happened ...'

Before the Sykes-Law engagement was announced officially, Keith took the opportunity to visit home. By the time of the press hoopla over 'The Politico-Aerial Wedding' – even the *New York Times* headline breathlessly described the couple's departure for their honeymoon by plane – Keith was well away.

7 THE PRINCE AND THE PRESSMAN

In August 2005, the *News of the World* published a seemingly innocuous item of gossip. 'Royal action man Prince William' had been left 'crocked by a ten-year-old during football training'. The fact that this private information had been gleaned from a voicemail helped raise the first suspicions over the practice of phone hacking. Seven years later, as his news empire faced the dual threats of statutory regulation and competition with unfettered online media, a defiant Rupert launched a return salvo. He reportedly ordered *The Sun* to splash a far more eye-catching story involving another prince: 'say to Leveson, we are doing it for press freedom'. The next day's front page was filled with a photo 'exclusive' of William's younger brother partying in Las Vegas under the headline: 'Heir it is! Pic of naked Harry you've already seen on the internet'. (The clearly drunk, then third-in-line to the throne, was at least 'covering his crown jewels with his hands'.) *The Sun* even parodied the traditionally sycophantic coverage of royal events and tours by stamping 'Souvenir Printed Edition' across its masthead.

This mutually dependent love-hate relationship between the press and the Palace, each needing the other for their own popularity, was nothing new. The connection between the Houses of Murdoch and Windsor had begun 90 years previously. The players then had been Rupert's father and the princes' party-loving great-great-uncle.

On 16 March 1920 Keith Murdoch again steamed back from England to Australia. Unlike his retreat home in 1909, this was a very different journey, for he was one of the four official press representatives accompanying the Prince of Wales on his empire tour to Australia and New Zealand aboard HMS *Renown*. He supplied detailed coverage not only for the 250 newspapers taking the United Cable Service, but also for Northcliffe's *Daily Mail* and *Times*. For Keith the tour provided a chance to air his opinions on Empire, Pacific and race relations and the need for improved networks of international communication.

Crucially, the trip to Australia would also allow Keith to negotiate the next stage in his career. Out of his control, however, would be an unexpected spotlight placed on his own growing fame. It would not only be Edward Windsor, Prince of Wales, making front-page news during the tour. Keith Murdoch, pressman, was about to become a man of renown in more ways than he had planned.

Though Keith's participation in the tour has previously been overlooked and primary records are scarce, the plethora of articles he wrote provides a rich source. They are most useful in illuminating Keith's ability to boost a cause and shape public opinion.

Following the long years of war and the fraught months of peace negotiations, the *Renown's* voyage to the southern world was trumpeted as a mark of thanks to the people of the Dominions. As with the wildly successful tour of Canada the previous year, it was hoped that fervour for the Crown and the continuing bonds of Empire would be reinvigorated. To this end, the newest communication forms and press techniques would be employed in a public relations operation capitalising on the celebrity of a cosmopolitan 'Modern Prince'.

In his later years as the exiled Duke of Windsor, the former Prince of Wales recalled of the tour: 'My job was to make myself pleasant, mingle with the war veterans, show myself to schoolchildren . . . cater to official social demands and in various ways remind my father's subjects of the kindly benefits attaching to the ties of Empire.' His casual approach contrasted with the blunt view of the King's private secretary at the time. Writing to the Australian governor-general, the private secretary emphasised the need for the trip to be taken as soon as possible after the troops returned from war. The governor-general had long feared a 'weakening of the sense of dependence on the Mother Country and a fostering of Republican sentiment'. The prince's visit, it was hoped, would prove an Imperial tonic to allay any stirrings of discontent.

With the tour party readying to leave Keith told his readers that this 'important mission' to the southern world was being undertaken by a new type of prince: one who had embraced the new 'co-equality' between the centre of the Empire and its periphery. A decade earlier, Keith had privately dismissed the 'beastly humbug' of archaic, London-centric Royal pageantry: now he declared the prince was shaping a new role. Edward Windsor was not a mere symbol, 'a stately puppet on a stately battleship'. Keith stressed to his readers: 'He wants to know You. He wants to be friends amongst friends, to become just as much a part of Australian life as he is a part of British life.'

Keith had prepared the public through a mounting public relations operation similar to that undertaken for Hughes. Whereas the Australian prime minister was now the 'Little Digger', defender and 'friend of the soldiers', His Royal Highness Edward Albert Christian George Andrew Patrick David of the house of Windsor (formerly Saxe-Coburg Gotha) had been rebranded as the 'Digger Prince': a 'modernised, democratised Prince' for the people. The personalising process, drawing on Keith's interaction with the royal personage, had started months before.

Writing in July 1919, almost a year before the *Renown*'s departure, Keith described the 'Diggers' Favourite' as 'a pleasant youth', still a boy at the age of twenty-five. He had bonded so strongly with the Australian soldiers during his visits to the Front that they had 'admitted him to the full comradeship of "diggerdom"'. Under the headline 'How the Prince Became a Digger', Keith detailed the royal embrace of Australian mateship. Fired with these happy memories, the prince had apparently confided to Keith his desire to visit Australia.

To round out the framing of the persona Keith added tales of the prince's passions for sport, animals, snappy dressing and a dash of romantic intrigue. The prince's features might not have been 'boldly handsome', conceded Keith, but they showed an 'engaging frankness' and 'an honesty that suggests good firm character'. (A somewhat ironic judgement given the decisions he would come to make in life.) Keith detected that the prince – who would later force on his introverted, stammer-afflicted brother Albert the burden of the throne – was himself possessed of a 'natural bashfulness . . . studiously suppressed'.

Now in 1920, about to return home to Australia for the first time in five years, Keith added a further burnish to his own reputation and strengthened his hand in the negotiations due with his employers. Ready to give to Denison and Fink on arrival were letters of praise from Lord Northcliffe, congratulating him on the operation of the United Cable Service during the war. Keith could claim to know these views better even than Northcliffe himself. A copy note to a secretary still to be found in the Northcliffe papers, but absent from the Murdoch collection, reveals that both letters had simply been 'drafted [by Keith] for the Chief to sign'. He responded in kind in a personal letter to Northcliffe that he buttressed with heavy flattery. Keith insisted he was 'certainly coming back' but even if he never met the press baron again he would 'retain this influence to the end of my life'.

The 800-foot-long *Renown*, a 'great white monster . . . glistening clean' as Keith described the 'wonder-ship', finally set off from a cold and stormy Portsmouth on 16 March 1920. This was to be the most fully documented, photographed and filmed royal tour yet. Joining Keith and the three other press correspondents on board were the official photographer Ernest Brooks (the Admiralty's photographer at Gallipoli who had helped Ashmead-Bartlett shoot his Aeroscope footage) and a 'cinema man', Captain Will Barker. The latter's 'topical reels' would eventually be spliced into a feature-length film, *50,000 Miles With the Prince of Wales*, described by its recent cataloguer at the Imperial War Museum as 'every bit as dreadful as its title suggests it might be'.

The tour was also to be the most rapidly disseminated in terms of news. With the advances in technology, updates could not only be cabled and wired but now radioed back and forth across large parts of the world, a situation contrasting markedly with the first royal tour mounted to Australia in 1868, four years before the completion of the Overland Telegraph Line. When unfortunate Alfred, 'the Sailor Prince', had been shot in an assassination attempt in Sydney, details of the incident took more than a month to reach London.

Keith was pleased to report that the prince 'spoke of the coming voyage with pleasure' and was in a 'buoyant and happy mood'. Edward wrote a different story to his mistress Freda Dudley Ward. He was already feeling in 'a complete and devastating hell' at the prospect of the trip, and had beaten a hasty retreat to his cabin to sob.

Ever the advocate, if not always a practitioner, of meritocracy, Keith was keen to emphasise that the prince's personal staff had been chosen 'for quality of brain and character rather than for titles, wealth and favour'. Undermining his point somewhat, he identified the 'Prince's Special Chum' as flag-lieutenant Lord Louis Mountbatten – formerly Prince Louis Frederick of Battenberg. Noting Mountbatten was only nineteen, charming 'and an exceedingly good-looking fellow to boot', Keith predicted great things for him.

For this trip the latest developments in communication and entertainment technologies had been marshalled, both to keep the world informed of the *Renown*'s mission and to prevent the young Prince from getting bored. Along with a printing press, a film projector had been installed, and Keith noted how the prince was 'the most regular attendant at the ship's bi-weekly cinema show'.

As the *Renown* ploughed on across the Atlantic, Keith was stirred by the power of one particularly modern form of immediate communication. He observed that the ship's wireless operators were getting little rest, given the greetings constantly being 'flashed' in.

A fortnight after setting off, the *Renown* reached its first official stop. As a local flotilla met the ship off Barbados in March 1920, Keith declared it 'the greatest day in the island's history since Nelson rid it of French rule'. He detailed how this 'veritable bee-hive of negroes' contained 'only 15,000 whites out of a population of 171,000', with the black population 'beginning to assert their claims of equality'. Issues of race aside, Keith was at pains to draw attention to the current deficiencies in technology and the need for investment: 'As in other parts of the Empire, the people of the West Indies are in desperate straits for communication with the rest of the globe.' A broken cable and an ineffective wireless service had meant the tour correspondents had to improvise.

Keith was doing his best to keep coverage of the tour constant and upbeat, but the prince himself was in desperate straits. Writing from Barbados, Edward confided to Freda Dudley Ward: 'Christ! How I'm loathing this trip; there isn't a single thing to it as far as I'm concerned as what's the use of it all!!' However, there was a diplomatic utility to the unusual westward course taken. The Colonial Secretary had advised Lloyd George that a stop in the West Indies would help reaffirm the ties loosened by the war and serve to 'most effectively discourage American aspirations in that quarter'.

As March 1920 drew to a close, the *Renown*'s huge bulk was carefully navigated through the narrow cut of the newly constructed Panama Canal, only in its sixth year of operation. For Keith, the canal stood as a symbol of the great civilising achievement of man and industry that was now pushing back the jungle: a brave new world of technological innovation and control. In purple prose, Keith wrote of how a 'swampy, fever-stricken, torpid place' had been reborn as the Canal Zone, 'extremely clean, beautiful, healthy, peopled by robust and contented families, fed, clothed, exercised, educated by a paternal Government. All works smoothly. Such is the skill and organization.'

The *Renown*'s stop at San Diego allowed the Californians to demonstrate their further skills for organisation – in this case for mass rallying aided by the latest technology with plenty of Hollywood pizzazz. The prince was driven through a tickertape parade to the huge open-air City Stadium where 40,000 had gathered. With aeroplanes buzzing overhead and cameras snapping, the media circus was intense. Keith recorded from his close vantage point that the prince had to deliver his speech with four film cameras 'turning and snarling within a few feet of him, and with the huge horns of the *magna vox* in front of his face'. As an acute observer and agent of political communication, Keith was deeply impressed. Unsurprisingly for someone who found speech a constant struggle he was also intimidated, predicting these 'electric expanders' would inevitably make Australian public meetings 'more terrible for the electioneer and the public speaker'.

Keith was also studying the Californian press, fascinated by their handling of the visit, the use of personalisation techniques and tabloid sensibility. For these correspondents, 'The Prince was a "regular guy," . . . a "democratic boy," "like Cousin Ed. Home from the naval academy"'. But Mountbatten was incensed by another example of American press methods when an enterprising reporter, seeing the prince leave the dance floor for a few minutes, claimed to have conducted an interview. The account ('a masterpiece of fabrication!'), 'duly appeared in the following day's edition of the *Sun*'.

In Honolulu, there was a demonstration of an early form of paparazzi action. Keith described the scene in the jaunty vernacular style of his American colleagues, though he added ballast to his reports with some stern political commentary on the future of the Pacific region. Keith's lengthy article, relayed across the Pacific 'By Courtesy of the Naval Wireless Service', and published 5,500 miles away the day after it had been written, related that the prince had been followed from the moment he landed by 'four stalking cinematographers', one of whom had chartered a boat in order to shadow the royal barge to shore. At first the prince had turned his back, but the photographer had pleaded with him: 'Be a good fellow, Your Highness, this is my bread and butter!' and he had consented and posed with them, remarking that this was a good example of American persistence.

The ultimate PR opportunity for the prince's party came with a visit to Waikiki beach where the prince made his first attempts at surfboarding and canoeing. The action footage, demonstrating more skill in filming from a parallel canoe than the prince showed with his surfing, took the prime slot in newsreels around the world.

But there was a political agenda too. While graceful natives danced a hula-hula to plaintive music, this struck Keith as 'the swan song of this disappearing race'. The romantic scene he described added poignancy to a stark political point: 'The Japanese in these islands now outnumber the natives by five to one.... And the Japanese increase rapidly.' While the United States was spending 'twenty million dollars on a great naval base' its government 'scruples about preventing the free ingress of a people against whom the base is unquestionably directed'.

Keith was sure that the sensitive prince would see the poignancy of this. However, Edward told Freda that 'The Hawaiian women who danced were too disappointing for words . . . though they knew how to wiggle their fat b---s!!'

On the trip down towards Fiji, the prince was again 'terribly depressed': 'everything looks so inky black ahead of me; starting real hard work again in N.Z. & Australia, which I'm dreading more than I can say'. He confided to Freda: 'who knows how much longer this monarchy stunt is going to last or how much longer I'll be P. of W.?' According to Keith, however, the prince was looking forward 'with boyish eagerness' to seeing the people of New Zealand and Australia.

The Times's lead editorial on the prince's safe arrival at Auckland praised 'Our Special Correspondent' and his 'glowing account of the hearty enthusiasm with which the Heir to the Throne was received'. It emphasised the power of the pressmen in making the effect of the Dominion tours Empire-wide and not just local: 'Publicity is of the essence'. In his own comments, Keith pointed to another key position. Just as important as the ninety uniformed policemen and Scotland Yard bodyguards protecting the prince was the manager of the telegraph department, who 'accompanies the pressmen to secure the promptest despatch of their messages'.

The pre-publicity operation had worked beautifully. Edward wrote privately of the huge, though 'amazingly respectful', crowds: 'they always call me 'Digger', which is the highest compliment they can give me!!' During the tour of New Zealand that followed, Keith's coverage took a distinctly saccharine turn. Front pages carried the expected stories of posies and flags, visits to injured soldiers and dances with pretty local girls. But Keith was also on the lookout for the personalising aside or unexpected moment that humanised the prince, in contrast to the pomposity of the official welcomes and endless speeches. The tale of Prince Charming coming to the aid of a 'lame girl' having trouble taking a snap of him with her new Kodak was typical.

The sheer volume of Keith's reports was phenomenal. Of the eighty paragraphs of text on the front page of the 27 April edition of the *Herald*, seventy-five were attributed to or directly relayed by him, and this was even before the prince had reached Australian shores. Embedded in the reams of print were some wry asides about the whipped-up enthusiasm. Keith mused on whether one rural town was 'going to follow the example' set by another 'and parade even its lunatics in the street' during its welcome pageant.

Just three days into the North Island leg of the New Zealand tour progress was derailed. A strike by the Locomotive Drivers' Union and the sabotage of the pilot train left the tour party 'Marooned in Maoriland'. While Edward was reduced to playing golf and otherwise 'twiddling his thumbs', Keith used the time to type a contemplative piece on modernity and the new order of things to come. He described that a group of Maori chiefs had presented the prince – who was decked out in his eponymous grey checked suit and Guards' tie, 'every inch of him' speaking of 'clean British manhood' – with one of their 'few remaining racial heirlooms':

> With something of that mystical sadness which is never far from the faces of these people they looked at the stripling Prince from the great country of teeming white men, and as he looked back at them with wistful, wondering eyes all felt that the different ages were meeting here across the span of the centuries.

Keith claimed the old chieftains 'knew of the contrast in that room and accepted it, bending low in obeisance to the fair-skinned and fair-eyed youth, eldest son of that great race whose sword had conquered their bodies and whose ploughs, wheels, schools, and laws had conquered their minds'.

Time for such wistfulness and reflection was suddenly removed with the abrupt end of the strike. The tour party left the station at night without public notice, and so only the railwaymen – whom Keith described as now 'eager to show their loyalty to the Empire and their friendliness toward the Prince' – and 'their girls' were there to give 'a warm send-off'. Harking back to the American newspaper coverage of a month before, Keith was keen to personalise the scene for his Australasian readership. He relayed how one man called out 'Hope we didn't disturb your arrangements too much, sir?', while the girls cooed 'Isn't he a peach . . . Fancy him walking, he's just like one of us'.

More than the railworkers and their girls could dare imagine, the prince wanted to be just like one of *them*. Writing to Freda, Edward declared 'the day for Kings & Princes is past'. The Prince of Wales, heir to the Imperial Crown, began signing his letters with the moniker 'Bolshie David'.

Unaware of this, The *Herald's* front page of 5 May boomed 'The Prince's Great Triumph'. The page also held a small article which was, for once during the tour, written by someone other than Keith. A parallel triumph was trumpeted under the headline '"Brilliant Journalist": Tribute to Mr K. Murdoch'. Illustrated with a photograph of Keith, the report relayed the praise heaped on him, as official correspondent of the tour, by dignitaries at the Australian Natives' Association dinner in London.

Glasses might have been raised in toast to Keith's name in the Mother Country, but he was receiving rougher treatment in left-leaning Antipodean newspapers.

'Mr Keith Murdoch's Lie: The Method of the Capitalist Press' ran one New Zealand headline above an article challenging the account of the rail strike. His tour coverage was attacked as being columns of 'sycophancy and snobbishness' beneath 'fantastic headlines'. More light-hearted yet still cutting criticism came from across the Tasman. The *Sunday Times* in Perth composed a special verse 'The Hapless Prince' in honour of Keith and his colleagues asserting that 'Australia owed a lot to these gifted chroniclers and assiduous gatherers of princely personalia':

In their repertoires there's scarcely a superlative remains,
Scarce a wire but drips with treacle that they shed,
The most-trivial occurrence sets them racking of their brains
To put another halo round his head.

Keith was scarcely immune to criticism from the other end of the spectrum either. Mountbatten recorded that there had been private complaints about a long article headed 'The Unpunctual Prince' that blamed the prince for always being late. The tour leaders were furious that such insinuations should be made against H.R.H. 'by one who has been an honoured guest on board throughout the trip'. Keith was absolved after explaining – somewhat disingenuously – that a local correspondent should be blamed. However, Keith's nickname stuck, rankling so much that three decades later the now Duke of Windsor recalled bitterly that each delay in the tour's schedule had added 'to the growing legend of the *Unpunctual Prince*'.

But a far more serious – and this time public – criticism of Keith came with an attack that would make headlines around the world. Back in London General Ian Hamilton had published his diary. The serialisation rights had been obtained by the UCS's bitter rivals, the APA: it was the Melbourne *Argus* that printed Hamilton's justification for breaking his silence over the events at Gallipoli.

Hamilton gave it both barrels. Keith's letter to Fisher, he wrote, had been a 'Guy Fawkes epistle' of 'irresponsible statements made by an ignorant man ... reckless scraps of hearsay'. From the other side of the world, Keith marshalled his own defence in a hurried counter-attack of cables sent via Christchurch. Under the headline 'Keith Murdoch Replies to Critics', the *Herald* set aside the middle third of its front page for Keith's version of 'the facts'. In 'Gallipoli's Story: Secret Page Opened', Keith claimed Lloyd George had told him his 'report' had 'led to General Hamilton's recall, [and] thus to the evacuation'. The great Lord Northcliffe had also backed Keith 'at every point'.

Keith even invoked a historical parallel, citing the case of Sir William Howard Russell, special *Times* correspondent, during the Crimean war. Russell's career and actions do bear remarkable similarities with Keith's, though not always in the positive way the latter perhaps had in mind. Russell had landed with the army at Gallipoli in 1854 on the way to cover the conflict in the Crimea. There he made a name for himself with his vivid despatches and exposure of army mismanagement. But he had also been accused of 'unjustly scapegoating' certain generals and senior officers.

The *Western Argus*, under the headline 'Post-War Controversies', explored the 'comparatively modern institution' of the war correspondent. It was 'difficult to over-estimate his powers in influencing public opinion and he has very seldom been accused of abusing them'. But the newspaper noted that 'Mr Murdoch was 'quite as downright as his accuser and uses the same big stick methods'. The *Sunday Times* in Perth, noting how Keith had recently been described as the only Australian journalist in London who was on terms of intimacy with Cabinet ministers, questioned whether his influence extended to getting military commanders dismissed. Hamilton's recollection that Keith had made him 'feel almost embarrassed by his elaborate explanations of why his duty to Australia could be better done with the pen than the sword' was, for the *Sunday Times*, 'surely the most biting sentence that has ever been flung at a war correspondent'.

In mounting his fight back, one of Keith's first actions had been to fire off a cable to Northcliffe: 'Hamilton savagely attacks me in diary ... would be infinitely obliged if you would reply my behalf in Times Mail.' Northcliffe responded pithily: 'Book dead but will expose in Mail.' A letter to *The Times*'s editor defending the 'eminent Australian journalist' was subsequently printed under the pseudonym 'AN AUSTRALIAN SOLDIER, British Empire Club, St James's Square'. In Melbourne the *Herald* quoted extensively from this letter. Hamilton had his own rejoinder published in *The Times* the next day, rebutting point by point the mysterious Australian soldier's assertions. By this stage, Keith's original source had waded in to the melee: an interview under the headline 'Sir Ian Hamilton Answered: Criticism by Ashmead-Bartlett: Mr Murdoch's Action Justified' was splashed across the *Herald*'s front page.

As the New Zealand leg of the royal tour drew to an end, probing questions were being asked in the Australian Parliament regarding the background to Keith's 'Mission' on behalf of the government in 1915, including the terms of his visit and how much he had been paid. And the sketch-writers had a new character to weave into their satirical takes on the workings of power. One disclosed what purported to be the text of 'another of President Wilson's telegrams to the British Admiralty': 'Daniels states, that Page states, that Churchill states, that Andrew Fisher states, that Keith Murdoch states, that there is no one in England with a big enough brain to run your navy ...'

On 26 May 1920 the royal party stepped onto the Port Melbourne pier before a grand procession led by two state carriages progressed through the city. Mountbatten thought the 'motor cars containing the press correspondents' bringing up the rear 'looked very incongruous and out of place'. However, the scale and mania of a crowd estimated at 750,000 – evidence of a PR job well done – meant that Keith could feel secure in his status.

Keith told his *Times* readers that the throngs of well-wishers were unprecedented - though 'possibly you are tired of reading about them!' Yet for Keith the 'most impressive sight' of the whole tour came with the drill display mounted by 10,000 children at the Melbourne Cricket Ground. It was 'a brilliant spectacle, resembling those modern pictures whose effect is obtained by the assembly of a myriad of infinitesimal dots of colour'. He was stirred not only to thoughts of art and pointillism but to visions of military precision as 'this army of children' moved to the sound of the trumpet 'with the ordered discipline of veterans'. It was not simply the children's good behaviour that struck Keith, however. The man who would later be drawn to eugenics, as we shall see, observed: 'The great majority were fair-haired, witnessing that they were probably of the purest Anglo-Saxon stock in the world today.'

Discipline, organisation and order might have been on display in the massed ranks of the Dominion's children, but their golden-haired prince privately felt so stale that he had 'ceased to worry now' about the tour. Edward told Freda: '[I] just drift along from minute to minute & hardly ever look at the programme & often haven't the least idea of where I'm going . . . Thank God!'

Already drunk after attending a twelve-course naval dinner served at a table shaped like a boomerang, he had drifted along to a smoke social at the Grand Hotel. The event provided an opportunity for Australian journalists to meet their British colleagues accompanying the prince. As Keith would be peeling away from the tour now, the social also toasted his achievements as an official correspondent. One editor waxed lyrical on how 'Mr Keith Murdoch belonged to a younger generation of journalists, and he was known as a man who would go far, although, perhaps, it was never thought that he would "live to mould a mighty State's decrees and shape the whisper of a throne." (Laughter) But he did it!'

When Prime Minister Hughes spoke, Keith was again singled out. Hughes recalled having left Keith 'engaged in shaping the destinies of our mighty Empire'. As the toasts flowed, Hughes let loose with the hyperbole: the journalists had come 'to write a new Odyssey. A more wonderful journey had never been made by any man at any time'.

Keith stood to speak, summoning strength to control his stammer before what must still have been a daunting audience: 300 professional colleagues, including competitors and not a few detractors. Though 'some of the things that he had done while away had possibly been open to criticism', they were done 'for the good of Australia'. Keith moved on to reinforce the points he'd previously made in a speech to pressmen in New Zealand, where he had impressed the 'assembled inkslingers' with 'humorous allusions' to the time when he and their prime minister 'were much together at the Peace Conference'. Keith emphasised the need to gain 'experience by travel' and 'strongly urged that there should be regular interchanges of journalists'. One newspaper reported how his 'world-wide reputation, invested his remarks with a peculiar degree of interest'. In Keith's view, Fleet Street was 'the very centre of the press of the world'; any 'eager man' who went there 'with some of the Anzac spirit' would win through:

> I think the younger men in particular should be encouraged to go to Fleet Street for a short time. I think the press is increasing in power. The London press is far more powerful than it was five years ago, [i.e. before the War] and it has never failed in any crusade which it has undertaken.

One report on the event included a perceptive account of Keith's 'meteoric' 'rise to fame' during the war: 'Keith Murdoch's success has been mainly due to a faculty for "getting there" where others failed. The barriers of messengers and lower officials surrounding Cabinet Ministers and other important personages never succeeded in keeping him out when he wanted to get in'.

On 16 June the *Renown* steamed into Sydney Harbour. The prince's tour would continue around Australia despite another enforced break, when he finally succumbed to the physical and nervous breakdown that had loomed throughout.

A week later the *SS Niagara* steamed out through the Sydney Heads. Keith was aboard with his rival employers, Denison and Fink, and a gaggle of the other most powerful figures in Australian journalism, all bound for the Second Imperial Press Conference in Canada. The month-long voyage across the Pacific to Canada would provide time for Keith to negotiate and forge the secret deal that would set his future career firmly in Australia. However, on arriving in Vancouver he bypassed the conference, carrying straight on back to London. There was a crucially important and influential relationship for Keith to tap before he returned home for good.

8 LESSONS FROM A MADMAN'S BIBLE

'I believe the independent newspaper to be one of the future forms of government.'

LORD NORTHCLIFFE

As Keith Murdoch returned to his desk in the *Times* office at Printing House Square in August 1920, a handwritten note greeted him: 'All Hail to you, and may I get after you at golf soon. N.'

On board the *Niagara* Keith had gained a confidential assurance from Theodore Fink that his ambition to re-enter the Australian press at the level of editor of the *Herald* back in the city of his birth would soon be fulfilled. Keith had honed his skills over the last five years by managing a cable news office. But before departing London again he wanted to absorb how to edit and reform a newspaper so that it became a circulation success with mass appeal. Northcliffe's brain would be mined for all its worth – even though, in Fleet Street and Whitehall, the soundness of that mind was increasingly being questioned.

A decade earlier Keith had been desperate to gather up whatever crumbs he could in the centre of world journalism before returning to Australia. Now, confident and assertive, with success and his name made, he was not only feasting at the table: soon he would be the subject of the toast. But it was not just Keith who had changed since 1909.

Northcliffe, the silent, 'simple and kind' man in unassuming steel spectacles whom Keith had witnessed from the sidelines at the first Imperial Press Conference had become bloated with power and pomposity, a change noted by the Australian journalist and politician Sir John Kirwan: having been 'seemingly shy and retiring', Northcliffe had now 'grown coarse and bulky, whilst in manner he was talkative, self-assertive, impatient and almost aggressive. He did not want to listen to others, but talk himself.' There was a darker strain to all this. Even the official history of

The Times records that 'as early as 1910 there had been whisperings that the Chief was not always in his right mind'. From 1912 he had exploited the paper to promote 'his own personal influence and personal importance', as his 'first "brainstorms", then occasional and slight in their incidence, brought with them a marked degree of megalomania'. Keith was so close in Northcliffe's affections that he could jovially barge into his office without hindrance whenever he wished. (Indeed, according to Charles Sayers, 'The influence of Northcliffe on Murdoch was almost obsessive. His admiration of the man amounted to flattery, unashamed.') It was this proximity that gave Keith an insight into Northcliffe's deteriorating mind and, as Keith conceded, increasingly erratic allegiances.

Previous biographers have glossed over the issue of Keith's awareness of his mentor's declining mental state. The carefully selected Murdoch Papers reveal little. But there are signs to be found elsewhere. The American correspondent Edward Price Bell recalled a Sunday afternoon gathering at Northcliffe's country home, which descended into a 'cauterizing outburst' aimed at Keith. Discussing the modern media, Northcliffe had railed with 'flaming words against all who "soil the souls of children"', declaring:

> I see a girl or boy, a young woman or man, reading a diseased book or watching a diseased picture or play, and I'm a murderer at heart. It's the only time homicide looks really good to me. I yearn to punish the producer and circulator of the stuff. I don't want to assassinate him; I want to stand up to him face to face and *cut him down*.

Bell and Murdoch listened mute as Northcliffe's onslaught continued:

> For what is the wretch doing? Poisoning the wells! Bringing feebleness, misery, decay, death to the individual and to the race! Let these basest of the enemies of mankind beware! I tell them, whoever they may be, they are engendering an appalling Nemesis!

Breaking the silence that followed, and displaying the pluck that had in former times endeared him to the most powerful man in Fleet Street, Keith began: 'But, Lord Northcliffe, the writers and publishers of "diseased" matter argue they only are giving the public what it wants.' Keith's pragmatic rationality prompted a 'thunder-cloud' response from Northcliffe: 'Even if what they say were true – and I say it is not – is one to give a baby arsenic because the baby cries for it?' As a Max Beerbohm caricature of the period illustrated, Keith was not alone in feeling Northcliffe's perplexing wrath at 'the demons of sensationalism'.

Despite Northcliffe's protestations of principle, it was his lessons in exploiting both female beauty and man's ugliest acts that proved the most useful to Keith. In the meantime, however, Keith found that the Pacific Question, maintaining

Australia's security in the face of Japan's growing influence and the sanctity of the 'Anglo-Saxon race' were two issues on which Northcliffe's fevered mind could stay fixed. This cemented their bond and ensured their contact even when, as was soon to be the case, they were at other ends of the globe.

On Australia Day, 26 January 1921, *The Times* published a lengthy polemic by the 'well-known Australian journalist' Keith Murdoch. Although Keith acknowledged that the day of Australia's 'Foundation' was now thought to be less important for the 'birth of Australia' than Anzac Day, it was an apt occasion for considering Australia's prospects. Keith drew an Arcadian scene of the country's development and people: 'Australia has the purest stock in the Empire. And do you not think that the world's cleverest breeders of sheep know the value of it?' However, there was suddenly 'a black query mark' demanding an answer. The great question Britain needed to ask itself was 'will she, if needs be, fight – for a White Australia?' In Keith's view the answer must be an emphatic yes:

> Racial purity is the sacred object, far more sacred to the new generation of Australians than any other worldly tie. Certainly to-day it has become more sacred than the tie with Britain. Can you doubt that it should be so, you who are a great family people and have seen in so many parts of the world the horrors of merging a coloured race with white?

Five years previously, one of Keith's first published scoops on arriving in London had been an interview with Rider Haggard. The famous novelist and fervent imperialist had been researching plans for post-war resettlement of white Britons. Keith explained that the author of *She* and *King Solomon's Mines* had 'asked Australia' through Keith's newspapers 'to regard Anglo-Saxonism as so sacred a doctrine as to justify every possible sacrifice and effort'. Even so, now in 1921, Haggard recorded in his diary that Keith had written what was 'rather an excited article' in *The Times* on the 'white Australia' policy.

Keith had fully intended to provoke debate with what he admitted at the end of the piece was a 'bold summarizing of the issue'. It was followed by a supportive editorial and was republished not just in Australia but in Ireland and even India. Northcliffe sent Keith a congratulatory note. Debate indeed followed, not only through exchanges in the letters page of *The Times* but in private correspondence to Keith from a disgruntled Hugh Denison, who refused to publish the piece in the *Sun* due to its inflammatory nature and, he alleged, inaccuracies. Responding to Denison, Keith defended his article, citing the support and coverage it had gained. In the spring edition of the *Review of Reviews* Keith reinforced his call, stressing the 'great ideal' of 'Race purity': 'Australians would rather their adventure end than compromise by one jot or tittle upon it.' As he boasted, the subject had 'become so lively that every review has an article on it this month'.

In mid-February, Keith accepted with 'great glee' Northcliffe's invitation to join him at his villa in the south of France: 'Lovely girls, golf, and one week more of yourself before I set sail for Australia – irresistible!' Six handpicked others, mainly bright young sparks from the *Daily Mail* and *Evening News*, would make up the group. The stuffier *Times* men were left off the list. Writing to Fink, Keith explained that, despite his sister's very recent arrival in Britain, his priority was to get away for the week with Northcliffe: 'So many questions to get his opinion on, and so fine a chance to interest him thoroughly in my new work.'

The party travelled down in style by the Riviera Express, with Keith entrusted to convey the replenishing stock of cigars for 'the Chief'. Teasingly he warned Northcliffe his golf form was 'plus 2!' Tom Clarke, later to be brought out to Melbourne by Keith to work on the *Herald*, gave an insight into the trip in his *Northcliffe Diary*. The men were treated as 'young millionaires' for a week, Northcliffe handing out francs for the casino as well as advice on 'the problems of the newspaper game'. Amid the 'marble halls, terraces, and gardens', Keith impressed as 'a big, hefty Australian, as jolly and mischievous as a schoolboy'. Clarke observed, 'As he is housed in the *Times* office, he comes in frequent touch with Northcliffe, who has developed a warm personal regard for him which augurs well for his future.'

Northcliffe imparted his knowledge and experience to Keith during walks through the gardens, on the golf course at Mont Agel overlooking the azure Mediterranean and from his eccentric reverse position in bed, feet to the wall. He was most animated that week when conveying the importance of crime news. The police were 'such peculiar cattle' from the top down that a paper had 'to get well-trained crime investigators with a big sense of responsibility, and the faculty of gaining confidence of high and low in the force, and dispelling that suspicion of the Press'. Getting that 'first-class scoop' over your competitors was all. And although Northcliffe's highly paid and well-connected *Daily Mail* team were 'in a position to know better than any of their rivals what is going on', he was still nervous every morning on opening his papers to check they hadn't been scooped:

> We must have more and more exclusives . . . and tell the public so in the story – and tell it them again the next day, and the next day after that, too. Crime exclusives are *noticed* by the public more than any other sort of news. They attract attention, which is the secret of newspaper success. They are the sort of dramatic news that the public always affects to criticise but is always in the greatest hurry to read.

With this attention came boosts to circulation, a key lesson that Keith would absorb and follow to the full nine months later back in Melbourne: 'Watch the sales during a big murder mystery', stressed Northcliffe, 'especially if there is a woman in it.' In the sage of Fleet Street's experience, this was a sure-fire way of capturing 'casual buyers stirred by the big story'. An editor at such a time must put his 'best leg forward to turn out the best possible paper' above and beyond the crime story itself.

The evenings on the Riviera provided a lesson, if one were needed, on the attraction of female beauty, together with the potential benefit in pandering to an employer's whims. (Particularly the case if one's host had fathered at least six illegitimate children, with four women. A son born to the family maid when Northcliffe was aged seventeen, technically his heir, was later placed on his newspaper staff but proved 'an embarrassment' and so was shipped to Australia, where he died in an asylum.) After taking the party to Monte Carlo's Café de Paris to watch the young people dancing, the Chief pointed out that the 'prettiest girl I have seen in the South of France' did not have a partner. Both Clarke and Keith gallantly raced to her aid. Clarke beat Keith to the girl, while Keith quipped under his breath, 'That'll mean a rise in salary for you.' Nonetheless, ever tenacious, Keith would later trump Clarke. He was able to regale Northcliffe with the gossip that on his return via Nice, he had 'found the girl, and she was very kind. We danced a good deal and it was not easy to set off to Paris'.

In his account of the week to Fink, Keith was keen to emphasise that he had joined the trip 'largely because I thought the experience would be useful in my new work'. He had managed to hand over a selection of back issues of Australian newspapers to Northcliffe, who was now writing a long assessment of them. Ever mindful of his future and eager to keep Fink on his toes, Keith told Fink that the Chief had insisted on giving him a letter 'saying that a position awaited me in London whenever I liked to return to it'. With this none-too- subtle, pre-emptive shot across the bows, Keith explained that he would be spending his remaining months in Europe in Northcliffe's various offices, including 'the picture paper offices'. Keith was already overhauling the selection of European papers sent on to the *Herald*, ordering 'more picture papers', which, he stressed to Fink, were 'useful for freshening our minds'. French papers 'which often have good ideas in make-up and show the progress of illustration' were particularly instructive. And using the opportunity of returning through America, Keith would arrange for even more samples and syndicated copy: 'We must give our people good reading matter, and enough of it.'

While these were positive moves for the *Herald*, Keith's letters to Fink also displayed a cut-throat negativity and ability to stir the pot. He had shown Northcliffe a letter from the Sydney *Sun* querying his application for two months' leave, so prompting the press baron's indignation. Keith gloated: 'I fancy that our friend H. R. D. [Denison] will get a frigid welcome if he comes [to London]. It will take some of the starch out of him.' Keith went further, telling Fink of Denison's last letter 'in which he accuses you of unpartnerlike action', enclosing a copy for good measure. On hearing that Denison had registered the *Sun* title in Melbourne, a precursor to launching an evening rival to the *Herald*, Keith asserted that the move, 'coupled with the threats and foaming at the mouth, will lead us to take our own interests in our own hands and, maybe, attack'.

In his handwritten letter to 'My dear Chief' to thank him for the Riviera holiday, Keith explained: 'I address you as such as the Chief of All Journalists (of all ages) . . .'. It had been 'the greatest privilege that any aspiring young journalist could have'. Keith indicated that Northcliffe's commanding yet paternal management style had impressed him most:

> I did not realise before the extent of your own hold on your staff. You have reduced your control of your vast organisation to a set of coherent principles which these fellows follow and understand – it makes the whole organization coherent. By 'principles' I mean principles of newspaper production and of the craft.

By contrast, ever the operator, he more cynically told Fink that Northcliffe 'cannot resist making his employees feel that they are the puppets of his will'. Nevertheless, Keith produced a memo summarising the key points of advice he had absorbed. He sent a copy to Northcliffe, together with a request for the Chief's last half year's internal communiqués on *The Times*, *Daily Mail* and *Evening News*. Though Northcliffe sent these on, he warned Keith to take care: 'Some of them got into print once and were entirely misunderstood.' Keith would ignore the edict to destroy the copies.

The memo, a scattergun document of sound advice peppered with bizarrely specific examples, provided the framework for the changes Keith hoped to start making at the *Herald*:

> '**Make-Up** – Stop Press is needed . . . Must always contain some late interesting news . . . Make far more use of pictures, especially showing action' . . . 'No **Advertisements** should dominate . . .' In educating the advertiser 'an enterprising Jew draper will be useful'. '**Circulation** – Net sales the foundation of a journal's power'. '**Staff** – A staff is like an orchestra, the editor the conductor . . . Youth is essential, but don't get the old men against you . . . Every Australian journalist should spend three years in Europe and going slowly home through America'. '**Briefs** . . . Pack the news in – condense . . . You want an appearance of fullness and intensity'. '**Sports** – Exploit them. Prizes and Competitions. Pigeon racing (for example)'. '**Serial** – Must be good, or useless'. '**Women** – Run a page every day. Dresses, cookery, social gossip'. '[And in] **General** – Go very slow. "You Cannot run counter violently to the habits of a community . . .'''

Keith would apply these lessons within months back in Australia. The more shaded yet crucial point about the need for sole authority and operational independence would also be acted on – but exactly who was pulling the strings would become an increasingly sore point for those Keith was usurping and, in time, for Fink himself.

Keith spent his final couple of months in Europe soaking up as much experience as he could in the various offices of Northcliffe's empire. The Chief's reports on the selection of Australian newspapers given to him by Keith were annotated with rolling updates on the runaway circulation figures for the *Daily Mail*.

The celebration for the twenty-fifth anniversary of that newspaper on 1 May 1921 provided a public demonstration of Northcliffe's escalating megalomania. His 'gigantic gathering' of 7,000 guests, served by 945 waitresses, sat down to a luncheon at the Olympia Exhibition Hall – the venue for the *Mail*'s Ideal Home exhibitions. Before the meal began, the blessing was delivered 'through the agency of the radiomicrophone, which had been installed by the Marconi Company':

Thou hast endued Thy servant Alfred with many singular and excellent gifts. Grant him health and strength, wisdom and power from on high, that he may continue to serve his time and generation, holding ever aloft the torch of imperial faith, and guiding aright the destinies of this great Empire.

As special hybrid flags fusing the Stars and Stripes and Union Jack were waved, there was a further surreally omnipotent twist. Northcliffe sat closed-lipped at the high table, his beloved mother and long-suffering wife at his side, yet his voice still rang out. Owing to throat troubles, his speech had been recorded on a gramophone record now blaring out through the cavernous space via 'five trumpets of the Stentorphone'. Northcliffe left the lunch early, returning to the newsroom in order to dictate the precise facts and tone to be used in *The Times*'s coverage of the event.

A rather less ostentatious and smaller but no less impressive event was held precisely two months later. The farewell 'Luncheon to Mr Keith Murdoch – A Servant of the Empire', as *The Times* headlined its report, saw more than fifty of the key actors in Keith's career to date, the elite of press and politics, gather at Printing House Square.

The event was captured in what for Keith would remain an iconic photograph. He sits assured, paired in the centre spot with Northcliffe, both resting cigars in their right hands and on their left wrists sporting the modern wristwatches newly popularised by the war. Northcliffe clasps a Stetson while sucking on his spectacles' arm, his posture tense, stare fixed: a glimpse of the rapid deterioration of his mind to come. Immediately behind Keith amid the starched collars, pinstriped suits and pocket watch chains stand the most comfortable and jovial looking members of the group: 'My young friends Ross and Keith Smith ... splendid fellows with extraordinary experiences.' (Keith had been trying to stir Northcliffe's wavering interest in the newly knighted heroes' planned round-the-world flight.) Thomas Marlowe, editor of the *Daily Mail*, sits directly to Keith's right with Wickham Steed, editor of *The Times* and Murdoch's sometime golfing partner, a further seat along; this order perhaps reflects too the priority Keith allotted the publications in learning their techniques. Immediately to Northcliffe's left sits Billy Hughes, in Britain for the Imperial Conference, and Lord Burnham, the proprietor of the *Daily Telegraph*.

Cradled between Keith's knees is a set of golf clubs. Although not mentioned in the *Times* report, these were a parting gift from his friends in Fleet Street. More than the silver inkstand engraved with 'Printing House Square' he was also given that day, they indicated the informal power nexus Keith had entered and prospered in. Over these last weeks he had been consolidating useful links and gaining more informal advice on the golf course as a member of the *Times* Golfing Society. And with just days to go before his return to Australia Keith had been grabbing every last scrap of time he could with Northcliffe, accompanying him to the golf championship at St Andrews. Prominent in those attending the luncheon, listed only after the Australian and New Zealand leaders in the official roll call, was Lord Riddell, chairman of the Newspapers Proprietors' Association and owner of the *News of the World*.

A great patron of Lloyd George, Riddell had perfected the art of political–press interaction through his development of the Walton Heath Golf Club. He gifted the prime minister a country house on the Heath while the golf course itself became the real seat of power in the view of some insiders; one commentator quipped, 'The war is obviously being conducted from Walton's nineteenth hole.'

(Half a century later ownership of the club would pass briefly to Keith's son Rupert, 'an unexpected part of the *News of the World* empire' inherited through his acquisition of the newspaper. Later, an ambitious female editor of the paper would find that learning to play golf was an essential requirement for getting on within the News Corp family. As her star rose, Rebekah Brooks would add sailing and horsemanship to her skill set, lashing tight her bond with the Murdochs and their favoured politicians.)

As the lunch plates were cleared the speeches began. Northcliffe's toast to Keith, the 'brother of the pen' who had done so much during his six years in London, focused on the 'open secret that it was due to his initiative that the Australians and the rest of us were removed from Gallipoli'. Northcliffe's account played fast and loose with the truth and exaggerated his own role. In reply, his voice confident among friends, Keith stressed 'the need of improving vastly the supply of news to the outer Dominions' and 'maintaining London as the news centre of the world'. He described recently standing 'in the syndicating room of a great New York daily' with thirty desks 'each with its own private wire leading to many parts of the world' supplying cheap news. He also trumpeted the immigration work being undertaken by his friends and urged those present 'to look towards the Pacific and send us [Australia] men and women'.

Not to be outdone, and never one to pass up an opportunity, Billy Hughes delivered his own speech. He appealed to the pressmen present – 'you, who really control public opinion' – to push the claim he would be making during the Imperial Conference for cheaper cable rates as a way of uniting the Empire. Northcliffe replied that he might soon have an opportunity to confirm Hughes's reports on Australia's dedication. He would be heading to the country of 'splendid soldiers and gentle nurses' during the winter.

The farewell honour afforded to Keith would not only make headlines in Britain. He saw to it that a detailed report of Northcliffe's words of praise, of his Gallipoli revelations, career and the 'great future' now before him, was reproduced in Australia. Indeed, so full was the account that it ran to two lengthy – and expensive – press cables.

In mid-July 1921 Keith crossed the Atlantic on the *Mauretania*. In the USA again he wasted no time, trumpeting to Hughes that he had 'seen many representative people in New York, Boston and Washington', including the secretary of state and Herbert C. Hoover, then secretary of commerce. (Although not listed in his letter to Hughes, Keith would later claim to his readers that he had also interviewed President Harding in Washington, DC, this 'most thoughtful of American cities'.) Keith impressed on the Australian prime minister that the US administration was very keen for Hughes to be present at the upcoming Washington Naval Conference. Unable to resist offering a guiding hand, he sought to steer Hughes away from his continued support for the Anglo-Japanese naval alliance, outlining 'merely a few ordinary generalizations' (which ran to two close-typed pages). Whatever happened, Keith was confident that Hughes's presence in Washington would bring about 'first class publicity – very necessary publicity for Australia'. Following further stops for research in Philadelphia, Kansas City, Detroit, Chicago and San Francisco, Keith crossed the Pacific.

He arrived back in Australia to a rather grand, though stilted, reception, according to the barbed account published in the irreverent *Smith's Weekly*. In an earlier article *Smith's* had warned Keith of Fink's shifting allegiances made on the golf course: "'Oh, be careful of the crocodile – the crocodile will eat you" ... The advice still holds good, Keithy!' Denison had pointedly sent a copy to Keith. But in September 1921, as the cosmopolitan son made good returned to Melbourne, the power relations now appeared inverted. *Smith's* described the scene:

Assembled to meet the highest salaried journalist in Australia ... were two motor cars (one new) driven by two men in livery (also new), Fink, Chairman of Directors (in a painfully new suit) and [Arthur] Wise, the manager, with a ready-to-wear smile of cordiality for the newcomer.

The 'young Prince' announced he was not going to start work immediately as anticipated: no, he was off to play golf for the next two days. *Smith's* concluded: 'Evidently the Northcliffe–Murdoch golfing partnership has yielded instruction on both sides.'

Just over a month later it was Keith's turn to arrange a welcoming party. Northcliffe arrived after his own stopover in America where, Wickham Steed concluded, he really had been 'off his chump at times'. If the puffery in the pages of the *Herald* is to be believed, the Melbourne stage of Northcliffe's 'world whirl' almost rivalled the Prince of Wales's visit the previous year. The 'monarch of the press' was greeted by a lengthy profile in the *Herald*, 'The Man and his Work – A Romance of Newspapers', written by someone who chose to hide behind the enigmatic moniker 'X'. Curiously, the elements 'X' chose to emphasise when detailing the life and rise of 'at once the most admired and the most vilified man in England' paralleled much of Keith's own experience: the lack of a university education, diligent and tireless early work under 'cloddish bosses, who didn't appreciate good ideas', and thrift for future investment. There were two parts to Northcliffe's success and character. Most obvious was 'the master craftsman' with a 'genius for knowing what news is, fearlessness in presenting it, dynamic energy and thoroughness in organisation'. But crucially married with this was 'the master of affairs' who harnessed his printing presses to the 'nation's causes'. Northcliffe's 'handling of public policies, superimposed upon his genius for newspaper production' made 'him one of the greatest men of our times'.

This was the first in what would be a series of articles by 'X' throughout the week. Great minds were obviously thinking alike on the great problems of the day. 'X' described how he had 'busied' himself on the 'same puzzle' – the Pacific Question – that Northcliffe was investigating. Having just witnessed things for himself, 'X' noted that there were two different tints to the glasses through which the American mind viewed the Japanese. The US was conflicted between the 'Californian question' of the west coast (how it was becoming 'mixed in color' with an influx of Japanese) versus the east coast's blinkered focus on increasing trade with Asia. The view was further blurred by the 'dust and poison gas of the Hearst Press, whose fierce anti-British and anti-Japanese invective makes steady national judgement excessively difficult'. Hearst's success, 'X' argued, was due to his 'poison' working upon 'any illiterates who will stand yellow [press] methods'. While 'X' was glad to note most Anglo-Saxon households in America banned the Hearst newspapers, he stressed that their circulation was nevertheless still huge.

'X' ended his profile by noting that, though Northcliffe was already the subject of many books, 'the most valuable volume' on his work had not yet been written. That volume would detail 'his secrets' on bringing the newspaper 'into close contact with the life of nearly every person'. A personal glimpse into Northcliffe's workaholic day was also given. After waking at 5.00 am, he annotated the margins of all his papers from his bed, circulating memoranda to his staff, while exhausting the five secretaries who took his dictation on rotation throughout the day. It was this close contact, and the copies of Northcliffe's own notes, that Keith had sought and gained.

Over the coming months, as Northcliffe continued his tour and Keith attempted to implement the 'secrets', letters provided further evidence that all was not well in Northcliffe's mind. Indicators of this deterioration would also start to creep into his advice to Keith. Even within the restraints of the regimented five-day programme in Melbourne – luncheons, speeches, golf, photo call reunions with Dame Nellie Melba and tours of the *Herald* office and presses – he had displayed erratic behaviour. A private tour with a citizen of Melbourne who wrote up an account for the *Herald* verged on the surreal. Dropping in to Melbourne High School, Northcliffe mistook the person addressing the students for Asquith, the former British prime minister. Published with this report was a photograph of the 'talisman from his enemies' that Northcliffe was keen to show everyone: a German medallion, now his good-luck charm, without which he never played golf. On one side it featured 'an unflattering likeness, indeed' of Northcliffe; while on the other 'he was depicted as Satan sitting astride a world aflame and feeding the fire with many newspapers'. It was a rather 'strange talisman', the *Herald*'s reporter rightly concluded.

Northcliffe's speeches in Melbourne, which were boomed enthusiastically by the *Herald* if not by the rest of the press, focused on what he believed would be the key consideration for the Washington Naval Conference: whether it was 'possible to exclude Orientals from white countries'. In supporting the White Australia policy, Northcliffe pointed to the recently published polemic *The Rising Tide of Color Against White-World Supremacy* as 'a vital book'. The *Herald*'s mention of the book and Northcliffe's associated views prompted supportive letters to the editor.

An editorial picking up on Northcliffe's concerns, headlined 'Newspapers and the People' and most likely written by Keith himself, trumpeted the need for a free and 'fearless Press' following years of wartime censorship. In a barely veiled attack on Hughes, with whom Keith was increasingly disillusioned, it asserted that Australians were 'kept in the dark' on 'vital matters', even the Empire Conference: 'Salient facts as to the Japanese Treaty affecting the safety of our children are withheld, and other important matters sedulously concealed from Parliament and the public. All this absurdity springs from the political megalomania which obsesses Ministers.' (Ronald Younger, the biographer commissioned by the Murdoch family, writing at some length about Keith's campaign to send an Australian representative to the Washington conference – waged through the *Herald* with Northcliffe's backing – maintains that this was an early 'triumph . . . in his quest to influence national policy'.)

Keith had already absorbed a lesson in managing politicians, and more precisely prime ministers. Power could be exerted through withholding coverage as well as deploying it. When still in London, Keith had written to Northcliffe on Hughes: 'I hope he is going to be taught he cannot play fast and loose with his best friends here and that he won't get much personal publicity.'

While Northcliffe was being whisked around the city by obliging young reporters, Keith was preoccupied with editing the *Herald*. Only weeks into his new role he had to establish his authority. However, a private dinner at the Orient Hotel was held in order for the Murdoch family to meet the visiting Lord Northcliffe. This appears to have been a straightforward and convivial occasion according to family reminiscences and authorised accounts. But Northcliffe would subsequently write to Keith asking for his regards to be passed on to the family 'whom I was not allowed to speak to – you remember that night'. This is a cryptic comment, and it is difficult to establish what did or did not happen during the meal.

On the same pages of the *Herald* where Northcliffe's shrinking frame – the result of a self-prescribed extreme diet – appeared, photographs of the American cinema star Roscoe 'Fatty' Arbuckle beamed out. The sensational tale of the death of the young actress Virginia Rappe after a 'gin-jollification' in Arbuckle's hotel suite – a tragedy that the *Herald* reported the American papers were calling 'The biggest scandal in movie high life' – had just broken. The story marked a watershed in tabloid sensationalism and the vilification of an innocent man in the rush for circulation increases. Within six months Australia would have its own counterpart.

By October 1921 Northcliffe was heading north up the coast of Australia. He related his experiences in a close correspondence with Keith. Meanwhile, Keith set about establishing unilateral control of the HWT, as his mentor advised was essential. In a terse letter to Fink addressed 'Dear Sir', he described his role as that of 'Editor-in-Chief of all the Company's publications', in line with what he believed to have been the spirit of the assurances he had received previously. Keith had fallen out badly with Wise, the manager, and stressed to Fink that 'any interference on his part, or that of any other office, in those sections of the journals devoted to reading matter, or with their staffs, will constitute a crisis and entitle me to retire on compensation'. Keith also applied this pseudo-legalese to any disagreement that might arise between the 'Editor-in-Chief' and any member of the board, including Fink himself as chairman. Keith's ally on the board was William Baillieu, apparently encouraged by Northcliffe to back Murdoch as the surest way of making more money out of newspapers. Having read a scrappily dictated article titled 'Keith Murdoch and the Herald by Viscount Northcliffe', which extolled his protégé's ability in unrestrained terms, Baillieu conspiratorially advised publication as it would 'bring us out into the position that I have been suggesting as necessary'. As we shall see, growing suspicions over Keith and the Baillieu family's aspirations and business connections would come to trouble Fink, and with good reason. (Keith would soon be telling Northcliffe that he and William Baillieu were 'sworn partners and with a certain amount of humouring of Fink manage to do everything we want'.)

Northcliffe, as well as sending articles he hoped would help reinforce Keith's position, was peppering his letters from aboard ship with what at first sight appear nonsensical jottings: 'I hope you will not forget to say "Jim Keeley", three times every morning.' A handwritten annotation on one letter implored Keith to 'Chant thrice daily "Gracious Keeley"'. Another opened with the simple exclamation:

Jim Keeley!
Jim Keeley!
Jim Keeley!

Northcliffe, however, had sound reason for invoking the spirit of James Keeley, Anglo-American former editor of the *Chicago Tribune*. The 'short, bullet-headed man with limitless energy and a robust curiosity', as he was described by one biographer, had forged a career by means of scoops, particularly on crime cases: 'local vice, murder, and robbery, mixed liberally with affairs of the heart'. His initial success empowered the *Chicago Tribune* to declare itself 'The World's Greatest Newspaper'. Keeley had formulated a set of principles for the modern newspaper. It should give 'personal service' and serve the role of an impartial 'friend' to the people against the depersonalisation of the city. The modern newspaper, Keeley stated, 'must enter the everyday life of its readers, and, like the parish priest, be guide, counselor, and friend'. As early as 1895 he was asserting that 'News is a commodity, and for sale like any other commodity.' In a 1912 speech he declared the role of a newspaper publisher was 'to print what the people want to read'. (A view that, as we have seen, was shared more by Keith than Northcliffe.)

Keeley was a key member of the same wartime London press set that Keith moved in, and they are likely to have met. Certainly the international exchange of personnel was an ideal they held in common. Keeley had written a piece for *The Times* published on 4 July 1919 headlined 'The Newspaper Press – It Should Create Good Will – Suggestion for Exchange of Staffs', asserting that 'Knowledge is power, and such knowledge in a score of newspaper offices on both sides of the Atlantic would be a tremendous force toward the spiritual and material cohesion of the two nations.'

A postscript to a further letter from Northcliffe, which has been conspicuously sliced off from the original lodged with the Murdoch Papers but remains as a duplicate in the Northcliffe Papers, advised: 'When during your shaving hour you think about Jim Keeley, don't forget about Denison. Personally, I would rather work with him than anybody I met on the banks of the Yarra [i.e., in Melbourne].' Keith's ambitions were already extending to Sydney, although he viewed Denison as a rival rather than a partner.

In December 1921, just a fortnight after Northcliffe's positive remark about Denison, Keith cabled Northcliffe excitedly with news that he and his 'friends' had plans to seize control of the struggling *Evening News* in Sydney, so taking the fight to Denison's backyard. This was Keith's 'big chance'. He would put in £10,000 of his own money (an astonishing sum at the time) and he wanted Northcliffe to join in for a 'few thousands'. By the following day Keith had secured the backing of the HWT but was still 'most anxious' for Northcliffe's own assistance. He was therefore relieved to read the Chief's cable a couple of days later that he would 'gladlyest' invest £5,000 'as encouragement to others and proof [of] my complete confidence in you'. Northcliffe added that his own name should be published as an investor, providing the clout of backing, and that Keith should make sure he had 'complete control'. The emperor of the press emphasised that 'one man control' was essential in the newspaper business.

As 1921 came to an end Keith could report success in gaining 'big options' over *Evening News* shares as well as written undertakings from the Bennett family shareholders 'that they will vote as I wish'. He was confident that the paper could be 'toned up with the greatest ease'.

Keith would later describe the *Evening News* as having been 'remodelled largely on the *Daily Mail*'. A comparison of the paper before and after he took charge shows a marked increase in the size and number of photographs on the front page, a slashing of text-only boxed advertisements and the introduction of engaging headlines on more localised issues and campaigns. Girls and beauty would come to play a key part too.

Keith had been spending much of his time in Sydney and felt he had been doing 'better with the *News* than the *Herald*' because of the standard of journalists there. It was only once the circulation had been built for both newspapers, though, that Keith felt 'we will begin to make Australia talk'. He told Northcliffe: 'Great political influence and general influence will come in time. And part at least will be yours. That is a certain amount of return for you, isn't it?'

Denison's plan to launch a Melbourne edition of the *Sun* had been stymied when Keith managed to dig out a legally binding non-competition agreement, 'black with dust and forgotten by everyone'. Instead Denison proposed they team up. Though some on the *Herald* board favoured this, Keith was intent on retaining his independence and developing his power. He was already making headway. The 'improved *Herald*' was 'the talk of the town', though its circulation still needed to be higher. As with the *Evening News* Keith was moulding the *Herald* on the classic *Daily Mail* formula. He declared Northcliffe's notes were his 'bible . . . I go to them daily'. He had plans to run a crime fiction serial and mount a beauty competition, among other things. In a Keeley-worthy move, three campaigns – on hospitals, police and the tramways – had been launched. However, actual news, the key driver of circulation, had 'been dead'.

On the same day that Keith sat at his desk lamenting this fact, a Melbourne schoolgirl was due to deliver a parcel to an address a couple of blocks away. She never completed her task. Early the next morning she was found in a dead-end passage: Gun Alley. She had been raped and strangled – culprit unknown. Keith finally had his story.

The *Herald*'s front page on the last day of 1921 broke the news of the 'Brutal Murder in the City – Girl of 12 Strangled and Left in Lane'. It was this treatment of the crime that would give the *Herald* a desperately needed circulation boost and help confirm Keith's ascendancy within the HWT. As with the Son of Sam case exploited by Keith's son on taking the reins of the *New York Post* half a century later, it would also raise the spectre of media-driven moral panic and cynical 'law and order' politics.

Keith sent the New Year's Eve edition of the *Herald* that had first reported the murder of Alma Tirtschke to Northcliffe as an example of the changes he was making to the paper. In the Chief's detailed feedback the front page was 'excellent', the 'news contrast' good. Now with 'some big news … you will get all the new readers you want'. The 'big news' had arrived just in time. The narrative of the murder, the hunt for the killer and the trial would be skilfully broken down and teased out to fill page after page for the next four months. As Keith had recently learnt, pictures were key. As no recent photograph of the victim was initially available, an artist was commissioned to bring her likeness up to date, complete with school uniform. A photograph of the grim alley was also published on the front page, an 'X' marking the spot where her body had been found.

With no immediate leads to follow, the immigration and race agenda was poured into the vacuum, not least by the *Herald*. It claimed that 'features in connection with the crime' suggested 'the work of a foreigner', revealing to its readers that detectives were tracking the movements 'of certain men of foreign nationality – Chinese, Germans and Italians'. An exclusive interview with a doctor 'who has made a study of criminology' proposed that 'one or more members of an alien race may be responsible' as they were 'notorious for actions of this kind against white women, and even white children'; it was 'hard to imagine white men sharing in such a vile business'. The following day, the centre column of the front page declared 'Keeping White – Australia's Plan Assailed' above a report by the special representative Keith had sent to cover the Washington conference.

Heeding the Keeley mantra, Keith brought his readers into the hunt, with headlines declaring 'Public Eager to Help Police'. Letters published on the front page gave voice to the demands of apparent correspondents, bearing everyman monikers such as 'Father of One', that a substantial reward be offered for the capture of the murderer. As well as supporting this call, an editorial backed the 'excellent' idea suggested by a former detective during a *Herald* interview that the full strength of the police should be focused on the crime with 'minor matters … held over'. The following day's front page was dominated by a photograph of the three senior detectives, 'Hot on Murderer's Trail', who had been 'snapshotted as they were discussing the newest developments'. Bowing to the *Herald*'s push, the government put up £250 as a reward.

Beneath the headline 'Earning the Reward – Points to Remember – Help for Amateur Investigators', the *Herald* printed a bullet-pointed list drawn up by 'a student of criminology'. Readers were advised to watch in particular for any young lodgers who had kept to their rooms. The remarkably self-referential point '3.c.' was unlikely to narrow the field of suspects:

Criminals are avid newspaper readers, particularly after they have committed an unusual crime. This desire for news is actuated by fear and vanity. Has any lodger displayed any unusual interest in newspapers since Saturday last by sending out for all the editions, or going out to buy them?

After ten days with no arrests made, the *Herald* raised the stakes by announcing it was matching the government's 'miserly' reward. The front-page story directly underneath indicated the kind of fevered mania to which the populace had been stirred. 'Australia's Accusing Fingers – Use of Concentrated Will-Power Suggested' relayed one correspondent's idea that if on a given signal everyone in the Commonwealth directed their attention to Melbourne, pointed their fingers and stated, 'Give yourself up and confess', the 'irresistible tidal wave of energy directed toward the murderer' would be impossible to resist. A very real and effective pressure was, however, being exerted by Keith through the *Herald* on the government, which was forced to increase the reward fourfold. 'The first offer was utterly inadequate, and it was necessary to tell the authorities so,' an editorial declared. With developments drying up, Keith turned his fire on the initial conduct of the police and their treatment of the Tirtschke family.

Following two days of intense criticism, the police suddenly arrested a suspect: Colin Ross, licensee of the Australian Wine Cafe in the Eastern Arcade near where Alma's body had been found. The *Herald* announced the breakthrough with a full-width headline. Its account of Ross's arrest and questioning included a description of a photographer being frustrated in trying to take a picture by a 'Sympathetic' detective stepping in front of the suspect and waving his hand. (The police would not again attempt to shield Ross from the snappers.) Not to be thwarted, the following day the *Herald* published a courtroom sketch of Ross at the inquest into the death and the day after that the paper managed to present a 'recent photograph' on its front page, unconcerned that this might compromise a fair trial.

As the inquest continued, Ross's face would be juxtaposed with a blown-up and embellished image of Alma taken from a recent school photograph the *Herald* had now managed to track down. Another prominently used *Herald* image would help frame the public's perception of Ross: a shot of the suspect handcuffed, being led from the police van.

On 20 February 1922 the trial began. The *Herald* split its front page between a light-hearted account of the 'wild rush' of the thousands who had queued to gain the few places in the public gallery and a full 'List of Jurymen', together with their addresses and occupations. This unusual move would draw criticism from many quarters for the pressure it placed upon the jurors.

With perfectly planned timing by Keith, the bumper edition of the newspaper covering the first day of the trial also saw the launch of the new serial story secured from the *Daily Mail*. Filling a full page, 'The Vengeance of Henry Jarroman' was ideally suited to Melbourne's current obsession with crime. The story opened with its protagonist, who had escaped the hangman's noose after being sentenced to death, declaring, 'I have been in prison for twenty years for a crime I did not commit.' Irony would be heaped on irony. As the deeply flawed trial of Ross proceeded, the *Herald*'s readers would also follow Jarroman's exciting quest for natural justice.

The *Herald* on the opening day of the trial also saw Keith reach out to the thousands of new readers with two powerful editorials. Both were on matters of 'public affairs' close to his and Northcliffe's heart: a call to 'Safeguard White Australia by Immigration' and an attack on the postal department, asserting that 'the wonderful inter-communication facility that Edison and Bell gave to the Community', the telephone, was 'Wanted by the Thousand'.

As the trial continued the cast of characters provided perfect news fodder, with aggrieved barmaids, mystery witnesses, and a fortune teller named Madam Gurkha who coincidentally advertised her services in the *Herald*'s classifieds every afternoon. Colin Ross presented a solid alibi backed by his family. His defence counsel George Maxwell took to task witnesses for the prosecution – including a barmaid Ross had sacked and a prison cellmate who claimed to have heard his confession – for changing their evidence after reading details in the newspapers. Maxwell pointed to the 'press and public insisting the crime must be sheeted home' to someone, combined with the rewards, as motivating the 'disreputable quintette' of witnesses.

Even before his appointment and the start of the trial, Maxwell had been compelled to write to Keith complaining of the hate mail he was receiving following the *Herald*'s report that he might be Ross's counsel. Keith chose to publish excerpts of the letters from Maxwell.

On 24 February 1922, the day of the judge's summing up, a photograph of the 'jury being shepherded to a hotel for lunch', their faces clearly visible, dominated the *Herald*'s front page. As they retired at 5.20 pm Keith, fearing being trumped by the morning papers, primed the presses and advised his readers that 'If the jury's verdict in the Ross trial is given this evening a Special Edition of "The Herald" will be published'. But it was midday the next day when the verdict of 'Wilful Murder' was returned and the sentence of death passed. Though Ross would proclaim his innocence to his end, the *Herald* declared that the tragic drama had 'reached its sternly logical conclusion'. It reproduced the embellished photograph of Alma under a single-word headline, 'AVENGED'.

The story rumbled on for another couple of months as Ross mounted a desperate appeal. Some prominent figures already regarded the trial as a severe miscarriage of justice. In a swiftly published book on the case, Ross's barrister T. C. Brennan regarded the trial as 'lynch law'. He warned that in future juries must be 'reminded of the necessity of never being stampeded by newspaper or popular clamor into preconceived ideas of the guilt of any man'. A. J. Buchanan, a figure who straddled the legal and newspaper worlds, stated in the book's preface that public opinion had been 'inflamed as it has not been inflamed within the memory of this generation'.

An insight into Keith's concern to dampen the passions he had stoked and to draw a line under the story is given by the journalist C. R. Bradish, then working for the *Bulletin*. Bradish described bumping into the ambitious editor and being asked what he thought should be the proper way to report the execution of Ross due to take place on the following Monday. Bradish replied that the *Herald* 'had reached a new "high" in penny-catching hysteria on a particularly loathsome crime' and that Keith could now 'safely drop to a sober pianissimo'. On 24 April 1922 the *Herald*'s headline declared simply 'Ross Executed – Statement on Scaffold – Protested His Innocence'. Its account that 'death was instantaneous' glossed the grim truth. The drop from the scaffold had been neither quick nor quiet.

Keith's editorial on the day of the execution acknowledged that those opposed to capital punishment had rallied to Ross's side, as they did for 'every condemned criminal'. However, the feeling of the 'general public' in this case, that the sentence of death had been a 'hateful but imperative duty', was correct.

Musing on the case, Bradish observed that Keith 'found the keenest joy in asking an assortment of the populace' from window cleaners to tram guards and mothers 'just what they felt on any subject that was stirring the public weal'. The concern over the presentation of Ross's execution – shown by the new editor who would soon start mounting plebiscites through his press and later pioneer the introduction of opinion polling in Australia – was, Bradish concluded, 'really an advertisement of the passionate integrity of Murdoch's Gallupised mind'. But there was a recurrent pattern here, a cognitive dissonance. Keith could both seek to lead and stoke his readership, acknowledging the power of this influence, and at the same time absolve himself from the possible public reaction.

Keith ended his editorial in unwavering terms: Ross had received 'a fair and exhaustive trial' and 'was rightfully convicted and condemned'. But the man, who had been condemned by the *Herald* and received an excruciatingly slow death by strangulation, the hanging botched, was innocent.

Ross's family would have to wait eighty years before his name was cleared. Kevin Morgan, a librarian, felt compelled to study not only the trial but the contemporary coverage of the crime. He soon realised that it would have been impossible for the jury not to have been swayed or influenced by the reports in the newspapers. Morgan argued that this was one of the first high-profile Australian cases in which it could rightly be said that trial by media had occurred.

Morgan's diligence led to the remarkable discovery of surviving samples of hair from the actual murderer. A forensic analysis including DNA testing proved incontrovertibly that they were not Ross's. For all the whipped-up public panic over immigrants, seedy bar owners and the danger of crazed strangers, the likely culprit was a relative of the victim. In 2008 Colin Ross finally received an official pardon.

(Ironically, Rupert Murdoch would strike an early breakthrough in his career by championing the case of a man found guilty of murdering a nine-year-old girl and condemned to die after an unfair trial. Rupert directed *The News*, the Adelaide newspaper he had inherited, to campaign against the legal and political establishment that had pushed for the conviction of Max Stuart, an indigenous Australian.)

Keith found Northcliffe's letters assessing the *Herald* during the period of the Gun Alley crime coverage to be a 'Godsend'. He reported to his mentor that circulation had rocketed by nearly 40 per cent from the day he had taken the reins as editor. The key reason for this was clear to Keith:

> You remarked 'When a sensation comes you will get all the new readers you want.' Perfectly true. I had only put on about 8,000 when we got a mystery murder – an unprecedented one, leading to such scenes as mounted police having to be called out to check the crowds about the residence of the supposed murderer. That left us with a steady 125,000. Then came the trial, when we were averaging 230,000 or thereabouts, counting our sporting edition. I started the Jarroman serial. Unfortunately I was in Sydney and the serial was not sufficiently boomed. But here we are today with a steady 144,000 [despite] no murder news . . .

He signed off this letter stressing how it 'was great luck getting the murder story, and I doubt if I would have had nearly as good a report to make on sales if some such thing had not happened along'.

In his next letter to Northcliffe, Keith acknowledged that rival papers had attacked him for being a 'Yellow Journalist'. The *West Australian*, at the very outset of the Gun Alley coverage, had described the 'crude sensationalism' of the *Herald*: its pandering to 'the morbid cravings of a section of its readers . . . an outrage of decent journalism'. Another publication had charged him with bringing '*Daily Mail* journalism to Australia'. 'I wish I had!' exclaimed Keith.

Following the trial, this publication argued the experience 'must convince every reasonable citizen of the necessity of limiting the licence of the press in such matters'. The *Herald* had 'acted in a manner that was an excitement to public passion' so that 'the accused was already convicted in the minds of most of the populace before a word had been heard in his defence'. Jury members had been put under intense strain given the 'mob thirst for blood', compounded by the loss of their anonymity: 'The printing of their full names and addresses in thick type was little less than an outrage.'

The *Herald*, however, was already prospering from the crime. Previously construction work on its new greatly expanded Flinders Street home had been halted. But a month into the Gun Alley sensation, its circulation and confidence now booming, building had recommenced. The timing of this success and its dubious foundations, as one of Keith's protégés Cecil Edwards later recalled, meant 'detractors christened our new office the Gun Alley Memorial'. Others personalised it more fittingly as the 'Colin Ross Memorial'.

Northcliffe praised Keith's coverage of the murder and trial: it had been 'extremely well done'. In the same letter he confirmed the runaway success of the newspaper model that Keith was aping. The *Daily Mail* back in Britain was now near 'uncontrollable' in its appeal; Northcliffe's company was literally unable to print enough copies to satisfy demand.

But more ominous asides were slipping into the advice from Northcliffe. He was starting to hurl accusations that would become increasingly unhinged. He thought that Hughes was 'going crazy', pontificating with unintended irony that 'Like many self-made men, he is apt to be dictatorish.' Keith's straightforward request for an engineer to oversee the installation of the *Herald*'s new plant equipment prompted a terse and paranoid refusal. Back in London now, his 'world whirl' over, the press baron cryptically wrote of hearing 'curious rumours here' about Keith.

Through his cables and letters, Keith tried to continue the good humour with conspiratorial updates in a Northcliffean vein: he had 'routed' his enemies at the *Herald* by becoming 'chief officer' of the company. However, he was left perplexed as to why Northcliffe's answers were taking so long. Keith's attempt to control the *Evening News* was now unravelling – both with a shareholder counter-move in Sydney and what appeared to be Northcliffe's sudden unwillingness to offer further funds. Keith implored, 'Don't leave me in lurch Chief', but to no avail.

On 25 June 1922 Keith sat down to write a long letter to his mentor who, he had finally learnt through private cables from friends, was gravely ill. He explained that the triumph in asserting his authority over Wise had been due to the 'increase in circulation by 30,000 a day and the great growth of the *Herald* in popular esteem'. It had been 'a very heavy fight', having to take on 'director after director' but he had been 'greatly helped by the Baillieu party'.

In Sydney Keith remained proud of the remodelled *Evening News*. Although it had 'leapt up 10,000 in circulation', it still needed 'some striking event to lift it higher' – another Gun Alley-type crime would no doubt have proved just the ticket. Once the advertisements had been banished from the front page, he was confident that it would then 'in make-up be the best thing in Australia'.

Keith assured Northcliffe he was reading 'my "bible", your communiqués ... every night'. But the *Evening News* was still 'entirely spoilt' by the advertisements and would remain so until Keith could get his 'teeth in good and hard on the directors'. He signed off by hoping for Northcliffe's 'full recovery, and a long life of good work ahead for you', perhaps even a meeting the following year when Keith thought he might return to England.

Northcliffe never read the letter. While travelling to Cologne at the end of May, he had entered the final, violent stage of his heightened mania. He was brought back to London and his doctor quarantined him within the safety of a makeshift hut on the roof of his house, where it was hoped the breeze would cool his fevered mind. As planes tried out the latest gimmick in advertising, looping '*Daily Mail, Daily Mail*' in smoke trails above, Northcliffe's strength and sense dissipated below. He railed at having been craftily poisoned by German ice cream ('I took a risk going there; they got me'). But even in the flux of his madness, his life's passion and nose for news remained. Fearing eavesdroppers on the line, the Chief whispered down the telephone to the office, 'I hear they are saying I am mad . . . Send down the best reporter for the story.'

On 14 August, so the Fleet Street legend goes, Northcliffe – still 'stalked by phantom Huns' – succumbed to his mysterious illness, 'with a Colt revolver in one hand, a Bible in the other'. The mentor was dead. But the protégé would retain the knowledge imparted and follow the example set. As the 1920s unfolded, Keith Murdoch – 'Lord Southcliffe' – would rise.

9 HEALTHY COMPETITION

The 'survival of the fittest' principle is good because the fittest become very fit indeed.'

KEITH MURDOCH *to his father, 1908*

Edinburgh International Television Festival, 28 August 2009. A century after Keith's letter to his father on the benefits of natural selection, his grandson James Rupert Murdoch delivered a controversial lecture: 'The Absence of Trust'. James attacked the stifling of free-market competition by both over-regulation and the privileged position enjoyed by state-sponsored media, particularly the BBC, which was 'bad for customers and society'. He illustrated the key thrust of his argument with a timely theme:

> This year is the 150th anniversary of Darwin's *The Origin of Species*. It is argued that the most dramatic evolutionary changes can occur through an entirely natural process. Darwin proved that evolution is unmanaged ... The right path is all about trusting and empowering consumers. It is about embracing private enterprise and profit as a driver of investment, innovation and independence.

Within months James would face the consequences of the free reign News International titles had been given in the pursuit of competition-beating exclusives. The revelations of the hacking scandal were perhaps proof that *devolution*, of standards and ethics, also thrived when 'unmanaged'.

Lord Northcliffe, the mentor who stressed the importance of competition against which to fight and so improve, had been dead barely a month when Keith was faced with a new rival to the Melbourne newspaper market. On 11 September 1922 Hugh Denison launched the *Sun News-Pictorial*: a morning tabloid with a light touch and heavy with photographs. The greater threat of an afternoon version of the *Sun* loomed for Keith at the *Herald*. For this first skirmish and throughout the next seven years Keith's editorial intuition, business acumen and populist strategies would be tested and honed. There were to be failures as well as successes, but with drive, dedication and ambition he would come to dominate the battle.

As the decade progressed Keith cultivated an aura of power, augmented by a newly acquired and studiously maintained cultural refinement. During these years of rapid development in technology and improvements in living standards he sought to build optimism and inspire ideals to elevate the population. His publications would trumpet beauty, youth, health and efficiency. At the same time Keith hoped to engage and capture a growing readership with related promotions and features: stories of the motor car, architecture, property and, most significantly, the wireless.

Harnessing celebrity, populism and sensationalism while promoting an almost religiously charged higher purpose of cultural advancement would prove a considerable balancing act. Popular competitions igniting circulation increases would be elevated by the use of fine artists as judges. Potentially controversial articles on social policies would bear the stamp of scientific and academic authority. The competition, Keith felt within, was not always one he could reconcile neatly or without contradiction: a will to succeed coupled with a sensitivity to mitigate or play down more outlandish initiatives.

By the midpoint of the 1920s, keenly aware he was entering middle age, the bachelor editor would also feel the pressure to select and finally win a young woman.

As Keith directed operations from his desk on the third floor of the new *Herald* building, Northcliffe looked down from the photograph taken at the London leaving party. This framed print would remain on the wall of Keith's office for the rest of his life.

Northcliffe's advice, preserved in the copies of 'Messages from the Chief' so precious to Keith, provided the guiding battle plan in the circulation war: first with the *Sun News-Pictorial* and from April 1923 against its stablemate the *Evening Sun* (the *Herald*'s direct competitor). Exclusives, competitions, crosswords, campaigns, comics, serials, sports results and court cases were the ammunition deployed with the aim of gaining new sales ('the basis of our work' as Keith emphasised) and crushing rivals into submission. Advertising layout was revolutionised.

Skirmishes also happened off the page: accountants were tasked to produce verified circulation tallies and selling agents were persuaded to sign exclusivity contracts. Rival newspapers were monitored so that, for instance, their trucks did not break the agreed rules of engagement on delivery times and on the notice period required before publication of 'special editions'. In the view of thwarted biographer Charles Sayers, some of Keith's actions 'bordered on absurdity'. Ridiculous or not, the results would please Fink. For the moment, at least, he could take pride in Keith who would soon be doing extremely well and 'making mince-meat of his opposition'.

As the demands of guiding the HWT's publications increased to the detriment of day-to-day contact with staff, Keith began circulating his own 'Managing Editor's Notes'. (Keith was happily using this new title of 'Managing Editor', reflecting his spreading power, before the official approval of the role by the HWT board in March 1924.) Key lieutenants were kept fully apprised of his reactions to that day's *Herald*, given instructions for the next and treated with nuggets of wisdom on the crafting of news. The remaining copies of these notes provide a fascinating insight into Keith's strategies in the fight for circulation and supremacy.

During 1923 a committee of Melbourne's good and great, including Keith's old foe General John Monash, conducted a competition to design a war memorial for the state of Victoria. Though the winning design for an imposing shrine was greeted with rapturous approval by most newspapers, in early 1924 the *Herald* launched a campaign attacking it. The resulting furore was an object lesson in designing what Keith termed the 'pebbles' that newspapers needed to throw into the pond to 'stir the public'.

The launch of the *Herald*'s 'War Memorial Plebiscite', described since as 'a remarkable experiment in popular democracy', was an early example of what would develop into Keith's passion for and recognition of power in public polling. Readers were asked to cut out the 'Voting Coupons' printed in the paper or, in a doubly profitable alliance for both the *Herald* and its key advertisers, to cast their ballots in the special booths set up in specific department stores. Supposedly representative examples of filled-in coupons were published under the headline 'What People Think'. The 'avalanche of letters' was evidence of 'the people's eagerness to express their opinion'.

Politicians were given a salutary lesson on ways in which the public mind could be whipped up and marshalled on matters other than sensational crimes. Keith had no hesitation in tightening the screws, urging that the campaign should be continued until the Cabinet decision.

Fighting the challenge from the *Sun News-Pictorial*, with its emphasis on photographs and human interest, required a broad front. Eager to lighten the *Herald* and widen its appeal, Keith had introduced a second news photographer. By 1923 he had added a third. He also hoped to lure new readers, both young and old, with the best daily comic Australia could produce.

Advertising proved a key battleground, with Keith impressing on his staff that 'all possible advertising revenue is vital to us'. He greeted the technical achievement of printing a double-page advertisement without a break across two pages (which people had called 'the impossible') with euphoria: 'This means revenue, It means also that the *Herald* leads again.'

Claiming the moral high ground, and with no apparent sense of irony, Keith attacked the *Evening Sun* for pursuing the 'Sydney formula' of 'Sport and Crime'. When it came to covering crime stories, however, the *Herald* journalists and subs were in for a confusing time. Perhaps still stung by the Gun Alley backlash, Keith conceded in an editor's note of April 1924 that it was his fault the paper had not led, as its rivals had, with the story of a man, Angus Murray, controversially set to hang the following day. 'We cannot encourage mob justice, but we must give full prominence to the people's talking point,' was how he expressed this. His writers followed the advice to be 'most reserved' about the execution. But their output was summed up by Keith 'in three words – informative, but dull'.

One of Keith's key actions on returning to Melbourne was to launch a bi-weekly sporting paper. The *Sporting Globe* was printed on pink paper in an echo of Fleet Street's *Sporting Times* (also known as *The Pink 'Un*). The *Sporting Globe* proved an immediate success, marking the first of what would become many profitable engagements with sports coverage for Keith and his descendants.

Across all of his publications Keith warned his staff against the risks 'of "settling down" – that is, becoming stodgy and losing punch'. Internal competitions and prizes were used to attract ideas for articles and innovations. Readers were also drawn into the world of the newspaper with competitions for billboard writing, crossword designing, short stories and essays, recipe competitions and hints for housewives. A racier inspiration, however, had encouraged women to untie their aprons and strike a pose.

When Rupert Murdoch took over the British *Sun* in 1969, it is claimed he told the assembled staff three elements would sell the paper: 'Sex, sport and contests.' In private, his decree was reportedly more forthright: 'I want a tearaway paper with a lot of tit . . '. The readers were told that the *Sun* would be 'the paper that CARES – passionately – about truth, and beauty and justice . . . And about the kind of world we would like our children to live in.' While the front page of the relaunched newspaper led with a 'HORSE DOPE SENSATION' and news of the Prince of Wales's latest girlfriend, the contents box tempted readers to look inside for the 'SUN EXCLUSIVE': 'BEAUTIFUL WOMEN'. Photographs of bare-breasted girls on its third page would soon follow, further boosting the *Sun*'s explosion in circulation. The 'Page Three Idol' competition to find a new model from among hopeful female readers would become a yearly staple, its entry requirements emphasising the healthy and 'all natural – no implants' body images it supposedly promoted. (At the Leveson Inquiry in 2012, the *Sun*'s editor Dominic Mohan defended the paper's 'Page 3 girl' on the grounds that she was meant to represent 'youth and freshness' and to celebrate 'natural beauty'.)

Half a century earlier Rupert's father Keith had shaken up the *Evening News* in Sydney by running a beauty competition. Its winner, the first Murdoch beauty girl, was aptly named Eve.

In one of his excitable communications Northcliffe had told Keith there were not 'enough stockings' in the *Herald*. Although Northcliffe's eagerness during his 1921–22 world trip to offer his views on 'chewing-gum, free love and women's stockings' had led to a ribbing by the American press, Keith took the advice to heart.

(Northcliffe had even sent Keith a saucily annotated postcard from Port Said of a Bedouin girl with a pencilled arrow pointing to her nipple, slyly exposed by the artist.) A few weeks later Keith was able to tell his mentor that he had run 'a beauty competition in Sydney, as you advised, and am now running one in Melbourne to find a beauty to match the Sydney beauty – great fun and great interest'.

In May 1922 the *Evening News* had assembled a 'committee of world-famed artists' as judges to give its winning result what the paper called 'The Stamp of Authority'. After sifting through 2,000 entries of demurely posed head shots, the artists brought together by Keith in Sydney decided unanimously on Miss Eve Gray, a twenty-one year-old stage actress with 'a most delightful complexion, fair hair and blue eyes'.

Following the beauty competition's runaway success in Sydney, in June Keith transferred the concept to the *Herald* in Melbourne as a key offensive in the battle against the *Sun News-Pictorial*. Interstate rivalry had already been cranked up so that it seemed as if the Melbourne public were generating the desire for the competition themselves. Excitement was built with reports of the 'Mailbags of Beauty' arriving in the *Herald* offices. Again, 'Leaders in the Australian art world' were selected as judges.

The competition was spun out over nearly three months with daily photographs and reports on the latest entrants. Bets were wagered on the result; the *Herald* boasted it was 'the one question exercising the minds of the people more than anything else' throughout the state. An exhibition of photographs of finalists at a city-centre gallery proved enormously popular.

To Keith's relief, the eventual winner in straitlaced Melbourne was a securely married woman, happy to take her husband's name and remain at home, shunning the lure of the bright lights. (The racier Sydney victor, Eve, had already adopted a stage name in her quest for Hollywood stardom.)

Just over a year later the intense newspaper rivalry in Melbourne caused by the launch of the *Evening Sun* led to the staging of another beauty competition. This time, however, Keith's sense of probity would be offended. A canny shift in title to 'The Ideal Holiday Girl' and a fivefold increase in the money for the first prize led to a massive response. Instead of demure headshots, entrants were requested to submit photographs of themselves 'in various poses of play and activity'. The lovelies of Melbourne took the hint and shed their clothes with gusto. Again, the handpicked judges were mainly artists, but they expressed po-faced criticism at the nature of many of the shots. In his summing up, one scolded that 'many competitors missed the spirit of the competition' with the posed 'studio pictures of bathing girls, of which there were many' containing 'little or no suggestion of a holiday'. Still, the winning girl apparently met the requirement of holiday spontaneity. She might have been wearing a bathing suit, but she was at least pictured outdoors. That day Keith declared in his note to staff: 'we must all be glad to see the end of this defacement of our paper. Still we would have been unhappy had we not tried out this competition. It has been a lesson in real values.'

Just a couple of days after the result of the 'The Ideal Holiday Girl', Keith threw his full-hearted support behind a new competition, presented as Australia's chance in a 'unique quest'. The *Herald*'s front page posed a question: the 'Best Baby in the British Empire – Where Is It?' The accompanying article explained that this would be no mere beauty competition because the 'health aspect of child development' would be emphasised. Readers were asked to submit 'unclothed and full length' photographs of their children. If selected for the London stage of the competition, 'medical testimony on the physical features of the competing babies' would be required.

Over the next six weeks the *Herald* would conduct the Australian arm of the British Empire Exhibition competition, filling its pages with pictures of the hopeful infants. Keith set up a 'qualified local committee' in Melbourne to determine just who the country's best baby was.

But this time around the judges selected by the *Herald* would not only number famous artists; the committee was to be headed by the vociferous eugenicist R. J. Berry, professor of anatomy at the University of Melbourne. Berry had previously received 'generous financial assistance' from the *Herald* for research measuring the heads of thousands of children as part of his quest for a system to detect 'aments', that is, children with mental disabilities. Sir James Barrett, an academic rival in the field, was the judging panel's deputy chair. Only photographs submitted with the paper's 'Score Sheet' questionnaire pasted on the back would be accepted. The *Herald* warned parents that the question 'Does Baby show any sign of Mental or Physical Defects' was 'of Vital Importance, and MUST be Answered Correctly'. With less than a fortnight until the closing date parents were exhorted to act quickly, as all the photographic studios in the city had a four-day backlog and 'the majority of family physicians [would] be very busy with requests to countersign score sheets'.

Having successfully stretched out the coverage of all the competition stages, the *Herald* finally revealed on 30 July 1924 that Melbourne's winner had triumphed over 60,000 other competitors from around the globe to be named Empire Champion in London. Mere photographs, it claimed, could not do justice to the 'full beauty' of 'little Pat Wilson' with her 'milk-white skin, rosy apple cheeks, blue eyes and rich golden curly hair'. The judging committee's 'reliance on purely eugenic and hereditary factors' had been vindicated, it seemed: 'In little Pat's case, beauty of mind appears to be combined with her physical excellence, and we are all very glad that she has won.' The 'cabled eulogy' from London on the exceptional standard of all the Australian finalists was for Professor Berry 'a remarkable commentary on the theory that the strongest are likely to be the most beautiful'. Keith was delighted, declaring that the competition had put the *Herald* far ahead of other papers. 'The *Herald*'s staff had set out to win the Empire competition, and did so.' The baby quest acted as a springboard for a wider campaign of health and societal betterment run by the *Herald* throughout the year.

Keith wanted the *Herald* to shape and elevate 'public thought' not only through the leader and news pages but also through specially commissioned features and articles. As parents across the city waited to hear the judgement on their offspring in the first stage of the competition, the *Herald* published what it described as a 'strong and powerful article', entitled 'The Problem of the Unfit', by Professor Berry. He posed questions in disarmingly homely Australian terms – 'What cattle-breeder rears his animals from degenerate stock?' – and claimed 'the bolstering up of the unfit at the expense of the fit is the worst form of national gambling'. An accompanying editorial note drew readers' particular attention to 'the constructive proposals' listed towards the end of the article:

1. The creation of the necessary research laboratories for the study of the human product.

2. The foundation of special village communities to which the less fit could be removed ... Harsh though it may sound, there are still others who would be happier in a lethal chamber or allowed to pass through life in a completely sterile condition ...

Berry concluded with a call for legislation to implement these plans, together with a final 'word of wisdom':

Punch's celebrated advice to those about to marry ['Don't'] might perhaps be extended to read, don't marry a moron and don't mistake a disease for a man, for even the Greeks knew that the 'gods visit the sins of the fathers upon the children.'

Driven by concerns over a declining birth rate and how best to improve the quality and health of the population, eugenic theory's promise of a 'managed evolution' gained a foothold in Australia over the next decade. But even before the extent of the grotesque practices carried out in the name of eugenics by Nazi Germany came to light, many critics railed against the theory. Not least among these was Keith's Uncle Walter, a man who would retain his socially liberal and enlightened views throughout his long life, while others hardened in theirs. Nevertheless, in 1936 like minds from Melbourne's elite founded the Eugenics Society of Victoria. The society entered an enforced hiatus during World War II and lay low as the world learnt of the atrocities carried out by the Nazis. But in 1947 the society's secretary was relieved to report back to the head of the international grouping that the branch in Victoria was 'having a vigorous rebirth' as new members joined. Prime among this select, discrete band, the secretary confided, was 'Sir Keith

Murdoch, the most influential newspaper man in Australia'. Keith duly paid his ten shillings for annual membership.

As the climax to its 'Great Health Drive', on 2 October 1924 the 'Herald Health Exhibition' opened at the Melbourne Town Hall. Even the *Herald*'s rivals conceded the event was a huge success. The campaign and exhibition aimed to secure nothing less than '100 per cent health, and therefore 100 per cent efficiency, for Australia'. One of the most popular stalls proved to consist of cots of newborn babies from the foundling hospital. A varied programme of lectures ranged from Dr Grace Boelke's 'Corsets in Relation to Women's Welfare' to Professor Berry's 'The Problems of the Subnormal Mind'.

(The Herald had kept Berry and his theories in the public mind with quotes and comment on events and crimes. Two years after the murder of Alma Tirtschke, another schoolchild was found mutilated. Berry stressed the perpetrator would be a degenerate specimen, 'most likely of the Continental type' rather than of Anglo-Saxon stock. The Herald again gave free reign to Berry's preaching on "The remedy": 'Purify your community by ruthless and constant weeding out of the unfit'.)

In the mould of Northcliffe's *Daily Mail* Ideal Home exhibitions, the Health Exhibition also served as a trade show for the products of *Herald* advertisers, representing 'all the latest labor-saving and hygienic appliances for the modern home'. The crowds were also exposed to demonstrations of the latest communication technology. Pathé Frères unveiled their new 'moving picture apparatus' that delivered an image viewable in daylight.

Another attention-grabbing exhibit presented at the Health Exhibition had been the wireless set specially fitted for 'the hygienic kitchen'. The *Herald* claimed that it would 'enable the housewife to hear broadcast music while she prepares meals – an innovation which will appreciably relieve the tedium of kitchen work'. That same week the *Herald* gave front-page prominence to a new competition: the 'Wireless Voice Search' for an announcer who would become 'better known to Australians than any other public man' when his voice is heard 'daily through the magic ether'.

Earlier in 1924, the HWT board had approved the erection of a broadcasting station on the *Herald*'s roof. The *Herald* declared it would 'mark a new era in world progress': 'Wireless is the Open Sesame to the world of modern miracle.'

As Health Week drew to an end, interest was directed to the opening of the 3LO radio studio, with its 'direct lines to "The Herald" and the various theatres that will provide news and other items for the daily programmes'. Over the ensuing days listeners were presented with a number of firsts, but the main coup was billed as a last: Dame Nellie Melba's farewell performance. (It was actually the first of her many last performances.)

Under the full-page-width banner headline, 'Victorian Broadcasting Begins Today', the *Herald* reminded its readers of Melba's Marconi broadcast that had started the 'boom' four years previously. (In a stunt backed by Northcliffe's *Daily*

Mail, on 15 June 1920 Melba had participated in what was billed as the first ever broadcast of popular entertainment. It was reported her trilling of *Home Sweet Home* at the Marconi station in Chelmsford, Essex, had been heard as far away as Canada.) A further article, ringed by pages of advertisements for receiving sets, batteries and valves, promoted the launch of the *Herald* 'Wireless News Service' for the following day, with details of times to listen to the reports of stocks, markets, weather, news and sport.

Keith was delighted with the blanket coverage: 'Our Melba matter showed that we know how to do Big things Big.'

At the start of 1925, with his new radio station firmly established despite some initial teething problems and a new generation of enthusiasts eager for up-to-date information, Keith launched a weekly radio programme magazine, the *Listener In*. He was proud to announce that 'our baby ... had a happy birth', though, in a somewhat unsettling mixing of metaphors, he cautioned that 'Detailed dissection must wait'. The glossy cover of the launch edition bore a single photograph. Squeezed to the side of a cot, sporting headphones and a wide grin (with a bulky receiver sagging into the quilt), sat a toddler: 'Pat Wilson, the Empire's champion baby, listens-in to bedtime stories.' One gossipy news item inside prompts contemporary reflection: during the broadcast of a church service, conversation snippets 'of a private nature' had been accidentally transmitted. They were most definitely 'not intended for eavesdroppers all over Australia'. It was claimed that even the Prince of Wales had been caught out recently, letting slip after a speech with an aside that 'certainly was not intended for the ether-waves'.

The *Listener In* proved a sellout. Keith added extra print runs and made the periodical fatter: 'When we get a success, let us make it a great success.' Within a month, the *Listener In* had launched a 'Choose Your Own Programme' competition. Entrants had the chance to win prizes, while valuable information on listeners' preferences was guaranteed for the fledgling broadcasters.

In this new uncharted territory populism would prove to be the driver. A *Herald* feature explored the problem that station heads and schedulers faced in connecting with the public. It proposed arranging 'the bulk of the programmes to suit middle-brow listeners' but above all emphasised that 'brighter broadcasting was necessary, which meant getting rid of dreary talks'. Racy photographs of beauties in bathing suits made the leap from the pages of the *Herald* to the *Listener In*. One girl was pictured demonstrating, rather questionably, how clasping 'an old broom to hold an aerial' allowed her 'to listen-in from the surf'.

Given the *Herald*'s recent experience, the *Listener In* was predictably soon promoting its search to find 'The 3LO Girl'. This followed the phenomenal but controversial success of the station's 'Prettiest September Bride' competition. It had culminated in the live broadcast of the winner's wedding, with an excited crowd of nearly 20,000 surrounding the church. In the pandemonium, female fans were pushed under the wheels of the bridal car and the broadcast delayed.

The wedding had already nearly been pulled from the airwaves when the Anglican archbishop refused his permission for the stunt. While he claimed that he did not object to broadcasting a sermon that might do some good, he was opposed to 'broadcasting a strictly domestic ceremony and turning it into an advertisement'. A shift in denomination, location and date kept the irreverent stunt on the air. Keith and his commercial sponsors certainly had a great day, even if the bride's memories were probably less than wonderful. Confronted with the crowd surge, she had 'screamed and fainted at the Church door'. When the service eventually got underway, those radio fans lucky enough to have been among the 1,600 to get inside stood on the pews and behaved 'in an outrageous manner', according to a rival newspaper.

For Keith, however, the pinnacle of the campaign to excite the public about the possibilities of radio (and to steal a march on his competition) came with 'the wireless exclusive' that linked Australia with America at the end of January 1925. This experiment, conducted over three days, promised 'to inaugurate a new era in broadcasting'. The *Herald* again asked listeners to assist by reporting the reception quality of the specially tailored broadcasts from a Pittsburgh station, KDKA. The *Listener In* reported that the words 'To the Melbourne Herald, Australia . . . Stand by for music' had been delivered 'in nasal accents' before 'a saxophone solo, very distant, but wonderfully clear'. Australia and America, already linked in blood, common ideals and language, were 'now linked in voice'. Keith would continue to forge links between Australia and the US for the rest of his life.

In his notes to staff Keith declared that 'boldly constructive idealism' should be deployed to inspire the population. The *Listener In*'s readers were now subjected to an object lesson in the art. The American tests had given 'a little picture of a new world' where the spread of radio would foster peace and unity: 'when national and racial barriers will disappear, when all mankind will be linked up by a vast network of communication and when to know all will be to forgive all'. The *Listener In*'s optimistic columnist foresaw the possibility of a lecture on 'Feeding Babies', uniting mothers in whatever country they inhabited, and doing 'more to spread the doctrine of peace on earth, good will to men, than all the conferences and protocols in the world'. Another commentator was captivated by the romance of it all, predicting that the very 'conditions of life' would be revolutionised: 'the really up-to-date wireless man will never be absolutely separated from his best girl, and soon it will be possible to send half way round the world, if need be, a wireless kiss or an ether-borne cuddle'.

Keith was ecstatic about the results of the wireless experiments, declaring it had 'opened up a new field for us', while the *Herald*'s coverage had been a model of print media, all done in the 'best London style'. In the fight for circulation and influence, he assured his staff, the wireless news 'puts us on a little wave to unquestionable superiority'. To underline the point, Keith had added a number of magazines to the ranks of the HWT during 1924, including the society weekly magazine *Table Talk*.

By the end of 1924 commentators were pointing to the 'journalist snatching and stunting' breaking out in Melbourne as the 'Newspaper War' entered its final stages. Keith was resorting to blatant cross-promotion, pleased to note the *Herald* being 'very kind' to another new purchase, *Punch* magazine.

The war of attrition was soon nearing its costly end. First casualty was the *Evening Sun*. Total victory came in August 1925 with Denison's capitulation and sale of the *Sun News-Pictorial* to the HWT. Keith brokered the deal with his old boss and now had possession of a profitable and successful paper that could only grow. It was an exciting time for Keith, marking his ascendancy in the newspaper world and strengthening his hand within the HWT: a media company now with a range of print titles and developing interests in the new field of wireless. Soon expansion would reach beyond the state.

Before taking control of the society gossip magazine *Table Talk*, Keith had criticised the *Herald*'s coverage of 'unimportant viceregal happenings' for offending the 'many thousands of democratic readers'. An anti-establishment feeling appeared to linger in him: 'We should talk of "society" people very rarely indeed. There is no "society" in Australia, and we do not want to create such distinctions.' Yet he was soon increasing his own social status, playing royal tennis, hosting refined dinner parties and moving in ever more elevated and influential circles.

Keith was mindful of the views of his new set. A typical note conveyed that some 'friendly and acute critics at a dinner I attended tonight said that the "Herald" is too frivolous'. Keith was inclined to agree, feeling 'we are apt to give too much prominence to poor matter'. (His staff would learn to guess with whom 'The Chief' had dined the evening before by the sudden instructions on matters to cover in that day's edition.) Often he would have a hangover of queasy distaste. The prominence given to a 'sordid story' of an alcoholic mother whose baby had starved was particularly repulsive: 'Constantly, such items make me ask, Why? Why? Why? ... We have better things to do.' On another occasion, Keith was riled by a placard announcing the news of a hearse that had upturned: 'Why sensationalise a minor, gruesome, nasty happening? Everyone naturally thinks we live like rats on scourings.' Instead, he stressed that the *Herald*'s house-to-house canvassing had revealed a 'hunger amongst women for more recipes, for hints about renovating furniture and caring for babies, and how-to-make matter about children's clothing – these things are life'. Without missing a beat, he added, 'So are court stories, which we are at present without.'

In society and celebrity terms, one woman would outsing all others in Melbourne during the 1920s. Dame Nellie Melba and Keith Murdoch had struck up a mutually beneficial friendship shortly after they both returned from their expatriate lives in London. In her younger days, Melba had had 'an insatiable appetite for virile young men'. Now in her sixties, the ageing diva preferred the company of attractive, artistic men ('young people with talent and ambition') – such as her assistant and ghostwriter Beverley Nichols. These were men more interested in burnishing her image and bathing in its reflected glow than jumping into her bed.

Keith partied late into the night at Melba's country cottage, exchanged coquettish notes, liaised through Nichols and gained an exclusive series of articles that he syndicated around Australia. Readers from Queensland to Western Australia learnt just how Melba had coped with 'Dame Rumor'. She hoped that her slating of the Australian accent, as she mischievously told her 'Dear Mr "Keith"', would rattle the cages: 'great fun!' When it came to the most famous singer in the world, Keith's concerns over frivolity in the *Herald* were suddenly mute. One front-page headline boomed: 'Melba Hurt – Fingers Trapped in Car Door – Faint in Street.'

Art and dancing proved to be great bonds between the exquisitely dressed bachelor editor and 'the ageing prima donna who, for all the sagging of her face and the thickening of her body, remained a stupendous personality'. It seems Keith's interest in building a collection of paintings and *objets d'art* was encouraged by Melba. One artist close to him believed Keith had not been born with instinctive good taste but instead had worked hard to educate himself in order to 'indulge a growing taste for the best of everything in the way of furniture, glass, old silver, cars, horses and wines'.

In 1928 one of the HWT's new magazines published a gushing, lavishly illustrated feature titled 'A Bachelor's House in Melbourne'. Keith had previously pointed his staff to a lengthy opinion piece in the *Herald* by the supremely well-connected architect Harold Desbrowe Annear, calling for Melbourne's layout and buildings to be improved, an example of Keith's promotion of 'constructive idealism'. Now the *Australian Home Beautiful* (Keith had changed its title from *Home Builder* which he felt smacked of the 'technical journal') described Keith's home, entirely remodelled by the architect. Ancient Chinese ceramics jostled with Chippendale furniture in the drawing room while in the 'dignified masculine' dining room articles gathered in far-off countries conveyed the 'stamp of the owner's personality'. Silver decorated the table, with the oldest piece in Australia, it was dubiously claimed, 'a most beautiful and rare Elizabethan chalice' as the main talking point. 'All the great Australian artists' were represented on the walls.

Keith was not only cultivating his own image but elevating his family's standing. By 1927 he was sufficiently wealthy to commission portraits of his parents from the pre-eminent portraitists of the day. The painting of 'Mrs Annie Murdoch', resplendent in fox fur and glittering necklace, won Australia's most prestigious prize for art. The Murdochs had, very firmly, arrived.

The story of how Keith, the workaholic bachelor, first saw and fell in love with Elisabeth Greene is now the stuff of romantic legend. The tale goes that, checking through a copy of *Table Talk* at his desk, he became entranced by a photograph of the eighteen-year-old debutante. The rest is history – or, rather, a selective version of it.

And yet three years earlier, on 7 December 1923, the *Herald*'s 'Women's World' page had been dominated by a portrait of another serious-looking eighteen-year-old with bobbed hair: 'Miss Peggy Mills, whose engagement is announced today.' Readers were told that 'Margaret, daughter of the late Ainslie Mills of Uardry' was to marry 'Keith, son of the Rev P.J. and Mrs Murdoch'. The following week *Table Talk* (not yet under HWT control) was able to provide further information about the 'lunches, dinner, and dance given to celebrate the event'. The 'poor girl', however, had not been able to take part as she was bedridden, apparently 'still suffering from the effects of a motor accident'. Keith had carried on with the engagement celebrations alone, hosting 'a gay young people's dinner' at the Menzies Hotel before entertaining 'forty guests at a supper dance at Old Admiralty House'. (Peggy did not prove to be the healthy young woman Keith presumably wanted: she was forced to remain on her back in bed for much of the next three years.)

Keith's prospective mother-in-law Lorna Mills, one of Melbourne's 'most famous hostesses', had given a lunch at a select club where the announcement was made. With Scottish roots in one of the oldest lowland families through the patriarch Charles, the Mills clan were sheep-rearing royalty, famous for their highly advanced stud farm. The family's wealth and expertise in selective breeding were to become impressed, quite literally, on Australia: the image of their competition-winning Merino ram 'Uardry 0.1' would adorn the Australian shilling coin until the switch to decimal currency in 1966.

Keith had just celebrated his thirty-eighth birthday; Peggy was less than half his age, as *Punch* (also not yet under HWT control) tutted. In her excitement *Punch*'s social writer told her readers that the 'tremendously successful fellow Keith Murdoch, who contrives to be both an editor and a social lion', had found a 'chick indeed'.

In the recollections appended to her mother Elisabeth's biography, Helen Handbury gave a potential indication of a tale that, though well tidied before her birth, still trailed its threads: 'We lived such a sheltered childhood. I remember worrying, for some reason, that perhaps Dad had been married before. We were never told anything about his fiancée or that side of his life before he met Mum.'

As with the ending of Keith's attachment to Isabel Law, the exact reason for the breaking of Keith and Peggy's engagement and its date are probably lost to history. The connection with the Mills family continued, however. In September 1924, presumably while the pair were still engaged, Peggy's mother Lorna, who was suffering from a heart condition, drew up a new will appointing Keith as a joint trustee of her estate. He was named sole legal guardian of both Peggy and her younger brother in the event of their mother's death. Within half a year the social grande dame Lorna was dead. Thus for the first time in his life, Keith took on paternal responsibility, as guardian of his former (if no longer still) fiancée Peggy and her brother Ainslie, then still a schoolboy.

As late as March 1927 Keith and Peggy were listed next to each other in a report on a society wedding. Within the month, however, another oval photograph of another intense-looking girl with bobbed hair gained a more lasting significance. *Table Talk*'s head-and-shoulders shot of 'Miss Elisabeth Greene, the youngest daughter of Mr and Mrs Rupert Greene', soberly dressed in a high collar, contrasted with the full-length portraits on the same page. The other, older 'Debutantes at Vice-Regal Balls' displayed frilled frocks and fashionably scooped necklines. Perhaps it was this contrast that helped mark Elisabeth out against all the thousands of self-consciously posed images that had passed through Keith's office over the years. Elisabeth was two months past her eighteenth birthday, Keith now in his forty-third year.

A constant theme in Keith's editor's notes was criticism of any publicity given to gambling successes. Rupert Greene was a respected wool-trade expert and, more conspicuously, for three decades the starter for the greatest horse race in the southern hemisphere, the Melbourne Cup. His betting habit imposed a constant strain on the family finances. Elisabeth would later stress he was 'a good father', though conceded he was no way an easy man: short-tempered, 'rather egotistical and quite intolerant of any of our short comings.' Money was a constant worry and the family often ran into debt due to Rupert Greene's addiction to gambling. During his 'rages' he could be vicious and cruel. Elisabeth recalled being told 'I'm going to cut your mother up and put her in a little black box in the garden under the gardenia.' (In time, Elisabeth would come to believe her son had 'inherited his gambling instinct from my father', while Rupert Murdoch himself would stress how his father had dreaded Grandpa Greene's influence on him: 'it was one of my father's nightmares that I'd turn out like my grandfather, which I probably did, a bit.')

Looking back to the time of her engagement, Elisabeth could see she had been 'very innocent and unsophisticated': an 'active sporting type', excelling in 'anything to do with a ball game'. At their first brief Keith-organised meeting at a Toorak charity ball early in 1927, she detected his shyness. She found his eyes, which 'seemed to follow me around the room the rest of the evening', 'big, dark and compelling'. The enigmatic and mature Keith won out over Elisabeth's equally hopeful younger suitors.

A controversial courtship followed. Keith took Elisabeth on motoring trips to the fashionable Mornington Peninsula in his powerful open-topped Itala sports car. To placate the Greenes' concern about the age gap, the couple were often chaperoned by Keith's colleague Henry Gullett and his wife, who by this stage 'were awfully keen for him to be married'. Following a day at the beach with a picnic packed by his manservant, Keith proposed marriage. Elisabeth's immediate acceptance took him by surprise; he had not even bought an engagement ring. Despite saying 'yes', Elisabeth had found the proposal equally 'unexpected':

> In fact, I was still a bit puzzled why anyone would take a fancy to me after seeing my photograph. It really was most peculiar. I thought I was a gawky looking

creature and I had no confidence that I was the least bit attractive . . . there were all these raving beauties around, and Keith Murdoch had chosen me.

The engagement was announced in April 1928, with much less fanfare than Keith's previous one. Peggy Mills had become engaged for a second time in mid-1927, but again it did not lead to marriage. Instead, she decamped to London and stayed abroad for a year.

Elisabeth was conscious of the rumours of a 're-bound' match. She also faced the prospect that her shocked godfather John Riddoch would disinherit her. During a heated exchange, he claimed to Elisabeth's sister Sylvia that Keith was 'a philanderer', asking her, as he went to his library to get a dictionary, whether she actually knew what this meant. Sylvia explained her understanding it was 'a male flirt' – the 'very, very last thing' she would have thought Keith was – before she 'was completely made mincemeat of'. Family jewels had to be returned and Riddoch halted his payments to Elisabeth's bank account. Unsurprisingly, the break between Elisabeth and her godfather proved to be permanent.

Nevertheless, the wedding went ahead in early June. It was a relatively low-key affair, conducted by Keith's father. Gossip columnists were frustrated by the couple's decision to 'dodge publicity', with all arrangements 'kept strictly under the hat'. 'There had been so much controversy over my engagement that I just wanted to keep it quiet and simple,' Elisabeth later recalled.

One prominent guest among the hundred or so was conspicuous because of her ostentatious trilling during the hymns. Melba had been sore about the match, while Elisabeth 'resented the rather proprietorial attitude she took to Keith', always making a 'great fuss of him'. When Keith hosted Melba at his house everything had 'to be laid on' for her, and Elisabeth believed that Melba 'made use of' him. Still, Elisabeth did not have to put up with the diva and her ways for long. Melba died a couple of years later from septicaemia, most likely the result of a botched facelift.

A *Herald* driver behind the wheel of Keith's new Sunbeam took the couple to the honeymoon destination: the country property with a simple single-storey house that was his wedding gift to his wife. Its new name, Cruden Farm, had been chosen by Keith to mark his ancestral roots. But Elisabeth, despite her youth, soon asserted herself, taking command of the domestic staff from Keith's bachelor life and notably dismissing her husband's manservant, 'a little raw, low Scot named Alec'.

An insight into Keith's interior life and insecurities even following his marriage is given in the unpublished memoirs of one of his handpicked employees, C. R. Bradish. At their first meeting, Keith impressed only 'as a man of many hollow snobberies and pretences'. Looking back thirty years later, however, Bradish felt more charitably that 'the man's opulence and success were partly inspired by a hunger for money and position', but also by 'a desire to stifle and ultimately choke a lurking inferiority complex which caught him pitifully in sundry sad encounters'.

Bradish describes one of the 'little eccentricities of behaviour' demonstrated by his 'sensitive' employer. On one occasion when both were staying in Sydney's Hotel Australia, Keith telephoned his employee with the command 'to come down and see him at once':

It was 7 a.m. and, thought I, as I hurried into my clothes, surely this interruption to slumber means that the King is dead . . . But no. As I tapped on his door and diffidently entered I beheld the not over elevating spectacle of 'The Herald's' Managing Editor seated half-dressed before the long mirror in his room and glumly remarking as he surveyed the picture of his far from repulsive countenance: 'Don't you think, Bradish, that I am an ugly looking devil?' That was all. No more and no less!

After delivering the required reassurance, Bradish beat a hasty retreat.

Perhaps to try and overcome such introspection Keith distracted himself with plans for overhauling and extending not only the growing HWT empire but also his personal properties. A spell away on a lengthy business trip provided an opportunity for what Elisabeth at least understood would be simple renovations to Cruden Farm. They returned to discover that under the hands of the same fashionable architect who had previously redesigned Keith's bachelor home, the one-storeyed cottage had evolved into a 'commodious country house in the American Colonial style'. Elisabeth complained that the design, complete with Georgian portico, was far in excess of their apparently agreed instructions. Put on the spot by Elisabeth, Annear explained in his defence that he had been guided by a photograph that Keith had supplied some years before as representing his ideal house.

Although not mechanically minded and a woeful driver, Keith was greatly attracted to large luxurious motor cars and he assumed that his new wife would share this appreciation. As early as 1924 Keith happily reported that the *Herald* had 'become the recognised motor medium' of Melbourne. He predicted that Australia's 'development will soon follow the line of America – where every person in seven including babies, owns a car'. The new transportation craze provided not only lucrative advertising for expanding motoring sections in his newspapers but also exciting news copy and photographs. These included exclusive 'wreck news', complete with pictures from the scene of motor accidents. It also provided fodder for campaigns against government policy or inaction, such as tackling the novel problem of traffic jams. But when Keith arrived home one day in a Rolls-Royce, Northcliffe's favoured marque, Elisabeth exploded – 'Too ostentatious!' Insisting the car be returned to the dealer at once, she refused even a spin down the drive.

Just a few days after their first wedding anniversary came news of a car accident. In normal circumstances, Keith's papers would have gained the best photographs and emphasised the society connections of the young victims. But this event was a personal tragedy for Keith. The Mills sisters, Peggy and Betty, had been travelling with friends to Sydney for a polo match when the steering rod broke and their vehicle dropped three metres into a culvert. Peggy died at the scene.

10 KINGMAKER

At his Select Committee appearance during the phone-hacking scandal, Rupert Murdoch was asked to expand on his 'frequent meetings with Prime Ministers' throughout his career. He batted the question away with a weary retort, raising a laugh in the tense room: 'I wish they would leave me alone.'

Right from the beginning of Rupert's life, political leaders have been a constant presence. Indeed, he would be born in a home that for the preceding nine months had also been, in a sense, the secret nursery to a prime minister in the making. Even as Rupert's life began, an example of political selection through the management of the press and media had already been set.

Melbourne, 1929. In April Keith and Elisabeth had celebrated the arrival of their first child Helen. Not unusually for the period, Helen was to be left behind in Melbourne with a nanny while her parents undertook a whistle-stop world tour. Keith confided in his close subordinate Lloyd Dumas, the man he had installed that year to oversee the HWT's expanding interests in Adelaide, that he aimed to return from this 'dash away ... thoroughly supplied with fresh knowledge of the best ideas and methods of other parts of the world'. Just before they left, Cruden Investments Pty Ltd, the family holding company that would later form the bedrock of a multi-billion-dollar fortune, was established. It had a capital of £200,000 and Keith and Elisabeth were the sole shareholders.

The itinerary of the 1929 world trip included breaks for sightseeing, a drive around the homes of Hollywood stars, West End plays and a visit to the Louvre for Elisabeth's benefit. However, it mostly consisted of meetings. Keith toured newspaper offices and printing plants the breadth of the United States, from Hawaii to Chicago, Salt Lake City to Detroit. In Los Angeles he met with Roy Howard, the Scripps–Howard newspaper chief. That year Howard had unapologetically trumpeted the 'tremendous advances' and what he believed was the power for good of increasing newspaper syndication and chain operations. By 'a system of setting in action identical thought processes in all communities of the nation at almost identically the same time', increased centralisation had 'annihilated provincialism' and was contributing 'to the development of a true American hegemony that is the marvel of the rest of the world'.

One press powerbroker whom Keith did not meet was William Randolph Hearst. *Herald* readers had already been given a flavour of 'The "Devil-Man" of America' with an interview secured by Keith's special roaming interviewer Frank A. Russell. In Russell's view the power of this 'most feared, best hated' man in the United States, 'wielded through a group of newspapers that stretch from coast to coast', was 'in a way, greater than the President's'. Though it appears that Hearst and Murdoch never met in the flesh, before long they were spoken of in the same breath in private reports. (One Australian Broadcasting Commission (ABC) manager confided to a British colleague in 1937: 'Keith Murdoch with his chain of papers and his broadcasting stations is becoming something like Hearst in the United States and is likely to give any Governments some headaches'.)

Back in Australia, Keith had missed a surprise federal election that resulted in a change of government. James Scullin led the Labor Party to a landslide victory, putting it back in office for the first time in twelve years. But Keith and Elisabeth's three weeks in New York in 1929 coincided with a time that would be critical for the whole world: the Wall Street collapse that would lead to the Great Depression, misery for millions and a search by a self-elected few for new leaders to repair the economies of the world.

A week before the stock market crash of 'Black Thursday' the Murdochs were honoured with a dinner thrown by the Australian commissioner-general, together with Keith's 'staunchest supporter' W. L. Baillieu, deputy chairman of the HWT board, with whom they were travelling. William Lawrence Baillieu was 'the pivot around whom the great family fortune, and much else in Australia, turned'. The Baillieus held fast to their tradition of 'loyalty to the family as the highest duty of all', typified in the name of one holding company as Mutual Trust. They would emerge unscathed from the downturn and Keith, regarded as a virtual son since childhood, would forge ahead, powered by the support of their capital and backing. At one point the patriarch had hoped that Keith would become his son-in-law by marrying his daughter. Now Keith, settled with Elisabeth, was building two new families of his own.

Back in Melbourne appeared the first edition of the HWT's monthly internal magazine *House News*, created by Keith to build cohesion while reflecting the expansion and diversity of what he termed 'the House'. (One of Keith's employees, John Hetherington, would write cuttingly that the 'name signified his concept of what such an organization should be: a kind of feudal aristocracy in which everybody pulled together for the greater glory and profit of its ruler'.) This first front page of *House News* presented a somewhat unflattering photograph of a grinning Keith superimposed on the skyline of Manhattan. The 'Chief' had cabled his 'Greetings from New York':

We are fortunate in belonging to The Herald Family, and I hope we will go forward to greater things together. During these hurried travels I have had only one objective – to study where we can improve our journals and their production.

The bar of competition was set at an international level. Now elevated to managing director, Keith insisted: '[W]e must make a big stride forward in services to the public if we are to keep pace with the best papers here.' Inside the cover was a picture of a beaming Helen, the 'Most Talked-of Baby' in the House.

Elisabeth would recall how, during this trip and for the rest of his life, Keith 'always worked so very, very hard'. She had quickly discovered he was a workaholic, driven to absorb all he could, particularly when travelling. Reviewing Keith's manic schedule, Dumas warned 'the trouble is that you do too much'. In Washington Keith again met with W. L. Baillieu's friend Herbert Hoover, though this time Hoover's desk was in the Oval Office following his landslide victory as president. Even the Atlantic crossing to England was utilised for work, with Keith booking a separate day cabin for his books and typewriter. He did find time, however, to head to the ship's sauna in the middle of the night and hobnob in the heat with Winston Churchill, his wartime sparring partner, then returning from a speaking tour of America.

In London, W. L. Baillieu's son Clive, a friend of Keith's since their childhood, acted as host. As the economies of the world unravelled, Keith stocked up on handmade shoes and a rack of Savile Row suits and had Elisabeth fitted out with the finest riding clothes and boots. She winced at the extravagance of the mink coat Keith insisted she accept. There was perhaps a sense of ostentatious over-compensation for the business-heavy nature of the trip.

Business was always paramount for Keith. Even during their east coast honeymoon the previous year, he had suddenly shifted the itinerary to include Brisbane. Elisabeth, who from the start had accommodated his business plans, had agreed immediately. Keith hoped to invest personally in the city's *Daily Mail*. This involved striking a deal with the notorious millionaire John Wren, rumoured to have made his fortune through off-course bookmaking. Through her father Elisabeth was well aware of Wren's reputation but Keith allayed her moral qualms regarding his new business partner.

Another lesson Keith absorbed and applied to his own personal newspaper holdings (later also employed by his son Rupert) was the usefulness of engineering board control even where a minority of the shares were held. By 28 August 1933 Keith held the controlling interest of the newly merged *Courier-Mail* in Brisbane. The 'articles of association of the operating company provided that the Board' was to be nominated entirely by Murdoch, so giving him 'almost entire control of the whole company'.

Keith was welcomed back to Fleet Street in November 1929 with a luncheon in his honour thrown by the Journalists' Institute. His fellow golfing enthusiast, *News of the World* proprietor Lord Riddell, toasted the 'mystic bond of friendship [which] depended on not how often one saw a man, but how one felt'. Keith wrote to Lord Beaverbrook saying he was very sorry that having to depart from London meant he missed the date arranged for their meeting. The fault, he assured him, had not been his and he was eager to renew contact. Beaverbrook in response thanked Keith effusively for the 'splendid leader' article published by the *Herald* on his political agitation – 'our movement', as Beaverbrook termed his Empire Free Trade Crusade – for financial reform.

This right-wing, wildly vacillating campaign to destabilise the party political landscape and undermine the Conservative Party in particular was supported by Northcliffe's brother Viscount Rothermere. It would lead the defeated and exasperated British Prime Minister Stanley Baldwin to denounce the power of the press barons and their 'engines of propaganda' in famous terms (with Rudyard Kipling's aid): 'What the proprietorship of these papers is aiming at is power, and power without responsibility – the prerogative of the harlot throughout the ages.' While Hearst and Beaverbrook put themselves forward as the public faces of their own political ambitions Keith was content to remain in the shadows.

The 1929 British general election had just been fought against the backdrop of increasing unemployment and economic downturn. *Herald* readers had been told that the new techniques and 'Spectacular Methods' of 'Movies, Wireless and Women' were to be used to win seats. The use of microphones to relay speeches was described as one particularly crucial innovation. The contest proved to be close, but Labour won enough seats to form a minority government.

Now on the spot in London, Keith was able to digest the electoral aftermath and learn from a British experience that had been notable for the first bespoke party political broadcasts, and the BBC reporting election results faster than newspapers could.

A further *House News* report outlined that radio station 3DB, another 'baby of the Herald organisation', was attracting some attention. The station would soon be exercised for maximum political as well as commercial advantage. And in a foreshadowing of Keith's grandson James's attacks on the BBC eight decades later, a collision course had been set for Keith against what would become the Australian Broadcasting Commission and its state-funded model.

On his return to Australia Keith found himself under attack. An article titled 'The New Monopoly' had appeared in the short-lived 'independent' newspaper the *Sydney Opinion*:

In recent months the public have witnessed the formation of powerful newspaper combines both in Sydney and in Melbourne . . . each are spreading out their tentacles to secure control of newspapers in other capital cities of Australia . . . It may be doubted whether the people quite realise what this implies. Obviously, however, it amounts to the erection of a new monopoly designed to mould and control public opinion.

The fear was that 'only views agreeable to high finance' would soon 'find adequate expression in the daily press', with 'the practice of that sort of "psychology" which, in the business world, especially in America, is so successfully employed to persuade people that they want what they do not want'. The international situation was pointed to as showing the path – 'the Hearst group controls over a thousand newspapers, and in Great Britain, where the Harmsworth, Hulton and Beaverbrook groups are psychologising and controlling public opinion'. The article concluded with the charge that 'as a controller of government, as the imposer of machine-made opinion in the interests of sectional groups', the press was becoming 'a most powerful agent in the extinction of liberty'. It was a charge that would echo down the decades.

This was part of growing critical coverage against what by 1927, and in the furthest corners of the country, was nicknamed the Southcliffe Press. Following the HWT's strategic success in purchasing Melbourne's *Morning Post*, *Smith's Weekly* also railed against the latest victory for Keith in the Melbourne newspaper battle, calling it 'another death-blow to individuality in journalism'.

The chapter in Charles Sayers's unpublished biography dealing with the spread of what was increasingly dubbed the 'Murdoch Press' in the late 1920s and throughout the 1930s bore the pithy title 'Monopolist'. (The published biography by Ronald Younger does not even mention the term 'monopoly' in this context, instead stressing the benefits of 'amalgamation'.) Keith would rebut the charge by emphasising that the papers within the chain were 'democratic' in ownership, as shares were held by many varied interests: the HWT was 'one of the most democratic companies in the country, being composed of 2,200 small shareholders'. As Sayers points out, although the term 'Murdoch Press' was inaccurate as to ownership, 'it had substance as to editorial control' in relation to the effect on public discourse. This was a crucial qualifier. It was a view that would embed itself in public perceptions as the decade unfolded.

In a double-page spread exploring the dangers of a syndicated press, the *Sunday Times* (Perth) anticipated that the public would soon 'wake up to the fact' of Keith Murdoch's plan, 'now partly accomplished, to establish a chain of newspapers in all the capital cities of Australia, all parrot-voiced and Melbourne owned and inspired'. It argued he was 'copying exactly the methods of the Hearst Press … with its factory for turning out journalists trained on Hearst lines in New York and sent to various centres in the different States of the Union to broadcast the ideas of Mr Hearst'. Australia was only a few steps away from the point when 'Mr. Keith Murdoch will have attained his dream of a Press Dictatorship for all Australia with Murdoch-inspired leaders and Murdoch-trained reporters and special writers scurrying from capital to capital, obediently obeying his commands. A roseate vision!'

In 1929, with the backing of the Baillieus and HWT involvement, Keith had bought a failing newspaper in Adelaide: the *Register*. Keith's eye, however, was very firmly on its profitable competitor: the *Advertiser*. He slashed the cover price of the *Register* and installed one of his brightest journalists to perform an overhaul and to lift circulation. The desired effect was achieved when the octogenarian owner of the profitable *Advertiser* Sir Langdon Bonython took fright and sold up in January 1929. Keith installed the talented and trusted Lloyd Dumas as the managing editor of the newly formed Advertiser Newspapers Ltd.

Keith's private directives to Dumas on ways of forging ahead are far more candid than his managing editor's notes. They provide the best insight into Keith's real instructions when faced with a newspaper battle, unfettered by a concern about how they could be perceived publicly if those instructions were ever leaked as Northcliffe's notes had been. Decrying the lack of 'general interest reading matter' in the *Advertiser*, he set out a new diet to entice readers: 'We want crime, love, excitement and sensation. More of these essentials are undoubtedly required even to maintain sales. And why should not sales improve every Saturday with definite attractions of this very human nature.' Two months later he reinforced his call, ordering 'more sensation thoroughly suited to the popular taste' for all classes. Keith insisted Dumas serve up 'romance, mystery, crime – all three and plenty of them!'

The close of the *Register* in 1931, the same year Keith was negotiating a controlling interest in Adelaide's evening-printed *News*, meant that the city was soon sewn up as an HWT–Murdoch monopoly. Expansion into radio in South Australia would follow.

The Adelaide *News* was to be 'the small paper' that Rupert later described as his single inheritance from his father. The *News*'s holding company News Limited would become the progenitor of News Corporation. J. E. Davidson, an enterprising journalist and chronic alcoholic, had founded the company following his resignation in 1918 as general manager of the *Herald*. He had died in June 1930 amid a pile of empty bottles while attending the Fourth Imperial Press Conference in London, enabling Keith to at once begin negotiations for a buyout from his heirs. (New research by Professor Sally Young has uncovered the secret support Davidson had in establishing News Limited. His co-founders represented mining business interests who saw the new company and its papers as a means of 'shaking up' the labour-aligned press and disseminating beneficial 'propaganda' while maintaining a veneer of 'independence' and 'impartiality'.)

By the end of the year, Keith confided to Dumas, negotiations with the Baillieus about News Limited were going well: 'Keep this under your hat. We will emerge, I am sure, with complete control there on as satisfactory a basis as we could hope for.' Keith stressed how it was 'all to our interest' to have 'scattered little parcels' of News Limited shares in 'the hands of South Australian people', while detailing the 'lumps of shares' of which he was aiming to seize control. Keith was employing a practice he had earlier learnt, designed to avoid perceptions of one-party dominance over other shareholders.

By the start of 1931 the terms of the Adelaide buyout had been agreed, Dumas congratulating Keith on having got the Baillieu shares 'even cheaper than you thought'. Keith was nevertheless irked by an insistence on the disclosure of share control in the redrawn articles of News Limited. He said he had hoped for 'far less fuss'.

Keith was also soon aggravated by the accusations levelled in the Arbitration Court, as he described them, that 'the Melbourne *Herald* and the Adelaide *Advertiser* are owned by a "money group" whose ramifications extend throughout the commercial world and who use their newspapers to support their commercial interests'. Knowingly or not, Keith appeared blind to the grounds of the charge. Press campaigns would follow, with links to Baillieu family concerns and the closely associated group of companies, not least the Broken Hill Proprietary (BHP) and Zinc Corporation, the seeds of the BHP-Billiton and Rio Tinto mining giants.

In April 1931 Keith wrote to Dumas at the request of 'Melbourne friends' who were backing improvements in the England–Australia airmail service. Keith enlisted Dumas to help in giving the scheme 'a good deal of publicity and actually urging the public to use this service'. Dumas was happy to 'boost it for all it is worth'. Before the month's end Clive Baillieu was pleased to forward a cable of thanks for the press support from his business partner, the chairman of Imperial Airways. The issue of the aerial business tie-up and the Murdoch press's part in it would be revisited.

Keith might have profited from the Baillieus' trust in him but his relationship with the HWT's Chairman Theodore Fink increasingly descended into deep distrust. One HWT journalist recalled the time he saw Fink 'throw his silver-headed cane skidding across the boardroom table at Murdoch, causing Murdoch, whom the cane missed, to throw back his head and literally roar with laughter' – the only time the employee could remember the Chief registering humour with anything more than a smile. In a bitter private account intended as a corrective for posterity, Fink sniped that 'K.M. made a good deal of money' through his friendship with the Baillieu family, and had plotted to displace Fink's son Theodore, making the HWT 'entirely a Baillieu-K.M. concern'. (Fink would have found Keith's correspondence with Dumas illuminating on this point.) W. L. Baillieu's biographer poses an interesting question about how crucial this relationship ultimately proved to the Murdoch family fortunes: 'The consequences of WL's decision to back Keith Murdoch ahead of Thorold Fink to run the *Herald* . . . resonates to this day – would Rupert Murdoch now own the world's largest media empire if his father had been forced aside from the Melbourne *Herald* in the 1920s?'

Fink was seeking to have it both ways, however; he certainly benefited from Keith's expertise and management. Writing to a British friend in May 1931, Fink observed that despite the Depression the HWT was 'now a gigantic corporation . . . standing up splendidly and certain to emerge more important as a collection of journals than ever'. Fink was keen to forge his own dynastic line, handing power to his son. The question of Thorold's ascendancy within the HWT was therefore 'central to the breakdown' in relations with Keith. According to Fink's biographer, the Fink family would remain wary of Keith, referring to him as a 'fiend' and regarding him as 'the catalyst for the antagonism' in the boardroom.

While Theodore Fink stewed and plotted, Keith was keen to keep tabs on all negative comments levelled at him from outside the HWT board. He asked Dumas to send on any criticisms of the Adelaide enterprises, as well as 'public expressions of hostility, or other news affecting our interests'. As a close reading of the Dumas correspondence reveals, Keith had worked hard to build those interests, ruthlessly using the economic downturn to his advantage and deploying all the tried and tested techniques he had honed through the newspaper battles of the preceding decade. It would be a case of survival of the fittest, though the solid capital of the Baillieu family – together with the significant cash reserves that the HWT had stashed away from the boom period of the 1920s – stacked the odds. As Keith told Dumas in mid-1930, 'We are not worrying here. The whole show is on a very solid foundation.'

Keith had carried out a number of wily moves. The HWT's newsprint warehouses were re-designated 'bonded stores' in order to beat the 'vindictive duty' on paper imports imposed by the government. Having gained privileged information from his contacts at the highest levels in the banks and government, Keith advised Dumas of the need to play the currency exchange over the coming months. Tens of thousands of pounds were sent to London, to be converted and brought back at an extremely healthy profit when the devaluing measures had been implemented.

Although employee unrest at cuts to come loomed, Keith welcomed 1931 'as a year of great opportunity'. He saw his task ahead, as he confided to Dumas, as nothing less than 'to reconstruct the nation'. Keith's description of his hard bargaining with the print unions shows a moral duality: 'We will certainly get a 10% cut, perhaps more; in fact we can get whatever we hold out for. But to my mind anything more than 10% is hard on the men. In these days we have to be hard.' A 13 per cent reduction was subsequently agreed upon, although Keith at least succeeded in not having to let any men go. But as one of his star journalists Cecil Edwards recalled bitterly, 'a notice of dismissal' was sent to each member of the HWT staff with a rider 'that said, in effect: This notice will not necessarily apply to you personally but we must get costs down and we can do this by paying less to everyone or by dismissing some.' In Edwards's opinion it 'was one of the nastier forms of wage blackmail'.

Keeping hold of this pool of workers in readiness for an upturn in the economy was a canny business strategy. In the view of the Murdoch biographer Charles Sayers, also an employee at the time, Keith's attempt to protect workers and their livelihood was genuine, but 'the emphasis of sacrifice' had fallen 'mostly on those least able to bear it'.

Directors' fees, bonuses and executive salaries had been reduced as a mark of solidarity, but this economising affected Keith less than others. There was no need to rush to reinstate his full salary, he confided, as 'I am such a big shareholder that dividends matter a lot more'. Keith also extended the belt-tightening to his personal servants, 'the maids, the butler and Nanny. Having the situation explained to them and all agreeing to take a percentage wage cut'. Cruden Farm, soon to be a scene of political entertaining and hosting, benefited after a group of unemployed men turned up at the property begging for work. Keith set them to building the architect-designed stables and landscaping the grounds.

In more Machiavellian terms, Keith saw the threat of job losses to press workers as an 'excellent chance' of getting what he considered to be the vindictive newsprint duty reduced. Pressure at a remove was applied through the print union onto government and through sympathetic politicians to the Australian prime minister himself. Keith claimed a 'most satisfactory' victory, though it was 'no thanks to the other proprietors, who refused to assist in what I did'.

The straitened economic times also provided an opportunity for picking up radio stations and licences on the cheap. Keith urged Dumas to follow the *Herald*/3DB model and add a station to the Adelaide interests. Acquiring 3DB had been a 'distinctly wise move', and securing 5KA would mean being 'on the air with all our papers, and making goodwill everywhere'. Keith was soon putting the screws on the 'eager seller', but then backed out when a better deal could be forced elsewhere. He had the power and boldness to exert the squeeze both when buying and selling. He saw opportunities in beating down the price to be offered to a radio station seller 'as times pass and become worse', while in his next breath suggesting that the agents be charged another penny a dozen for his papers.

Keith was not fond of the regulatory requirements for providing substantial news services on Adelaide radio, but thought these could be interpreted 'in a reasonable way'. He swung Dumas into action to lobby politicians and gain the support of the South Australian government itself. Keith employed some direct lobbying, inviting the powerful secretary of the Postmaster General's (PMG) department for lunch. Dumas was tasked with despatching a correspondent to Canberra to get Scullin, Lyons and Daly (at this stage respectively the Labor prime minister, the Postmaster General and the leader of the Senate) interested in the application for a licence for 5AD (the call sign chosen to reflect both Adelaide and the *Advertiser*), before 'putting in a word with the politicians myself'. Keith was hopeful, declaring Daly 'a tower of strength to us'. The next crucial move was to get on to Lyons, who he said was also very friendly.

During this new stage of radio expansion, takeovers and consolidation, the PMG's department vetted licence applications, classifying them as 'suitable', 'doubtful' or 'unsuitable' on the basis of the applicants' financial history and broadcasting experience. Some applications for interstate licences were dismissed as 'doubtful' because 'the principle of granting more than one licence to the same company is not advisable': the first indicator of disquiet about the ownership of multiple radio stations. However, the department immediately ignored this policy by issuing a licence to the Adelaide *Advertiser*. Keith thanked Lyons for the way the application was handled by inviting him in August 1930 to open 5AD.

The licence approval process might have been handled smoothly, but the poor sound quality on the first night of transmission made for a rough experience for listeners. Keith chastised Dumas over it. Reflecting the power of the reach they now held, and the importance Keith placed in getting things right, he wrote that 'we had been caught out by a million people in a failure' when 3DB rebroadcast 5AD throughout Victoria.

When he returned to Australia from his 1929 world tour, Keith had begun carrying out the ideas and developments he had absorbed in America and Britain. Increasing synchronisation and cross-promotion of his newspapers and wireless stations was a key aim. Having set his staff to thinking and innovating along the same lines, Keith rewarded one employee with a guinea for proposing 3DB give nightly publicity to the photographs appearing in the *Sun News-Pictorial* and *Herald* of the following day. It was a case of sound pointing to imagery in a neat, early case of media cross-promotion. But there was another media form – one that combined the senses in itself – that Keith was keen to develop. It would be put to use in his mission of 'giving the public our news service in every possible form'.

For Keith, recent developments in film and sound synchronisation were proof that movies were becoming a great interest for, as he estimated it, 90 per cent of the population. He instructed his editors to give this interest much greater attention. Inspired by his experience overseas, where he had observed 'the close association of this form of entertainment [film] and service to the public', Keith pushed for the setting up of the *Herald*'s own newsreel.

Just as Keith arrived in America in September 1929, Hearst was producing sound newsreels for the first time in partnership with Fox under the banners of Fox Movietone News and the Hearst Metrotone News. Two years earlier, on 20 May 1927 (five months before the premiere of *The Jazz Singer*, the first 'talking picture'), Fox Movietone had delivered the first popular sensation in audible cinema, reproducing not only the sight but the accompanying sound of Charles Lindbergh taking off earlier that day on his historic solo flight to Paris. The capacity audience of New York's Roxy theatre had leapt to its feet and delivered a ten-minute standing ovation following this first presentation of a 'news event as it was breaking'. And ironically, given the future career of Keith's son, Fox Films had got there first, Down Under too. The 'Australian Fox Movietone' issue of 2 November 1930 featured a speech by Prime Minister Scullin.

With a regular edition of Movietone appearing by January 1931, the HWT was making every endeavour to catch up as quickly as possible. Following negotiations that included persuading Fox to keep away from Victorian newsreel production, the HWT announced in February that a deal had been struck to form Australian

Sound Films Pty Ltd. Keith's star interviewer Frank Russell was tasked with 'the descriptive talking'. Plans envisaged the newsreel expanding to the other states, to be named individually following the title of the newspaper in that part of the HWT group or its associated newspapers. Citing the examples of the Beaverbrook and Hearst press's arrangements in Britain and America, *House News* claimed that 'only newspapers with their expensive and intensive news gathering can properly supply the public with newsreels'.

A fire that destroyed the 3DB studio provided the perfect opportunity to refurbish it using 'specifications adopted by the National Broadcasting Company of New York'. Opened early in 1931 the new studio acted as a dual-purpose screening and recording facility that could be transformed from one purpose to the other within minutes. A special camera truck was under construction, while the best noiseless recording equipment available was on its way from Britain. This costly voyage into new media territory was presented to the workforce as an exciting development. However, the front page of the same edition of *House News* had consisted entirely of a 'candid talk' from the Chief on the necessity for an 'all-round reduction' in pay.

For Keith there was a crucial need for this investment: not only to steal a march on his rivals but also to broaden the scope for shaping public opinion to accept the need for economic reform and, as we shall see, to instil faith in a potential new leader. Keith would also recognise, from his previous experience in promoting the exploits of aviators, how the involvement of a celebrity flyer would heighten public interest and engagement.

These aerial explorers became the world's first media superstars, 'urged on by their publicity-seeking sponsors to achieve headline-grabbing firsts' and eagerly followed by the population on radio, via newspapers and now moving pictures. In 1928, Hearst had sponsored an Australian aviator to beat Roald Amundsen in the flying race to the South Pole. A year before, in 1927, Keith had sponsored Charles Kingsford Smith and Charles Ulm's record-breaking flight around Australia, his accompanying letter used for publicity purposes at the stops along the way. A couple of years later, the *Herald* was once again sponsoring a daring flight by the dashing Kingsford Smith, with exclusive story rights assured.

Keith's dedication to promoting aerial communication and endeavour was typified by the fact that once again the aviators carried a triumphant letter from him to be delivered at their destination. In it Keith trumpeted how the arrangements for the flight had been made with such 'elaborate care' that there was 'every reason to hope that this letter will have been carried from Melbourne to London far more quickly than any previous epistle'.

As with Harry Hawker's ditching in the Atlantic ten years earlier, the story and its coverage really took off when Kingsford Smith, flying his iconic Southern Cross, disappeared somewhere over the Northern Territory. The drama was milked for all it was worth, with Keith ordering his various titles to work closely together on building the narrative. He revelled in the fact that the popular mood had been captured all across the country and stressed that the story represented 'one of the greatest newspaper opportunities of the decade'. Though the aviator was lost, Keith predicted that they were leading up to (yet another) 'great *Herald* exclusive – Smith's own story'.

Keith oversaw the now tried and tested formula: incite public ire at the inadequacy of the government's response, in this case the lack of planes dedicated to a search of the interior and inhospitable coast, while stirring passionate approval for the HWT's own valiant independent efforts in chartering a rescue plane.

As it happened, Kingsford Smith had simply made an emergency landing, losing radio contact in the process. (The much-vaunted 'elaborate preparations' seem not to have extended to packing a backup radio.) However, one of the craft racing to scour the bush for Kingsford Smith did actually crash, killing two. Competing newspapers questioned whether the whole thing had been a publicity stunt cooked up between the pioneer and his backers.

In early 1931 Keith added *Aircraft* magazine to the HWT stable. By late September of that year a lavish twenty-part serialisation of the *Southern Cross* story was being syndicated throughout Australia. Its first instalment coincided with another attempt by Kingsford Smith to fly to England from Australia in the least time possible. In an echo of Northcliffe's earlier support for aviation, Kingsford Smith's cargo was reported to include a letter of goodwill and achievement from Keith Murdoch to Geoffrey Dawson, editor of *The Times*. Although 'Smithy' failed to 'recover the "aerial ashes" for Australia', this time he avoided a crash landing. This sponsored flight was hailed by *House News* as a breakthrough in multi-platform coverage.

The HWT handled the world rights for the newspaper serialisation and broadcasts. Before take-off, Kingsford Smith and Frank Russell had spoken over '3DB, The Herald Broadcasting Station' and the home of 'bright radio'. But in a mark of the latest communication developments, the first newsreel picture made by the HWT was also loaded into Kingsford Smith's aeroplane. It joined a 'sound film' of greeting to the British prime minister from the then Leader of the Opposition in Australia, J. A. Lyons, which assured the people of England of the intense interest of the Commonwealth in the efforts now being made to effect national reconstruction.

From his days as a pre-war political correspondent, through the war years and the campaigns for Billy Hughes, to his role as editor and then head of a multi-media chain, Keith displayed an unwavering confidence in picking and then promoting those who he believed should lead his fellow men. His preference was to act behind the scenes, whether alone or in tandem with other self-appointed powerbrokers. He assured himself he had Australia's best interests at heart. Perhaps in his messianic zeal he truly managed to remain blinkered to the business benefits that certain choices provided.

After Keith's death one anonymous commentator, who appears to have been close to him, addressed this question. Reviewing the 'pious act on the part of the Melbourne *Herald* to publish a concise and attractively produced memoir' on Keith's death in 1952, 'Observer' averred:

In a sense, all through his full life, Sir Keith Murdoch was a preacher and a worthy of that select order who are sons of the Manse. [He had] an ardent desire, in which he was doomed to be perpetually disappointed, to find the ideal Prime Minister. I think as the years passed he reluctantly brought himself to believe there was no such animal. That discovery did not weaken his missionary fervour to improve politicians; on the contrary it strengthened his zeal to correct the frailties of a succession of imperfect humans in the Prime Minister's lodge . . . Never since John Knox has the Kirk produced such a zealous corrector of men in great places.

By the end of June 1930, as public finances worsened, Keith was confiding to Dumas that 'our papers are approaching a time when they have a very serious and important duty to perform for the nation'. The bad position of the country's finances had to be set out together with the necessarily drastic reduction in government spending. Keith was confident that the public would respond to clear leadership based on the facts. These facts were to be reinforced for Keith by the visit of the financial expert Sir Otto Niemeyer from the Bank of England. Keith became convinced, following their private meetings including dinner at the Murdochs' Melbourne home, of the need to implement severe cuts and deflationary measures.

Keith instructed Dumas to 'keep hammering at the Federal Budget', his Adelaide satellite responding with cuttings and the meek line, 'I hope they are what you want.' Keith soon perceived the shift in the public mood intended by the coordinated dark warnings on finances. Relieved, he told Dumas that now 'we can infuse the different note into our writings'. However, Dumas was reminded to toe the line of *Herald* comment, Keith pressing the importance of keeping in step on all major issues. The hierarchy and driving position were clear: 'under the natural order of things the pace has got to be set in Melbourne'. It was a point that would be reinforced over the months and years to come.

Keith had spent time in Canberra vetting the current political leadership. On his return he advised Dumas to cease giving publicity to those politicians whom Keith thought not up to the mark, and to soft-pedal the coverage of others on whom he was yet to decide.

In Keith's view Prime Minister Scullin, although 'eloquent and honest', was simply 'not big enough for the tremendous job'. Keith felt they had to support the leader of the National Party, John Latham, with his reputation for being pro-business while taking a tough line with the unions, despite regarding him as 'thin-lipped and thin-voiced': 'We must set out to build up Latham with the public. We have to make him into a big man. We have to get him accepted as a true national leader.' Latham, an experienced politician, had attended the Paris Peace Conference with Billy Hughes, whose tactics and manner he disliked.

Soon, however, a stronger and more down-to-earth politician with a perfect voice for wireless came to Keith's attention as the man to boost. The new protégé was Joseph Aloysius Lyons, acting treasurer from August 1930, and later described, variously, as the 'Tame Tasmanian', the rat who split Labor, and 'the best prime minister Keith Murdoch ever had'. But as 1930 drew to an end the figure of 'Honest Joe' was being shaped. Together with his media-savvy wife Enid and their brood of eleven children, he was the perfect package on which to base a personality cult. The man who as Postmaster General had recently given the go-ahead for 5AD was also a consummate radio communicator.

A clandestine meeting at Cruden Farm between the Lyonses and Keith was arranged. More meetings at the Murdochs' home followed with representatives of the Baillieu family and the cabal of businessmen and big money backers sponsoring Lyons, known secretly as 'the Group'. Keith was thriving on the excitement. He felt that Lyons, as an acting treasurer standing firm in his respect for orthodox finance and balanced budgets against criticism from within his own party, was 'doing splendidly'.

Keith soon claimed to be central to the strategising. A trio of ministers including Lyons were now convinced of the need to push through a conservative economic programme. Keith described his chosen role: 'My job has been to stiffen them, and organise outside help so that there will be support for men who are excommunicated by their Labor people.' The success of the loan conversion campaign, when the acting treasurer at the end of 1930 joined with figures from the Opposition and powerful finance houses to raise tens of millions, became a Lyons moment. He had astutely used radio to get his message to as wide an audience as possible, with his voice becoming 'as well known as those of radio announcers'.

During the early 1930s Keith, reaching his zenith as a media controller, was becoming an increasingly influential player in politics. Involvement in political machinations re-energised Keith, as Sayers states in his unpublished biography:

He loved it, caressed every moment of its excitement; wooed the adherents of the things he believed in: detested the men who opposed those things. He may have felt that he was a king maker, that he was the originator of policies that were making that king, the conqueror of his opponents. But that, of course, was not so. For the first time he was the controller of a massive newspaper campaign; at last he was feeling the power that control of the machine operating that campaign gave. It was a bonny fight and he planned it as such, and saw it as such, using every weapon of pen and printer's ink: everyone knew that. Every dice that was thrown was loaded against Labour [sic].

Keith anticipated a great split to come in the government, noting the criticisms from within Labor. His prescription now was to appeal to what he called 'middle opinion'. The Labor Prime Minister James Scullin had controversially been absent for four months, attending the Imperial Conference in London. Pre-empting Scullin's return sweep through Adelaide in early January, Keith dictated the harsh terms of a leader article that he wanted Dumas to print to greet Scullin. The *Advertiser* should stress that the prime minister had the chance to take 'heroic' steps or go down in history 'as a betrayer of the whole existing organisation of the country'. Dumas duly obliged. Over the coming months and years, Dumas would get used to this prompting, and on some occasions correcting, from Melbourne as Keith yanked the chains of control tight from their centre.

In an echo of Northcliffe's slide from sanity Keith's great supporter and role model of dynastic power W. L. Baillieu was succumbing to what would become a total physical and mental collapse. Baillieu fretted that his fortune had slipped away and that his children would be left destitute; in reality his legacy would be seen in the rise of such giants as Rio Tinto. Nevertheless, in February 1931, the patriarch managed to write a brief note, signing off: 'My love Keith to you & Elisabeth. I hope she will find a little boy at her side very soon now.'

At midnight on 11 March 1931 that little boy was born. Writing the following day to Dumas, extraordinarily Keith made no mention of his new son; his preoccupation with work seemed total. The opening two paragraphs of his letter were wholly focused on a close analysis of varying italic types and the make-up of Dumas's newspapers. Keith's primary concern appeared to be organising a defence to accusations that his closure of the *Register* had been part of a monopoly-building strategy, not simply an economic casualty of the times.

Elisabeth's father Rupert had been proudly telling friends that his daughter had chosen to name her new son in his honour. However, Keith moved swiftly and personally registered the boy's name as Keith Rupert Murdoch. The front page of the newspaper that Rupert would later inherit, however, was dominated by the story of a different blessed event: 'Mr Lyons to Lead New Federal Party – Broken with Labor ... Now Hopelessly Divided' boomed the banner headline.

Keith's papers reported that Lyons had delivered a blistering attack in support of a motion of no confidence in the Labor government, of which he was technically still a member. Lyons had been emboldened by his shadowy supporters and the knowledge that a significant proportion of the press was behind him. He found himself the next day sitting in Keith's Melbourne office discussing plans for an upcoming publicity tour of the country.

Suspicious of Lyons's motives and fearing the risks involved in creating a new political party, Dumas questioned Keith on the defector's 'socialistic' tendencies, 'which could make it extremely embarrassing for us'. However, Keith was emphatic that Lyons was 'the man for the occasion'. His policies were sound, his leadership qualities 'undoubted':

He is more able, more shrewd, more sympathetic than anyone else outside the Labor Party, and he has great gifts of speaking. He has such an immense personal prestige already that the nation is demanding that he should lead it.

The fracturing of political parties in the process was 'a minor consideration' when set against the task of saving the country.

Keith's resolve held. He impressed on Dumas that their newspapers were not as free to promote other individuals now because they had stood by and encouraged Lyons 'for about nine months, and at times when his decisions were extremely difficult we told him what to do. . . . Our strength and future are wrapped up in our isolation from political parties, and our courageous standing out for the policies which we evolve for the public's good.' However, Keith could rest easy in the knowledge that this isolation would not last. The Nationalist Party and the All for Australia leagues were well on their way to accepting Lyons as the leader of what was to become the United Australia Party (UAP).

In his letter to Dumas, Keith expressed his confidence that Lyons was 'not a socialist in any form' and that he would 'put private enterprise first'. Looking further ahead, however, Keith was cautious about a return to democracy as normal:

> If Australia can afford to return to party politics after the mess has been cleaned up then let it do so. But for the next three years at least we will have to have a real clean up of the mess, even if it means disturbing large blocks of voters.

For now, the major consideration was the saving of the country from economic ruin and making sure that the 'heresies and abuses' of those with contrary political views were 'suppressed'.

Keith believed that 'the better part of the Labor Party' – although 'we could never support socialistic enterprise' – would be incorporated with the 'best thought of the Nationalists'. Keith insisted that over the coming year they must swing 'all public thought into vigorous support for intense individualistic effort throughout the country'. One charitable historian stresses Murdoch's championing of Lyons was primarily motivated by the public interest, though they concede the self-appointed king-making role was 'pure Northcliffe'.

The federal election Keith hoped for would not be called until the very end of the year. But campaigning effectively started straightaway with the opposing camps battling it out over the airwaves across the country. One Tasmanian newspaper claimed that the live broadcast of political addresses one after another by Lyons, Latham and their former Labor colleague, now rival, Ted Theodore was unique in the history of politics. 'In a striking address broadcast from 3DB' Lyons, going first, had made an appeal 'for sane and honest dealings'. More than a thousand miles north, the *Brisbane Courier* excitedly detailed the 'Radio Scoop'. Unsurprisingly, the left-wing press in Queensland presented a different view, under the headline

'Afraid of Theodore, Tories Arrange "Radio Sandwich"'. The *Worker* described significantly and pointedly that the 'main difference' in the broadcasts was that Theodore, the reinstated treasurer who supported a Keynesian solution to the financial crisis, was facing a huge Brisbane audience, while Lyons and Latham, who went last, merely had to talk quietly into the microphone at station 3DB Melbourne.

Falling into line as a convert to Lyons's cause, Dumas set about helping to consolidate support in Adelaide. The city, with its monopoly press and associated radio station, would prove a fascinating laboratory for a new form of synchronised political campaigning. In the run-up to Lyons's arrival for a round of events, and most importantly 5AD broadcasts, Dumas found the enthusiasm infectious. The 'radio trade' was delighted, having its busiest time for eighteen months with more radio sets sold than during the Test cricket matches.

In April 1931, a year after Lyons had approved the HWT's licence for 5AD, he was in Adelaide preparing to open his campaign for 'Honest Finance'. The newly merged *Advertiser and Register* reported that 'special arrangements have been made for the monster rally at the Exhibition Building' to be broadcast by 5AD, with loudspeakers installed for the thousands expected there. Those listening at the rally, the newspaper contended, 'comprised only about a fiftieth part of the invisible audience which filled halls, shops, cafes, and private houses, not only in this State, but also all over Australia'. It claimed that the broadcast, relayed by 3DB Melbourne and other radio stations, had reached three-quarters of a million listeners, and that 'no public man in Australia has ever spoken to such a tremendous audience'. Keith was delighted.

Not everyone was so enthusiastically swept along by the tide for Lyons. In Canberra a month later the Labor MP Jack Beasley had drawn parallels with Lyons's actions and Billy Hughes's splitting of the Labor party during the war. He told the House of Representatives how 'remarkable' it was that 'whenever this country faces a crisis of great magnitude, the anti-Labour [*sic*] forces are unable to find a leader within their own ranks, and have to look elsewhere for a man to do their job'. Having 'devised means of detaching men from the Labour party to do their dirty work', the new masters would have no compunction in disposing of the traitors once their purpose had been served. The government's policies were 'being framed, not by Cabinet, but in the office of the Melbourne *Herald*'.

The honorable member then came to Cabinet with a policy which was not that of the Labour party, but one inspired by the editor of an evening paper with which he has since been continually associated, and which has been boosting him for the last few months. It is known that the new leader was forced on the members of the Opposition. The pressure of the Melbourne press was so great that Nationalist members have been carried off their feet; their own judgment has been overruled, and like weaklings they have handed over the reins to a new leader of whom they know very little.

The next day, when Lyons moved that 'this House condemns the government for its failure to take steps which are within its power to safeguard the Commonwealth against national default, with its inevitable consequences of extension of unemployment, distress and suffering; and that accordingly the Government no longer possesses the confidence of this House', Beasley shouted out: 'Did Keith Murdoch write that out for you?' The motion was defeated by 34 votes to 32.

Keith was unconcerned by a few swipes from Labor firebrands. Writing to the chairman of Reuters back in London in mid-1931, he confided the details of the 'tremendous fight against flabby socialistic thought' that he had been waging:

We have won this fight entirely as regards opinion in the country, and if the Scullin-Theodore Government faced an election now it would be hopelessly defeated – in fact there would be a rout such as has never been seen in a British democracy. We have, however, failed to get them to the country although we have got their party split into fragments.

A month later he was happy to report to Jones that, even with the financial crisis, 'our group of newspapers has accommodated itself wonderfully well now, and we are on a very sound profit basis'.

This was despite the fact that in May the Melbourne Trades Hall Council had launched a boycott against HWT publications that would run for half a year. Although a standoff ensued, as a Council meeting heard, it was 'impossible to induce people who followed sport and court cases' to not buy the *Herald*. One speaker pathetically proposed that the Council, not being in control of any printing press or radio station, use chalk on pavements to communicate its message. Responding to the Trades Hall's charges gave Keith the opportunity to roll out his line about the HWT being 'one of the most democratic companies in the country'.

Keith met with the Council representatives in August 1931 and in a follow-up letter assured them that no bias in the political coverage of his press was intended. He qualified this contention by saying that 'the haste of newspaper work' meant that on occasion words that might be considered partisan had slipped into reports, but given the intensity of the last year that could not be prevented. Privately Keith told Dumas that the boycott had shown 'how important it is to give ample space and prominence to views and news of moderate Labor'. The boycott eventually petered out in mid-November. At the end of that month the date of the election was finally announced as 19 December. Keith was about to see the results of his multimedia campaign in support of Lyons.

The *Advertiser* revealed that Lyons the challenger and Scullin the prime minister would both deliver policy speeches via broadcasting stations, 'thus emphasising that this will be essentially a radio election'. The same phrase was proclaimed enthusiastically by the *Wireless Weekly*. The eagerness of the parties to buy time for their candidates proved a financial godsend for commercial stations: one remarked 'we could ask almost anything for our time in the evenings'. Even Lyons's campaign theme 'Tune in with Britain', expressing the idea that if elected his coalition government, as with the National government in the home country, would put nation before party, was a riff on the wireless theme.

It was unsurprising then that as the competing election campaigns started, the *Listener In* pointed to the prime minister resorting to the simple strategy of using radio to 'get in touch with the greatest number of people in the shortest amount of time'. But Scullin's campaign broadcasts were very much a calculated risk; certainly his dull monotone wasn't suited to the airwaves. Lyons, on the other hand, flourished. Keith had always been confident of his chosen candidate's skill as a 'great speaker'. Lyons had had months to practise the art of his delivery and get used to the new medium, most often broadcasting through Keith's main station, 3DB.

Lyons's embrace of the media explains much of his success and that of his party. A UAP film made for the 1931 election featured a confident prime ministerial aspirant speaking direct to camera. This 'talkie', shown throughout cinemas, had been organised and filmed by Keith's new newsreel company. Lyons had been involved with the *Herald Newsreel* from the moment of its launch in September 1931. The footage of Lyons speaking with Kingsford Smith, the hero of the skies, certainly helped his image by association, while the sound film of his greeting to the British prime minister by 'the leader of the Opposition' (transported by Kingsford Smith on his flight) helped to frame the presentation of Lyons as a prime minister in waiting.

The waiting was now over. The Labor Party's first preference vote crashed from 49 per cent to 27 per cent and Joseph Lyons became prime minister. The sense of success seems to have been infectious at the HWT. A correspondent suggested to the *House News* editor that a campaign should be launched 'to secure a Federal Government job for "Smithy"'. (It was probably just as well for Australian democracy that this wasn't pursued, given Kingsford Smith's secret membership of the fascist New Guard which had planned to overthrow the Labor government by force if it had remained in power.)

The *Herald Newsreel*'s footage of the new government's first Cabinet meeting was 'an exclusive' enlivened by the additional drama, perhaps not without symbolism for some viewers, of a policeman trapping and killing a black snake that had made its home under the sentry's box. In a neat tying up of a victorious campaign waged through the power of the press, newsreels and wireless, the footage of Lyons included him broadcasting a speech over the air introducing his Cabinet members to the nation. The shot lingered on the banks of radio equipment. During the ministers' next visit to Melbourne, a special screening was arranged for the Cabinet to view the reel at the 3DB studio. Lyons was presented with a copy before declaring that in years to come 'the film would be of historical record'.

Keith managed to buy further publicity for the *Herald Newsreel*, alongside a boost for investment in Australia, through placing prominent ads in the international editions of the *Christian Science Monitor*, detailing the message the victorious Lyons had sent 'through the new medium'.

Back in March Dumas left it a week before acknowledging Rupert's birth in a letter to Keith with a rather limp postscript, hoping 'Mrs M and the infant are getting along splendidly'. But on the subject of the election victory Dumas could barely contain his happiness, cabling Keith his '[w]armest personal congratulations. Consider Victorian landslide great personal triumph for yourself.' The following day Dumas wrote that 'We were all amazed at the wonderful swing in Victoria as the figures came through on Saturday night.' Keith 'must have been delighted to find the influence of "The Herald" and "The Sun Pictorial" in the industrial suburbs so strong':

> Looking back a few months, one can realise the part that the Melbourne 'Herald' and you personally have played in the success of the new Government. Your strong backing of Lyons was the decisive factor in his election to the leadership of the United Party, and everything that has happened since has hinged on that.

Keith already felt himself to be the proud father of a government and its prime minister, a man 'whom we chose and made'.

In July 2011, as Rupert made his appearance before the House of Commons select committee inquiry on phone hacking, outside a demonstrator enacted a version of the ties at the heart of the British government. Ventriloquist dummies representing the new Conservative prime minister and his media secretary danced as their strings were yanked by a puppet-master sporting a papier-mâché head mask of Rupert.

Seventy-five years earlier, when Rupert was still a young boy, a remarkably similar image had been published: a cartoon depicting Prime Minister Joseph Lyons and his Cabinet as marionettes dancing on a stage under the banner 'Government of the People, For the People, By the People'. Looming above them all, grinning as he pulled the strings, was Keith.

11 MEDIA EMPIRE

It is he today who launches the thunderbolts, and before whom terrified politicians . . . shrink. How can they be heard in the capitals except at his behest?

SMITH'S WEEKLY, *1933*

On 15 June 1933 a very public piece of art was unveiled across the crisp modernist façade of Newspaper House, the HWT's new outpost in the centre of Melbourne. Keith Murdoch and Theodore Fink, though increasingly at odds, had set aside their differences long enough to commission a coloured glass mosaic. In gold block capitals above, stretching the width of the building like a banner headline, was Puck's promise to Oberon from *A Midsummer Night's Dream*: 'I'LL PUT A GIRDLE ROUND ABOUT THE EARTH.'

A few months before in London, Lord Beaverbrook had unveiled two huge murals in the lobby of the new chrome-and-black-glass-sheathed *Daily Express* building on Fleet Street. One represented Britain, the other its Empire – a jumble of Indian elephants and African tribesmen, all topped by an Australian shearer tackling a horned merino ram. In Melbourne, the mosaic's artist had been given a clearer brief and, as it would turn out, a more farsighted subject. The design presented a media empire.

The opening of Newspaper House was a celebration of the power of the media, its mosaic depicting the latest as well as future forms of communication. Proceedings were broadcast live on 3DB. Keith, still afflicted at times by the stammer he would never completely master, was happy to leave the speaking to Fink and the old barnstormer Billy Hughes. They dwelt on the mosaic's title and the push towards ever more rapid and distance-shrinking communication in a modern world full of radio waves, motor cars and airships. Its design, embracing a smorgasbord of allegorical and classically charged imagery, was declared 'intentionally symbolic'.

Readers of that evening's *Herald* were told how the panels represented the 'symbols of the news'. The mosaic was designed to be read from right to left: from the four heads of the 'inspirational forces' of commerce and industry, idealism, the arts and the 'highest ideals', to the virile young architects 'who formulate the news'. Seated at its centre is the singular and all-powerful figure of the media itself, delivering a perpetual trumpet blast around a world in which distance is no longer a bar to communication. Finally, on the right are the 'receivers': a mother, father and their golden-haired child: the hope for the future.

On that evening in mid-1933, as Keith bid farewell to his distinguished guests he received his own personal congratulations. For ten days now he had been Sir Keith, knighted for his services to Australia; or perhaps, as critics put it, rewarded for installing Joe Lyons as prime minister. Keith told Lloyd Dumas how the news of his knighthood should be broken in the Adelaide newspapers under their control: 'I would be glad if in your notice you make the point that I am a working journalist'. Others were soon describing his role in less disingenuous terms.

In a typically biting assessment, the irreverent, independent magazine *Smith's Weekly* profiled Keith as the embodiment of a new Australian phenomenon: 'a Press dictator'. The *Smith's* correspondent wrote that this 'intimate of Lord Northcliffe' had studied 'the mechanism of the megaphone press' in London while his mentor and Lord Beaverbrook were forging their own 'mighty engines of popular expression'. His methods were no longer concealed, and now he was a 'candidate for control of the ether' too. *Smith's* hoped voters in the next election would 'look for the Murdoch puppets and note how they will be upheld by the blare of approval from his Press loud-speakers.'

Indicating the critical discourse among actual working journalists, on the day the mosaic was unveiled, Keith was warned that the journalists' union had floated a proposal in its circular: if the public were made aware that 'a small and cheap paper was being produced by journalists to tell what journalists really thought, unhampered by proprietorial strings, it might easily become a best seller'.

Following Lyons's victory at the end of 1931, Keith recommended the new prime minister take on one of his former journalists, Martyn Threlfall, as his political secretary. Threlfall started immediately. As Keith's main Canberra correspondent Joe Alexander was already close to Lyons, having been embedded in the campaign from the start, he was certainly kept well informed. Keith also remained in frequent personal contact with Lyons during the early 1930s. (The revolving door between Murdoch media roles and government positions continued to spin well into the 21st century, typified by the *News of the World*'s editor Andy Coulson who became Prime Minister David Cameron's spin doctor, and President Trump's head of White House communications, Hope Hicks, who found a new berth at Fox News's parent company in mid-2018. Her replacement in the White House, Bill Shine, was himself a Fox News producer and key executive.)

The surviving cables from Keith reveal the informality of their meetings: 'care lunch or dine with me quietly . . . will send car for you'. Lyons responded promptly and with keen enthusiasm: 'anxious to see you and will get in touch with you on arrival'. Lyons was one of the first to cable his sympathy on the sudden death of Keith's brother Frank.

The imbalance in the relationship, at this stage at least, was one that Lyons left unquestioned. Invariably it was the prime minister who travelled to Keith's office at the HWT or to the Murdoch family's new city home in the exclusive suburb of Toorak.

Heathfield which had belonged to the Baillieu family, had twenty-seven rooms, tennis courts, five acres of gardens and a vast dining room: a seat fit for a knight of the realm. As a child Keith had viewed it as the embodiment of success and now his possession of it stood as a physical marker of his ascendancy. As *Smith's Weekly* put it, Keith was now 'the owner of one of the 'Baillieu palaces' and would soon 'dwarf the biggest Baillieu'. With artful understatement, Keith told Lyons how to find it: 'Go to the Presbyterian Church on Toorak Hill, turn to the right. Our house is a rather big one standing back'. A description, perhaps, that summed up Keith's own travels in life so far.

Keith's links with the Baillieus and their network of business concerns were still prompting criticism. One member of the Opposition attacking the new government's 'rich man's Budget' in October 1933, pointed to the 'sinister influence' at work on behalf of the wealthy. He predicted that the history 'of the Baillieu group, showing its ramifications,' would one day be exposed: 'It is said the "Melbourne Herald" created this Ministry, which gave Keith Murdoch quid pro quo.' Another Labor member chipped in, 'They knighted Keith Murdoch.'

Keith was able to generate special attention to financial matters that could benefit his own various business interests. A month after the Budget Lyons responded to his request to see the HWT tax adviser and assistant manager with the assurance that the assistant treasurer would be looking into the 'question of exemptions from Sales Tax' for blocks and photographs involved in newspaper production.

Protecting the financial footing of the new radio side of the business would come to be an overriding preoccupation. In 1932 Keith feared the proposed terms of the Bill establishing the Australian Broadcasting Commission would affect his commercial stations and newspapers. He despatched Dumas to Canberra to meet an old employee, now minister for trade and customs. The following day the government tabled an amendment. During a subsequent committee debate, one Labor member of the House of Representatives highlighted this opportune timing and threw down a challenge:

A large newspaper combine, at the head of which is the Melbourne *Herald*, is making a determined effort to usurp the rights and powers of Parliament. Apparently, it is the ambition of Mr Keith Murdoch to become the Northcliffe or Beaverbrook of Australia, and dictate public policy.... I challenge the Minister for Trade and Customs to deny that [Dumas'] visit related to the Broadcasting Bill, particularly the clause now under consideration.

Unfazed, the minister replied: 'That may have been so; but what does that establish?' As the Labor member described how this showed 'the influence that was brought to bear on the Ministry to compel it to amend this clause', the minister delivered a 'loud guffaw': confirmation, for the Labor member at least, that his statement had touched on the truth.

Dumas was able to forward to Keith an inside view of how the Newspaper Proprietors' Association (NPA) in Britain was dealing with the issue of radio news, including the terms and operation of its agreement with the state broadcaster. Restrictive timing of bulletins was paramount: due to their prohibition until 6.00 pm, with a repeat at 9.00 pm, there was 'no effect on sales of evening papers in most towns'. Sports commentaries did have a considerable effect, however.

Dumas had further encouraging news to report. Though Sir John Reith at the BBC was very powerful, he was 'kept in good check' by the NPA, which had effectively full control over all the news agencies. Dumas' covering letter to Keith added that a visiting BBC representative had had big ideas about the broadcasting of news when it first started, but staggered by the cost of setting it up the BBC was glad to 'make an arrangement' with the newspaper owners to use newspapers' words in their bulletins.

The Australian proprietors pushed the new ABC to a harsh deal. Agreement was struck that for the next three years the ABC could for international news use up to 200 words of a newspaper article or Australian Associated Press (AAP) cable. For local news, however, evening bulletins could only be broadcast after 7.50 pm to avoid encroaching on evening newspapers' exclusivity. Keith's tough line towards the ABC was plainly intended to protect both his newspapers and his radio stations.

Lyons had been re-elected in September 1934 following a campaign in which air transport played a crucial role for the first time, with the aid of personal pilots including Charles Ulm and Smithy himself flying Lyons to campaign stops around Australia. The prime minister wasted no time in addressing a letter of thanks to 'the editor of the *Herald*'. This original message ended up in Keith's own personal papers. Lyons felt 'keen appreciation' for the 'great help' he and his party had been given, believing 'that the influence of "The Herald" had an immeasurable bearing upon the verdict recorded by the people'. But Keith was more concerned that Lyons, no longer holding an outright majority, may be swayable by others now. Keith told Dumas they should coordinate the pressure from their presses, proposing they adopt a pincer movement strategy to 'increase the effectiveness of any actions we take' on Lyons in future. Still, a week later Keith was content to report that he had 'had a good talk this morning with Lyons': 'The Cabinet is well launched.'

Keith's notorious battles with the ABC in the mid-1930s and beyond have received significant attention and critical assessment since at least the 1970s, though not necessarily by his former biographers. In 1935 the ABC attempted to negotiate new, freer terms regarding the broadcast of news. But it found the press, led in its campaign by Keith, so against this that for the first time the ABC considered starting a news gathering service of its own. In the same week that a Stan Cross cartoon depicting Murdoch and his marionettes appeared Keith wrote to Lyons, incensed at the proposed regulations. It was time to really pull some strings.

Keith was stung that ministers, including the PMG, had been describing the changes as 'designed to corner "Murdoch and his crowd"'. While he could 'understand a straight-out Socialistic policy' which aimed to limit commercial class stations while building up those funded by licence fees, surely this wasn't what was in Lyons's or his ministers' minds? Keith fired his shot across the bows: 'You were elected after a series of speeches which struck a very different note.'

Using a line of argument that his grandson James would echo eight decades later, Keith insisted that programmes would be improved only through chains of commercial stations rather than via government-supported stations that had 'immense revenues and yet cannot get the listeners'. The charge 'that "a monopoly of programme" has been created in America [home of a purely commercial sector] and is unwholesome' was 'truly ridiculous'. In Keith's view, the 'great American programmes' were 'the finest in the world'. He concluded this point by stressing that it was 'such a pity to see a Government based upon liberty for individual effort do such a dreadful thing as this regulation'.

Keith then turned the attack on to the ABC chairman and his attitude towards newspapers. In another line of argument that would also be echoed decades later with his son Rupert's attack on the 'piracy' of internet providers and their 'plain thievery' of news and entertainment, Keith claimed that the ABC was dishonourably intending to use newspapers' content and facilities 'without paying fairly for them'.

Lyons's five-page handwritten response from Canberra was defensive and showed signs of strain. He had hoped to be able to talk personally with Keith in Melbourne and had asked Joe Alexander to arrange this, but had been laid low with exhaustion. No Cabinet minister had attacked Keith personally, he wrote: 'Though ministers, like myself, might sometimes complain of criticism by the papers of your group they all realise only too well what the government party owe to those papers.' Every consideration had been given to the industry representatives regarding modification of the regulations and a promise made to continue hearing testimony. In exasperation Lyons asked, 'What more can we do?' The ABC, Lyons stressed, was 'to a great extent entirely independent of control by the government'. But he assured Keith he would look into the matter.

Keith responded forcefully, denying that he had wished to be given any special favours about the broadcasting regulations. He had not suggested for a moment that the ABC's head should be 'interfered with', though he added the intriguing rider: 'It may be impossible, and it may be unwise.' Another quietly arranged Lyons–Murdoch talk was proposed for when the prime minister was next in

Melbourne as the way of dealing with Keith's concerns over how 'things are drifting'. In the meantime he emphasised how 'in view of all our relationships, I thought it wise to let you know what has been in my mind for some time so that there should at least be frankness between us'.

One HWT copyboy during this time, tasked with bringing Keith his afternoon tea, heard him shout to his secretary, 'Get Lyons down here at once. Tell him I want to see him'. The Australian prime minister duly arrived at the Chief's office, having made the journey across town. As the young employee placed the tea down, Keith was still shouting, though now at Lyons who was standing before the desk. The copyboy beat a swift retreat, but not before witnessing a scene that would prove indelible in his memory:

> I turned and there, with his hat in his hand, like a man seeking a job, stood the Prime Minister before Murdoch's desk. As I shut the door, I heard the leader of the nation say: "Yes, sir."

The government duly substituted a more lenient set of broadcasting regulations, with Keith agreeing to the most mild of concessions: the evening news bulletin could start at around 7.30 pm instead of 7.50 pm. Plans for the ABC's own news service were dropped.

Although Lyons agreed with the ABC's head that 'Unfair newspaper opinion does not represent "public opinion"' and that across the political spectrum the public resented the press's machinations, his government's need to retain favourable press support in the lead-up to the 1937 election overcame this view. Robert Menzies, then attorney-general and later to be prime minister, would tell John Reith of the BBC that 'everyone had got cold feet about the next election'. Reith queried whether the Australian government would ever do anything about the increasing dominance of commercial stations. Menzies replied simply: 'We haven't the guts.'

The former journalist and now Labor leader of the Opposition John Curtin expressed his fear that 'this alliance of great newspapers and broadcasting stations' could 'so inflame public opinion as to make ordered government almost impossible'. When Keith's grandson James Murdoch delivered his lecture to the Edinburgh International Television Festival in September 2009 he attacked the BBC's supposed dominance and licence fee model. Mark Scott, the managing director of the ABC, suggested that James's antipathy to public broadcasting resembled the attitude of his grandfather: 'Sir Keith Murdoch's newspapers began calling for a reduction in the ABC's licence fee on the basis that an ABC news service would constitute "improper competition" . . . it's a phrase that has resonated for the family down through the years.' This was corroborated by the then head of the BBC, who observed that 'when people thought James sounded like his father – it goes back even further'.

In early 1937 an ABC manager wrote to his opposite number at the BBC, exasperated by the campaign against the issue of the broadcasting licence fee in Australia. The press's case against it, he said, was hidden behind 'the smug plea that their only interest was that of "the listening public"'. The manager took solace, however, in sensing that 'the Murdoch papers are now so notorious for their "disinterestedness" that the attack looks like falling down.'

Dumas tried to convince Keith that the HWT campaign against the ABC ran the risk of backfiring. Dumas stressed: 'It would be assumed, and not without some degree of justification, that we had personal or business ends to serve, and that we were using our papers and seeking to drag the private listener into our fight with the Broadcasting Commission, in the belief that he was fighting only for his own ends.'

In January Lyons had attended the launch of the HWT's latest radio station 3LK, the service that would widen 3DB's reception to the far country reaches of the state. Keith's speech of that evening was broadcast and recorded, resulting in a remarkable and rare recording of his voice. His delivery is measured but there is no hint of the stammer that had so affected his early life.

Thanking the politicians present for their attendance, Keith stressed that the *Herald* was 'one of the first newspapers in the world to develop the theory that newspaper work and broadcasting could be joined to the advantage of all concerned'. Lyons had to stand mute as Keith addressed the listeners directly, hammering a political point home. The broadcasting innovation had been expensive and risky for the company, with the costly programmes all going 'to you free over the air, for we get none of the listening fees you pay'. Defending the commercial model Keith cited the large, established audience of 3DB as proof of success. He promised that programme quality would improve, and so improve 'the artistic and cultural development of our life'.

By the end of 1933 Keith's schedule and levels of activity, such that he lamented to Dumas that there was no longer any use in bringing his golf sticks when travelling, were beginning to demand a price. As well as the general stress of running the HWT there was the burden of being self-appointed backseat driver of Australian federal politics.

The first of a series of health shocks came when Keith overexerted himself on the grass tennis court at Heathfield in a match against Neville Fraser, father of the future Liberal Party prime minister Malcolm. Despite being still only in his mid-forties, Keith apparently suffered a heart attack. The complications following the episode laid him low for weeks at a time, much to his frustration. Even Keith's antagonists expressed their concern and hope that he would slow down. The editor of *Smith's Weekly*, a man who held a sneaking regard for Keith, wrote urging him not to let 'them get you working at high pressure' again: 'You can take more out of yourself than you can give back in what passes for success. Anyway, what more do you want?'

One doctor assured Keith he had a good enough heart for another thirty years, but said he was tired and nervous and should go abroad for a rest and change of scene. But Keith needed to stay on the spot. Theodore Fink was plotting to manoeuvre his son Thorold into the line of succession at the HWT while ousting Keith from executive control.

By 1936 Elisabeth and Keith had not travelled together outside Australia for more than six years. Even rest and travel as a couple within Australia had been rare and precious. But now with Australia on the path out of Depression and Keith's business interests on a solid footing, the HWT boardroom putsch averted and the prospect of the next election far enough away in the future, Keith at last felt it was time for the long-delayed break with the family.

At the end of February, Keith and Elisabeth finally departed for Europe. In 1929 they had left baby Helen behind: this time (assured in the help of Nanny Russell) all their 'bairns' were with them: Helen now aged seven, Rupert aged five, and new arrival Anne, just four months old.

After happily wandering through Spain and France, including visits to 'lovely places, including the galleries and museums', they arrived in Britain. A quarter of a century earlier, alone and depressed in the city at the centre of the Empire, Keith had pined for 'bright children, faithful friends, and a comfortable home'. Though devotion to work and establishing a career had delayed these things, he now had them all, and had brought his longed-for children back with him to London.

For the next three months Keith based the family in a Westminster mansion flat next to St James's Park. But if Elisabeth had expected a rest she was destined to be disappointed, for Keith immediately embarked on 'a whirlwind of engagements'. However, amid the business meetings and networking, as part of what Elisabeth would later describe as their 'big spend up', they managed to fit in trips to tailors and shirtmakers, and shopping expeditions for furniture, antiques and art. A portrait of Rupert and Helen was commissioned. (Cherished by Elisabeth, it would be given pride of place in the drawing room of Cruden Farm for the rest of the century.) And in a decision that would come to be seminally important for the children, an English governess, Miss Joan Kimpton, was selected. 'Kimpo' would become an integral part of the family and a formative influence.

Still concerned by his health and keen to get a second opinion, Keith consulted the King's own physician. Sir Maurice Cassidy declared there was nothing wrong with Keith's heart, instead diagnosing that the 'illness was entirely due to overwork and overstrain'. Keith was told he could work hard when at work but when with his family he must learn to switch off and relax. But as he admitted to Dumas this was 'a most difficult formula for men like you and me, in fact, for all pressmen, because we have, all our lives, taken our problems home with us'.

Though he was in London with his family and away from the day-to-day concerns of the HWT, Keith could not resist making side trips. One of these was a six-day visit to Germany, where the Nazi Party had been in power for just over three years. Before setting off, Keith had made sure he was well briefed by the Foreign Office and Air Ministry. He had thought their gloomy view on Germany's expansionist ambitions was 'unduly pessimistic'. However, his stay would convince him otherwise.

In Berlin Keith mixed with the crowds that stood in front of Hitler's house 'crooning and saluting all day'. He was astonished to see that Hitler was 'almost worshipped'. After attending the opening of the controversial Olympic Games, Keith told Dumas that 'the German people have arrived at a state of mind in which they regard Hitler as their saviour and accept his teachings. These are hammered home by the discipline of concentration camps, and the newspapers are not only muzzled but are used in the cleverest way as sounding boards for the Hitler doctrine.'

Travelling on to Dresden near the border with Czechoslovakia, Keith found 'new aerodromes and bomb proof barracks' with 'vast numbers of airmen' everywhere. Keith was 'sure that soon the clarion call will have to go out through the Empire for a great effort in aerial defensive organisation.' The sobering experience of Nazi Germany created a lasting impression.

By August it was time for the Murdoch family to return home, though this time via a different route. *House News* in 1929 had pictured baby Helen alone, left back in Australia, but the front page of the September 1936 edition had a huge photograph of a beaming father and son: Keith holding the blond-haired Rupert at the window of the Southampton boat train as they prepared to leave for the USA on the last leg of their world voyage.

Once across the Atlantic, Keith broke off for a series of meetings in New York, Chicago, Seattle and San Francisco, while Elisabeth and the children travelled to the west coast to stay in a gated and guarded community on an island in Puget Sound. Memories of the Lindbergh kidnapping still fresh, friends thought Elisabeth would be glad of this safe haven. However, she seemed more concerned with the conduct of American servants, who she considered to be 'inclined to a somewhat pronounced free-and-easiness of manner'. While his family waited in safety, Keith was working. As he explained to one employee, he had to 'go through America and see the paper mills and paper men'. Keith was intent on establishing a pulp mill in Tasmania, so providing an independent newsprint supply safe from the whims of 'vindictive' government duty.

Interviewed by the *New York Times*, Keith explained that he was travelling to Seattle to see the results of the experiments undertaken on the eucalyptus samples he had sent north a year before. He also stated boldly that having spent $1 million on the enterprise, if successful he stood to save millions a year. It was no accident that the figure representing the power of the media in the Newspaper House mosaic sat on a throne made from a freshly hewn tree stump.

Having crossed the Pacific, where Elisabeth taught Rupert to swim by dunking him in the liner's pool, the family reached Australia and home in October 1936.

Keith, as he had hoped, felt refreshed and ready to work again. The trip had concentrated his mind on family as well as business matters, and he set to 'rearranging [his] affairs by establishing Trusts for the children'. On New Year's Day 1939, Elisabeth Janet was born, completing the Murdoch brood. Family friend Joan Lindsay – author of *Picnic at Hanging Rock* and, together with her artist husband Daryl, godparent to Rupert – described how the clan, out riding in the lanes near Cruden Farm on a Sunday morning, made for 'an unforgettable spectacle – a sort of medieval cavalcade of children, servants, outriders, horses and dogs … At the head of the gay motley procession rides Keith, mounted on a massive charger, an upright rather heavily built figure immaculate in English tweed and riding boots; proud and happy …'

Even amid this Arcadian childhood, Rupert found a way to hone a cutthroat commercial streak. He organised his sisters into helping him collect and sell manure from the horses. Sister Helen recalled 'I think he said it was for the Red Cross!' Rupert soon developed a lucrative sideline in rabbit pelts. Helen described how Rupert 'used to kill them and I used to stand by while he skinned them … we were always out there working with the men, rabbiting and helping them kill the chooks. I suppose we were pretty beastly really, Rupert and I. We used to quite enjoy gutting rabbits and saying "Ooh, look at all the baby rabbits inside."'

Family relations might have been closer following the world trip, but another relationship was unravelling. After a long catch-up talk with Lyons, Keith told Dumas in scathing terms that they 'may as well recognise that he is an unrepentant socialist'.

The prime minister and Keith had already clashed in their differing reactions to the conflict between Italy and Abyssinia (now Ethiopia): the former keen to tread carefully, the latter to attack Italy's aggression. Keith's experience in Germany had convinced him that Australia needed to wake up to the threat of war but Lyons did not agree, urging Keith to play down his papers' views of what was happening 'in the national interest'. By the end of 1936 their correspondence had taken a starchy, distant tone. But in line with Keith's actions during the previous war and particularly his machinations in the campaigns for conscription, he now joined those figures agitating to put Australia on a war footing.

By December of 1938, Keith's meetings with the prime minister were well and truly strained. While Lyons believed the public would not vote for compulsory military service, Keith believed that they would certainly do so 'if well led'. Writing at the start of 1939 to his friend Clive Baillieu back in London, he declared that while Lyons was adamantly against it, Australia 'should have compulsory military service, even if it is only for the national outlook it brings':

The present position is that Lyons and his wife are quite determined to remain in office. I do not think it would require a long continued demonstration to convince Lyons that he should get out, but he definitely wants to stay in. He has lost usefulness; he is a conciliator, a peace man and of course, a born rail-sitter.

To Dumas, Keith went so far as to say that 'we must campaign for a new Prime Minister'. Keith considered Lyons's lack of preparation for war so slack that he told Baillieu he was forming 'a very grave view of the future and think that revolutionary measures must be taken in this country'.

Keith now wasted no time in plotting to get rid of Lyons. Enid Lyons later recalled that a waiter in Melbourne had written to her after claiming to overhear Keith saying: 'I put him there ... and I'll put him out.' However, Lyons's sudden death of a heart attack on 7 April 1939, aged only fifty-nine, saved Keith the trouble.

Lyons was the first Australian prime minister to die in office and he left a succession vacuum. As the position of deputy leader of the UAP was currently vacant, a ballot was run. Robert Menzies won the leadership over Billy Hughes and became prime minister.

For Keith, everything was now pointing to conflict. But even as he was focusing his energies on politics he had been organising a remarkable first for Australia. As the world edged towards another civilisation-shattering war, a ship was steaming south from Europe to Australia. It was laden with twenty-eight crates of precious paintings and sculptures, the like of which had never been seen in the southern hemisphere. At the end of 1938 Keith had despatched his art critic to Europe on a mission to gather 'an educative exhibition of all significant painters from impressionist paintings to ultra-modern'. Keith had two objectives in the scheme: to bring 'great prestige' to his newspapers, and to prove 'a milestone in the progress of Australasian culture':

Gallipoli had given us one kind of maturity. A great *Herald* exhibition of contemporary French and British art would give us another kind of maturity.

On 16 October 1939 Keith was proud to see the exhibition declared open. The 217 works included canvases by Dalí and Picasso but the emphasis was heavily on French and British artists such as Cézanne, Gauguin, Matisse and Augustus John, Jacob Epstein and Walter Richard Sickert. German Expressionism was absent; the social satire of Max Beckmann and Otto Dix, so hated by the Nazis, was missing. Not that excellent examples would have been hard to obtain. The Nazis' purge of 'degenerate' works from German museums had 'produced a glut in the market for modern German works, offering unbelievable bargains'.

Keith used all his press resources to promote the *Herald* exhibition with scatter ads and daily news stories filling his papers, a special window display at Newspaper House and the Melbourne trams 'plastered with stickers, with the words "Modern Art Exhibition" in bold type'. The old art establishment loathed not only 'the advertising efforts that have been made to urge us to swallow this putrid meat' with 'pictures boosted like a cheap line of socks', but the works themselves: 'the product of degenerates and perverts . . . filth'.

It appeared Keith agreed with them in one case. Salvador Dalí's *La Mémoire de la Femme-Enfant*, with its focus on a single pert breast amid a tower of flesh, was in Keith's judgement 'an obscenity of the first order' and he asked for it to be omitted before the exhibition transferred to Sydney. He made sure that his views were known, and newspapers were besieged with letters from readers demanding its inclusion. It stayed on the wall and the public came in droves, crowding around this work more than any other. Keith's deployment of pragmatic risk and populism – family traits that would deepen with the generations to come – had won through. (Not to mention recognition of the mass appeal of bare breasts.) The collection, though delayed at times by the war, would go on to continue its successful procession around Australia, stirring, entertaining, shocking and uplifting the public as it went.

The 1939 exhibition, however, was not the start of the story. Even while swinging the country behind Lyons in 1931, Keith had still had the idea of organising an exhibition of high-quality colour prints of modern art, together with some key originals. Two years later, even while the Newspaper House façade was receiving its finishing touches two years later, the new building was already hosting exhibitions. Mirroring Keith's wide interests, the startling modern works of 'British Contemporary Art' collated by the exotically named Mrs Alleyne Zander had been given one floor, a more staidly traditional collection of Scottish antiques another. One review reported the confusion when an eager Scot attendee, having taken a turn off the staircase at the wrong level, complained 'he could not find the famous Culloden sword', instead discovering himself amid daring Jacob Epstein sketches and vivid cubist oils of semi-naked bathers.

When Newspaper House's façade was finally complete and its mosaic unveiled, some regarding the composition of its figures might have felt a similar sense of disorientation. The arrangement was remarkably similar to that of the Gallipoli gunners in the photograph given to Keith by Northcliffe, and which he had made famous. As the decade ended, with the world now at war again, Keith was about to re-embrace the role of propagandist. It would prove a costly move.

12 A GIRDLE ROUND ABOUT THE EARTH

Melbourne, 23 October 2014. The young co-chairman of the newly formed 21st Century Fox stepped up to a podium that bore the legend 'Keith Murdoch Oration'. Lachlan Keith Murdoch unfolded the text of his speech: 'A Free Media: Dependent On No One For Favours'. With an accent more American than Australian he began. Lachlan's message was delivered powerfully: he railed against the Australian government for its recent introduction of a law that could imprison journalists for reporting on special intelligence operations. As the frame for his argument, he invoked the example of his grandfather's career and particularly the Gallipoli letter. But in detailing Keith's life and legacy Lachlan omitted mention of a role that Keith had embraced during World War II. In a speech slamming governmental control and the strong-arming of a free press, it was a curious omission.

If Keith had hoped Lyons's replacement as prime minister would be as biddable as Lyons himself had been in the early days, he was mistaken. As the world entered into another war, Keith's hold on the reins of politics, and increasingly his judgement, were slipping.

Robert Menzies' secretary recalled his boss's views about Lyons and other ministers visiting Keith at his HWT power base to talk things over:

Menzies somehow felt this was wrong. I suppose partly he feared Murdoch, although they had a good deal in common in the sense that some members of their families had been friends in the generation behind, and so on. But he always pulled away from going and seeing Murdoch at the office, he did not think a Minister should be summoned by a tycoon . . . he had all the time this sort of sense of dignity.

Menzies was no fool. Perhaps understanding the need to pull Keith close to the government rather than allowing him to remain outside the fold and free to marshal his media in attack, Menzies made him an offer. In May 1940 he approached Keith and asked him to be the newly created director general of information (DGI). This would allow Menzies to remove himself from direct involvement in the operations and policy of the department. Now the so-called phony war was over, he regretted having added this responsibility to his own portfolio.

For Keith the attractions were manifold. As well as the main role overseeing all media output and information in the country, he would have access to the War Cabinet and be privy to the most confidential and classified papers.

The position of DGI undoubtedly appealed to his sense of service, but also perhaps to his vanity. He was following in the footsteps of Beaverbrook and Northcliffe in terms of the official positions they had been given in the last war. But there were possible problems. His uncle Walter Murdoch, the well-known academic and essayist who had exerted such a formative influence in Keith's youth, had warned in 1924 that in the next war 'the great success of the Beaverbrook–Northcliffe enterprise will not be forgotten ... the use of propaganda – which is a moral poison gas, more deadly than the other – will become a monstrous growth, darkening the world. It is an appalling prospect'.

On 8 June the appointment was announced. When the HWT staff were summoned to hear their boss's farewell speech, before Lloyd Dumas took over as acting managing director, Keith stated passionately that it was the imperative duty of newspapers during wartime to tell the truth. One key journalist, Cecil Edwards, found this difficult to square with his employer's previous instructions on managing public knowledge of, and indeed hiding the facts behind, a range of sensitive issues. Keith stressed to his staff that 'his new job was difficult and dangerous', admitting that his reputation, 'a lifetime career, could vanish in half-an-hour'.

In the immediate reorganising of the department of information, Keith greatly widened its reach and power. Its remit was extended to all forms of media in the country. Keith agonised over the drafting of an address to be broadcast nationally, justifying his role and the task of building up what he conceded was 'a ministry of a peculiar kind'. He invoked the spirit of the battlefields of two decades before, begging for the 'confidence and help' of those listening: 'I know you well, you men of the 1914/18 times, you earlier and later generations.'

One of Keith's first moves was to arrange for a national hook-up at 7.15 pm every evening of the week except Sunday for a programme of talks on the latest war developments and Australia's war effort to be broadcast on every single radio station, ABC and commercial. He further asserted that full use would be made of the press, the cinema, and war rallies in order to 'encourage, comfort and inform the people'.

On 19 July 2011 Rupert Murdoch told the committee of MPs who had summoned him to answer for his newspapers' actions in the phone-hacking scandal, that this was the 'most humble day' of his life. Seventy-one years earlier to the day, Keith had had to read the most brutal and humbling headlines of his career: 'A BLUDGEON FOR THE PRESS', a 'TOTALITARIAN TYRANNY'.

Over time he had become used, if never quite inured, to the predictable attacks from the left-wing press. But on 19 July 1940 the humiliation was all the more painful because these accusations had been made by his fellows and competitors in the newspaper world.

The press had spoken out en masse after the announcement of new regulations that would enable Keith's department to order the printing of enforced corrections. Taken to their logical conclusion these powers would result, the *Sydney Morning Herald* argued, in the Australian press being subject to 'a dictatorship as complete as that exercised by Dr Goebbels in Germany'. The *Argus* pointed out that Keith invited recollection of Pontius Pilate's 'famous question nineteen centuries ago, "What is truth?"' Keith is lauded to this day, and by figures as unexpected as Julian Assange, for having written the Gallipoli letter and daring to speak truth to power. But in 1940 he was condemned by those who valued a media free of government control, blasted for seeking to 'out-Goebbels Goebbels'.

Perhaps the hardest and most embarrassing criticism that Keith had to face came from close to home, delivered by the HWT chairman Theodore Fink. In a blistering statement from his sickbed Fink declared that he was thoroughly against censorship control, and dissociated himself from the views expressed in the publications of the HWT in favour of the regulation.

Those close to Keith saw how hard the storm of criticism hit him. Cecil Edwards believed Keith's consternation at its intensity was genuine. Edwards also saw that Keith's line of defence – that he had never intended to use the sweeping powers granted him by the regulations – did not convince his critics. As Edwards summarised it: 'If a man borrows an axe and, asked what he wants it for, replies: "To crack an egg," it is natural to say: "Then why didn't you ask for a teaspoon?"' Edwards was convinced that over the years Keith had grown 'so remote from public opinion that he came to regard his views as those of the people'. In a persuasive analysis, Edwards tracked this back to Keith's upbringing and character:

His Presbyterianism convinced him that, as he could desire only what was right, those who opposed him must be wrong and, for their own good, must be forced into the paths of righteousness. Having little power of reflection, he proceeded by a kind of instinct that, like Northcliffe's, was often right in the early days but had become stale by lack of contact with what people said and thought.

In November 1940 Keith announced, with a hefty tilt of spin, that he had achieved what he had been asked to do and would therefore be stepping down from the role of DGI. If he had hoped he could retreat quietly, he was mistaken. The confirmation of his fall from grace even made the international news. *Time* magazine devoted a long profile piece to the resignation of 'Australia's Lord Northcliffe', the 'tall, hearty man of military bearing' who 'lives in a big U.S. Colonial home outside Melbourne'. It quoted a front-page editorial by the Sydney *Telegraph*:

He is so used to getting a docile 'Yes, Sir Keith' from those who trot at his beck and call in Melbourne ... that he expected the whole Australian people to bow down humbly and submit in the same way.

The Leader of the Opposition John Curtin claimed that Keith's appointment had achieved his ambition to exercise control over Australian public opinion. The regulations had given 'a power over Press, radio and motion picture productions that went far beyond anything in any British country'. Curtin promised that a Labor government would 're-organise the whole department so that its function will be to tell more and to restrain less'.

There might have been another entirely understandable reason contributing to Keith's errors in judgement around this time. On 1 July 1940 his father Patrick had died.

Seated in his favourite wicker chair at family gatherings and picnics, pipe always in hand, Patrick had long been a source of patriarchal gravitas for the clan. Rupert as a young boy would be questioned teasingly by his father on his comprehension of the mini sermons Patrick had delivered at the family dinner table. Even in retirement, Patrick had written a weekly column for the *Presbyterian Messenger*, and according to his son had reached the age of ninety 'with clear mind and contentment'. There would be further cause for mourning five years later when Keith's mother Annie died, aged eighty-eight, in February 1945.

Many years later Keith's widow Elisabeth recalled the 'horrid time' her husband had endured as DGI. In her view, he had been persuaded ('I didn't think Menzies behaved very well over that') to take the role that would be considered 'his greatest mistake in life'.

As the newly appointed DGI, Keith had entered his first War Cabinet meeting determined to reorganise the department of information. Through his networks he was already able to access the views of the elite: two days previously he had told Menzies privately that he had sounded opinion in five states. Bringing to mind his push for conscription during World War I, the main conclusion Keith emphasised was that the country 'would get a great rallying point if the Government asked for 200,000 men at once'. But as he joined the Cabinet table he had a crucial initiative to push, as the minutes stamped 'SECRET' reveal:

It would be valuable to establish a service for ascertaining what a typical cross-section of the public mind is thinking on important questions. It would be necessary to do this in an obscure manner and for the information to be ascertained by a non-Government authority ...

Keith's concerns were well placed, as events in Britain would soon show. There in July a furore was unleashed when the press discovered that the Ministry of

Information, headed by Churchill's friend Duff Cooper, had been conducting a secret social survey using mass observation techniques. The home intelligence division operatives, dubbed 'Cooper's Snoopers', were attacked for bringing 'the shadow of the Gestapo over honest and loyal creatures' with their 'house- to-house questioning'. Australian newspapers soon picked up on the political backlash and relayed it to their readers in front-page stories. But Keith's private plans, already underway, would continue apace.

Back in April 1940 Keith had arranged for an ambitious young employee, Roy Morgan, to head to America and gain experience with the pollster George Gallup of the American Institute of Public Opinion at Princeton University. Four years before, when Keith travelled through America, the presidential election had been taking place. Two very different opinion poll methods were being used, each predicting a different result. The poll produced by the *Literary Digest* following its mass balloting of readers was a much-anticipated, regular event at election time. This time round, the *Literary Digest* called the result for the Republican Alf Landon – and by a landslide too. But the accuracy of Gallup's innovative new technique of extrapolating results from a small representative sample was apparently proved when he correctly predicted Roosevelt's own landslide victory.

Morgan returned to Australia in October to become managing director of Australian Public Opinion Polls (The Gallup Method). Though this new company was to be jointly owned by newspapers representing each of the state capitals, it was effectively controlled by the HWT with Morgan reporting to its general manager.

In September 1941 history was made when the first Australian public opinion poll was published in the *Herald*, revealing that 59 per cent of the public were in favour of women receiving the same wages as men. The trailblazing move proved politically controversial, however. Labor politicians, unions and the left-wing press in particular attacked the 'Yankee stunt' by the Murdoch press.

Menzies had been in Britain during the first half of 1941 while back home his support was leaching away. He returned to Australia to discover his position was untenable, resigning as prime minister on 27 August. The UAP could offer only Billy Hughes, now nearly eighty, so a fill-in was chosen to head the Coalition. He lasted barely forty days. Two supporters of Menzies, disgusted by his treatment and eager for stable government, crossed the floor of Parliament and told the governor-general they would now support Labor's John Curtin as prime minister, who was duly sworn in. After a decade of UAP–Coalition rule, Australia had a Labor government again.

Soon Keith was marshalling a counter-attack with instructions for Dumas:

I think it is essential to follow our conscience as regards the Federal Government and criticise soundly in the way I have been doing here. If the present drift continues, the Nation will never do its best in the war … And if it does get through there will be a tremendous vote for the Labor Party which definitely is a big trend towards proletarian dictatorship. I believe all this can be stopped if we follow my lines of criticism.

During this period Keith was party to the plots and meetings with figures, including his Sydney press magnate counterpart Frank Packer, who wanted to 'rebuild Menzies' as the alternative prime minister. But though Keith conceded Menzies might well be 'the only one we have', he still remained 'short of some valuable qualities'. Keith told Dumas, 'his gifts are very superficial and . . . he cannot lead this country.' (Menzies would go on to set the record as Australia's longest-serving prime minister.)

Keith was eager to act as kingmaker again but by mid-1942 felt frustrated in his task. One well-informed Canberra reporter recalled Curtin saying he thought Sir Keith Murdoch was very disappointed that 'he could not find a leader – "even from our camp. He had hopes of me for a while."' Keith might have felt there was no viable alternative leader to Curtin but that did not stop him from trying to destabilise the incumbent government.

On 4 December 1942, Keith had to open his speech to the annual meeting of the HWT with a eulogy to two people: Theodore Fink and his son Captain Thorold Fink. The former died aged eighty-six after a long illness; the latter was tragically killed just a few months later while on army duty when his jeep overturned. Keith delivered a suitably glowing account of the pair's contribution, their 'kindly qualities', full lives and the sadness that had greeted their passing. But in respect of Theodore's send-off he told Dumas privately, 'I confess that I have never been so unmoved at a funeral.' The threat of a rival dynasty had been snuffed out.

Keith was now chairman as well as managing director of the HWT, yet despite all the pressures on his time this dual role entailed, he also reinvented himself as one of its most prolific writers. Keith was reliving the glory days of his youth, fighting the war in the way he thought best: assembling 3,000-word articles that he could march out across columns and columns of his newspapers.

But to many his output appeared disjointed and suspect. In March 1942 Cecil Edwards confided to his diary that Keith had risen to his 'most Messianic mood' yet, producing 'long exhortatory articles which include peculiar phrases': 'dear brown robins' for the army, 'brave blue fliers' for the air force and 'spray boys and sharpshooters of the seas' for the navy, all while praying that we may not 'emerge from our ordeal with dross befouling us'. Edwards was tickled to read that a compositor, as cynical as he was, had managed to slip an error into Keith's rousing line 'while our brave boys are fighting for our shores', turning the last word into 'shares'! The diplomat Frederic Eggleston in Chungking, after reading a stack of *Herald* back copies containing what he considered were inaccurate and overly pessimistic articles, concluded that the 'panic-stricken' Keith had 'gone nuts': 'He must think that the Japs will knock 3d off the *Herald* dividend.'

By September Keith had adopted the mantle of spiritual guardian for the country. He made sure his call for a renewal of faith – 'the greatest need of the nation today' – was widely published. He even penned a new creed to raise Australia 'on to one common ground for inspiration and notion':

I believe in the good purpose of life, in the beauty of the universe, and the high destiny of men.
I believe in the power of the spirit and the triumph of the good in heart.
I believe in rule by just law and liberty within the law.
I believe in the ethics of the Christian Church.
And I dedicate myself to war without stint until victory . . .

At around this time Keith himself received some slightly more light-hearted religious doggerel, sent to him by Lionel Lindsay, brother of Daryl, Rupert's godfather:

O God, Creator of all Sports and Pastimes
Protect thy people.
Protect thy especial glory the noble Racehorse, and the swift grey-hound,
And the cunning hare of tin.
Give us our Daily Dope: our Sensational Press and The Pictures and Radio,
That we may not be forced to think,
And preserve our motor-cars which are as angels in our sight.
Lord; save our Lottery; save the football and the cricket-ball and especially the golf ball which keeps us pure of heart through play.
Protect Big Business and all holy profits made in thy name. . . .

(Rupert, asked three decades later what he believed, would describe: 'The old Protestant ethic – hard work, professionalism, some sort of idealism about the world, the ability to bring out the goodness of people.' And on receiving the Inaugural Legend Award from the American Australian Association in October 2018, Rupert ended his acceptance speech by quoting the first three lines of his father's wartime creed from the podium.)

After Keith wrote an article attacking the army minister and the government's war policy, Curtin, unprompted, delivered 'an amazing outburst' during one of his off-the-record briefings to the Canberra press gallery. A contemporary note by one of those attending records Curtin as saying Keith's article was 'silly and unfair' and certainly 'no good for public morale'. Curtin continued: 'I do not like Sir Keith Murdoch. I do not trust him. He is utterly unscrupulous in the way he conducts his newspapers.'

In May 1943 Curtin again briefed the press gallery on yet another 'dirty stinking article' by Keith, which explored the relationship between the Australian prime minister, Churchill and Roosevelt. The briefing then turned to the attack, led by Keith, on the chief publicity censor, in whom the prime minister had the utmost confidence:

> Curtin added that Murdoch was a bastard because as Director General of Information he was an entirely different person from Murdoch as a newspaper director and member of the Press Censorship Committee in that he recommended the doing of certain things, some of them most drastic. He was now condemning some of these same things. 'Apparently,' added Curtin, 'they were approved as Director because they did not hit his own papers, but now that they do he is squealing. . . . One of these days I'll tell him exactly what I think.'

Keith certainly had strong views on Curtin's administration that he was able to promote through his press, but 1943 offered the chance for the electorate to deliver its own verdict.

As the federal election neared Keith cabled Dumas that it was 'our duty to make people thoroughly conscious of [the] grave issues involved'. On the issue of election advertising in their newspapers, Keith instructed that provided Labor got an 'adequate share' he did not 'regard equal distribution essential'. A follow-up letter stressed that as 'Labor is not wanting space at present' there was 'no need to limit' the Opposition and that 'at all costs soap and other advertising should be put out of the paper, to make room for good interest-making electioneering material'. Keith believed that 'the best service to Australia would be for the country thoroughly to defeat the existing government'.

Despite all his efforts and predictions, the record-breaking landslide victory for Labor astonished Keith. Chastened and shocked by the results, he could only add a forlorn postscript to his letter to Dumas: 'Do you have any complaints that my articles "overdid it"?'

As well as fearing Labor was not aggressive enough in its commitment to the war, Keith was deeply concerned at the societal changes underway and the prospect of a new economic settlement to come with the peace. One critic on the left published a pamphlet in ironic gothic type, presenting Keith as 'The Modern Don Quixote'. The reply to Keith's 'Criticism of the New Order' depicted him on its frontispiece as the misguided knight on his charger, complete with the legend 'Defend ye Ancient Orders and Estates. Sir Keith of ye "Herald", Valiant Knighte to ye rescue.'

Dumas kept Keith well briefed on any attacks aimed at him, forwarding a memo he had received quoting a public lecture in Adelaide given by a professor of history and political science. To ironical cheers the professor had told his audience: 'A few days ago Jove thundered down from Mount Olympus . . . in other words, Sir Keith Murdoch spoke to us through his papers.'

In his 1944 chairman's speech at the HWT annual meeting Keith stressed to the assembled shareholders that the company had 'weathered the war years better than our most optimistic hopes'. But he also seized the opportunity to vent against his critics, and at some length:

Business interests, loosely condemned as 'vested interests' and then bracketed with Satan's forces as money-grubbers and self-seekers, are all today under attack in some quarters. Newspapers are particularly castigated . . . But just as I would lay it down that our newspapers attempt to be disinterested seekers of the public good, so would I lay it down that it is our duty to make them pay.

Keith concluded by stressing that no media organisation could be perfect, 'we may have been affected by passions and prejudices'. Mistakes would always be made, but 'so far as these things can be exorcised they are exorcised and we try always to serve the public with truth, sincerity and a vigorous regard for its interest'. Keith emphasised that '[w]e must remain actively disliked by those whom in duty bound we watch and criticize, but the newspapers must stand as one of the guardians of public rights and interests'. As the company passed into what would hopefully be the constructive years of peace, Keith emphasised that the press's 'vital and historic role' must be carried out more strongly than ever: 'Those great principles we believe in must be rigorously espoused, but we must seek the greater confidence of the people and their full trust in our honesty and disinterested truthfulness.'

During World War I Keith had been part of the secretive group of business leaders in London who had orchestrated the conscription and pro-war electoral campaigns. Now, along with Dumas, he was a leading founder member of a new group that sought to reframe the debate in Australia in opposition to what they felt was a socialistic drift to the left: the Institute of Public Affairs (IPA).

With the backing of Keith's contacts in big business, not least BHP, the IPA would go on to become, and today remains, the key free-market pressure group in Australia. Typical of its recent campaigns are a crusade defending what it terms 'Western Civilisation', and calls for the country to exit the Paris Agreement on climate change.

Keith helped facilitate the group's 'skilful and persistent propaganda' in its general campaign to orientate the climate of opinion towards the benefits that business and the capitalist system would bring. Within a couple of years, the IPA's views would help form the basis for the programme of a new right-of-centre party.

In May 1943 an Australia-wide Gallup poll revealed that support for the main parties was evenly divided. But crucially, it also showed that nearly one quarter of the electorate were turning their back on these established parties and giving 'other parties' as their preference.

Keith and Menzies were keen to unpick this phenonemon. Menzies as leader of the UAP realised that if he was to have any hope of ever regaining office he would have to form a new umbrella party. In 1944 the Liberal Party was formed. The conservative base of politics in Australia had been recast for decades to come.

In 1918 Keith had written a plea for 'closer relationships' between Australia and America. Just before the Armistice he had given his readers a colourful portrait of the American soldiers who had joined with their Australian colleagues. ('Their physique is undisputable and far better than the European.') Now a second global conflict was taking place, but the American public was still far from receptive to entering another war in a faraway theatre. In January 1940 R. G. Casey had been sent to Washington, DC to take up Australia's first diplomatic post as 'Australian Minister in Washington'. On arrival he had explained that his task as head of the legation there was to promote 'Australian-American friendship and understanding'. When Keith took up the role of DGI, he had immediately made moves to establish a bureau for disseminating information about Australia in America. It finally opened its office in New York in February 1941.

In 1920, while on tour with the *Renown*, Keith had seen the great new American naval base at Pearl Harbor and dwelt on the threat posed by Japan's expansionist aims. Two decades later, on 7 December 1941, that base was attacked. The following day, America declared war on Japan – and entered the conflict in the Pacific. US troops were soon arriving in Australia.

In March 1942 General Douglas MacArthur arrived in Melbourne to become the supreme commander of the South-West Pacific. His authority extended to all allied naval, land and air forces, including those of Australia. Soon Keith asked MacArthur whether he could break with custom and make an appearance at a sports ground. The newly formed Australian–American Co-operation Movement, of which Keith was chairman, had organised for exhibition matches of American football and baseball to 'celebrate the new relationship' between the countries. Keith even wondered whether the general would 'be good enough to pitch the first ball'. MacArthur declined but told Keith he was 'gratified to see the proverbial ties of friendship between our two countries molded into activity in so salubrious and delightful a manner'.

A contemporary briefing note in the MacArthur archives on 'Australian Personalities' reveals the kind of information MacArthur would have been given even before he met Keith. It makes the point that Keith's father was a Presbyterian minister and describes Keith himself as 'a little fanatical, and insurrectionist in a mild form, agin the Government and very pro-British ... He is prone to vacillate'. MacArthur's wife Jean would later recall her admiration for Keith: 'I know the General liked him very, very much and had a great deal of conversations to and fro with him because he was the leading newspaper man.' But the trail of correspondence left by the general, a complex and authoritarian character himself, reveals a very different view.

In September 1942 MacArthur had written to Curtin enclosing one of Keith's censor-braving articles with the comment that there was 'no military intelligence source through which the enemy could receive such complete and accurate information of our forces'. As Keith continued in his one-man mission to undermine and counter what he believed were the over-confident and misleading official accounts of the war's conduct, MacArthur intensified his attacks. One of Keith's assertions, MacArthur claimed, was a 'vicious audacious lie' for which he should be called before the prime minister. MacArthur's PR officer declared the whole series of articles 'masterpieces of implication, suggestion and innuendo'. For MacArthur, Keith was a quisling needing to be censored.

Keith may have railed at the censoring of his articles but he seems to have been active with his own blue pencil. In the World War II government file about Keith Murdoch there is a note commenting on the curious edit applied by the Melbourne *Herald* and the *Sun News-Pictorial* to their otherwise full reports on the radio-savvy President Roosevelt's world broadcast of 13 October. The president had stressed that Allied military plans were 'not being decided by the typewriter strategists who expound their views in the Press or on the radio', wryly going on to quote the old adage that all the best generals apparently work in newspapers rather than the army. The file note points out that these lines 'were deleted, not by the Censor' but by the editors of the two papers. Never one to let a potential attack against Keith pass, Arthur Calwell, a Labor MP now serving as minister for information himself, cited the example in a speech:

No censorship conducted by this or any previous government has been as drastic as that operated by the newspapers themselves. Sir Keith Murdoch, for example, recently censored the President of the United States.

Keith might have seen his standing undermined in Australia, but on the international stage his stock remained high. He might have baulked at the idea of formally entering politics but many abroad regarded Sir Keith Murdoch as a lay statesman for the nation, a role that did little to harm his business interests.

In March 1944 the British high commissioner to Canberra asked Anthony Eden, secretary of state for war and later British prime minister, to see 'the one and only big newspaper owner in Australia ... he is very keen to have a talk with you and he is important enough to us for me to ask you to see him. He is a Tory, self-made, a good Empire man and friend of ours ... keen on Australian–United States friendship.' Next in consideration came Curtin, 'perfectly pleasant' though 'his former little Australian mind may at moments assert itself in some excessively local viewpoint'.

Keith's 1944 trip echoed Northcliffe's frenetic round-the-world whirl. Keith took the difficult route from Perth to Colombo by Catalina flying boat before stopping off to visit his old acquaintance from the *Renown* tour (now Admiral) Mountbatten, at his South-East Asia command headquarters in Kandy, India. Next he went north to London where he penned an article for Northcliffe's old powerhouse, the *Daily Mail* itself. Keith opened with the observation that he had gained 'more than a birdseye view of some Empire problems in my recent long distance air journeys' as 'one characteristic of the air age is that speed in a long hop gives one time on land'. The main point of his article – while stressing that Australia wished to continue 'her development within the orbit of the British Empire' and that her 'main body of sentiment is stoutly and uncompromisingly British' – was to highlight that a new co-operative relationship was needed:

> The truth is clear that in the Pacific Ocean British, Americans and Australians – those who live and think our way – can survive and develop only by working together. They have about them a thousand millions who live, think and aspire differently.

On his way home Keith developed his point in a speech to the Foreign Press Association in New York, asserting that his countrymen sought 'the closest strategic and material unions between Britain, Australia and America'. His three weeks in America were crammed with meetings and functions with the leading figures in business, banking, art, the press and not least politics, including a private appointment and 'pleasant chat' with President Roosevelt. Generously, Keith assured his countrymen that as well as 'finding out about' the United States, 'I am putting in a good word for Australia' in Washington.

Despite Keith's volatile relations with MacArthur, his regard for the Americans and their contribution remained high throughout the war. The embrace would continue to grow. As a secret report for the British War Cabinet noted in early 1943, perhaps with not a little concern, Keith had even written an article advocating the granting of Australian citizenship to American soldiers who had fought in the South-West Pacific. Considering that at the time Australian citizens were also British subjects, such a suggestion would certainly have been unwelcome.

With peace came reflection. For Keith, the developments during the war consolidated his own view that – notwithstanding his apparent rejection of Curtin's famous declaration – America now served as the most powerful inspiration and useful guide for Australia's development. The name of the organisation Keith headed changed from the Australian–American Co-operation Movement to the Australian American Association. In 1946 the AAA's newly launched *Pacific Neighbours* magazine was proud to present a message from the new President Truman praising the association's 'splendid objectives' and wishing it success in its 'new and promising venture in the promotion of better understanding between our two countries'. The AAA's letterhead would bear the innocuous legend 'For the better understanding, mutual appreciation and friendly co-operation of two great Pacific democracies'. But Keith's mining magnate friend W. S. Robinson described the AAA as 'an important propaganda centre, favouring the economic beliefs which made the United States great and, Australians hope, will make their own country equally so'. Douglas Brass would note how 'with a shrewd eye on the future' Keith nurtured relationships with 'men of influence and talent in the United States'.

The Murdoch family's close involvement with not only the AAA but also its counterpart the American Australian Association continues to this day; they are the sponsors of the latter's Sir Keith Murdoch Fellowship. In 1996 Keith's grandson and Princeton graduate Lachlan Keith Murdoch was invited to address a meeting of the AAA. Lachlan used his speech to argue that nations embracing other cultures profit 'from hybrid vigour'. He held up the example of News Corporation as 'uniquely placed to symbolise and celebrate the union of energies and talents from Australia and America'. Hybrid vigour? It appeared pure bloodlines still held the greatest sway. Lachlan Murdoch had just been appointed managing director of News Limited at the age of twenty-five.

13 BY PHONE AND CLONE

St James's Place, London, 10 July 2011. The gaggle of TV cameramen and paparazzi suddenly sprang to life as Rupert Murdoch stepped from the entrance to his apartment building. The eighty-year-old media boss had landed in Britain earlier that day to take charge of the response to the phone-hacking scandal. Isolate, contain, fix. He had closed the *News of the World*; surely senior heads would now roll. One reporter managed to make himself heard over the clamour, shouting, 'What's your priority?' The British outpost of the empire lay besieged, Rupert's reputation was taking a battering like never before and 200 journalists' jobs lay in the balance. Yet he pointed to the red-haired woman at his side and answered, 'This one.'

She was Rebekah Brooks, his protégée, and it has been said that Rupert regards her almost as a daughter. Determined, ambitious and driven, Brooks entered the Murdoch fold as a researcher for the *News of the World* magazine. Rupert, noticing her drive and talent, encouraged her on and upwards. At the age of twenty-seven she was promoted to the role of deputy editor of the paper and by thirty-one was its editor. Still only thirty-four she reached the pinnacle of tabloid power when Rupert made her editor of his cherished *Sun*. Her appointment as CEO of the entire News International operation at barely forty-one crowned her rise. Her discretion and devotion to her boss would remain total: and vice versa. Though the building pressure of the *News of the World* scandal left her with no option but to resign, she would be cleared of all charges related to phone hacking in 2014 and reinstalled as head of Rupert's rebranded News UK just over a year later.

Keith's devotion to handpicking and grooming young talent for his papers had begun at the outset of his career, inspired by the example of Lord Northcliffe. In 1922, getting to grips with his new role as editor of the Melbourne *Herald*, Keith told his mentor that the office was 'now well supplied with youngsters of the well-educated fighting type that makes fine journalists'. In 1934, a father himself now with a toddler son, Keith told Lloyd Dumas that he felt 'old enough now to take an almost sentimental interest in the progress of the young'. Keith was doing his bit for the old Scots links, having benefited from them himself as a young man. He had just arranged a posting for the son of his pre-war prime ministerial friend Andrew Fisher.

Though some aggrieved employees would deride the revolving door of what they nicknamed the 'sons of famous fathers department' at the HWT, Keith was nevertheless establishing a global network of talented young men on meritocratic as well as dynastic lines. Those not possessed of a famous or influential father could win him over by demonstrating bold initiative and a passionate interest in international travel. This was a formula employed to great effect by Phillip Knightley, the renowned investigative journalist and author, just one of the successful reporters and writers who secured his first chance in this way. Keith even used the Newspaper House mosaic as part of a combined observation and literary test for promising cadets. One recalled being asked to return to the Chief once he had worked out why 'we in Australia ... valued *A Midsummer Night's Dream'*. Perplexed to begin with, the candidate eventually looked up one day, spotted the mosaic, clocked the reference and hastened his path up the ladder.

One of Keith's employees, Keith Dunstan recalled that Keith was 'unlike any newspaper proprietor' he would encounter during the rest of his career: 'He was the omnipotent, even ruthless, chief, but at the same time he wanted to be the benevolent, paternal father of us all.' Being a child of the Chief wasn't easy, however. Dunstan experienced first-hand the resentment against Keith and his papers, not only when covering the union scene but in straightforward street inquiries. Asking for information on a run-of-the-mill robbery, Dunstan had the door slammed in his face with the words, 'I won't speak to any Murdoch cunt.'

But John Hetherington, one former favourite who came to despise Keith, observed that the 'ever-changing group of promising journalists' known throughout the industry as 'Keith Murdoch's Young Men' had 'nothing in common with Mr Ziegfeld's Young Ladies [the showgirls of the Broadway Follies] except their constant liability to fall from the graces of the master'. Hetherington recalled his master's wistful explanation for the tireless 'search for human material': 'You young fellows will have to carry on when I am gone!'

Keith's handpicked favourites, those with the most potential, were asked to accompany him on tours of the Empire. While they were on a plane Dunstan recalled that his boss had handed him a pile of weighty reports and HWT accounts to digest with the words, 'Here, study these. See how they work. You will need to understand all this before long.'

New cadets were groomed and cultivated, handed presents of books on the great editors. But they were also given strict instructions about their appearance. Hats were to be worn at all times and, in common with other men in Keith's employment, growing a beard was forbidden. Northcliffe's advice – 'Always dress well ... and never spoil the picture by being in the wrong costume. I like the appearance of my young men to be a credit to the profession' – had stuck. (The high sartorial standards would be passed on again down the Murdoch line. Rupert's second wife was surprised to discover that he insisted on having his own dressing room, making him 'a very Victorian gentleman' with an attitude that came from his father. Rupert also repeated the rule against staff beards.)

Keith also did a spot of covert investigation to get the measure of a hopeful applicant's appearance and conduct before granting an interview. One young man was astonished to realise that Keith had visited the shop that was his current workplace, having to buy a belt in the process in order to look him over.

Keith's complete trust in his secretaries and personal staff did not extend to paying them overly well. In particular, he did not believe in paying women high salaries. It was ironic, then, that the first question in Keith's new 1941 Australian Gallup poll was on the issue of equal pay for women. Keith's ambition for a male secretary, preferably a graduate, would remain thwarted. He tried out several but had to concede that women secretaries were better for diary management and all his personal and confidential typing. Though often hidden behind the front of a man serving the role of 'first secretary', the trusty 'Miss Demello' served Keith with skill and complete dedication to the end of his life. (Rupert had his own devoted gatekeeper Dot Wyndoe who served him for over half a century; while Donald Trump relied on the discretion of his executive assistant Rhona Graff for over three decades.)

While Keith allowed his men to circulate around parts of the HWT empire and his own holdings to gain experience, he encouraged them to stay in touch and write back to him. Decades later, Rupert would use such lines of communication and feelings of obligation to develop a whole system of informal control over his own empire. In the words of one of his editors, Rupert conveys his will not by issuing diktats, but more subtly 'by phone and clone'. (The academic David McKnight has investigated the phenomenon, pointing to the account by Andrew Neil, former editor of the *Sunday Times*, of the sudden and unpredictable phone calls with their ominous silences. The former editor of *The Sun*, David Yelland, described how though 'you don't admit it to yourself that you're being influenced', as an employee you nevertheless end up agreeing with everything he says: 'Most Murdoch editors wake up in the morning, switch on the radio, hear that something has happened ... and think, "What would Rupert think about this?"' A former News Corp executive described this pattern of behaviour as 'anticipatory compliance'. Another former insider explained that Rupert is 'less hands-on than people assume ... It's not done in a direct way where he issues instructions. [Rather,] it's a bunch of people running around trying to please him.')

However, Keith was not averse to gifting his young men to others, particularly when the flow of information in return would be useful. He had given Joe Lyons Martyn Threlfall in 1931, and as far back as 1925 he had agreed to Prime Minister Stanley Bruce's request for Cecil Edwards, then federal roundsman for the *Sun News-Pictorial*, to become the 'press officer in the election tour'. *Smith's Weekly* had greeted the deal with the headline 'Melbourne Herald Lends Bruce Its Boy Poet'. Edwards wrote Bruce's speeches and acted as adviser during the 22,000-kilometre campaign tour, at the end of which he felt confident he was 'closer than other newspapermen to the Prime Minister'. Long before Andy Coulson, the disgraced former *News of the World* editor, was hired by David Cameron, or Bill Shine hopped from his role as co-president of Fox News to head up communications at the Trump White House, Keith had forged the way, discovering the usefulness of lending spin doctors to leaders.

As well as exposing his young men to the world of politics, Keith was keen to put them in touch with the latest thinking and to elevate their social skills. They would be invited to join the regular lunches in the private dining room on the executive floor of the HWT, finding themselves alongside fellow guests from the elites of the business and cultural worlds. The guest list would invariably include any important visitor from overseas who was then in Melbourne. Some of these guests themselves were young, and having the right parentage helped. On one occasion the honoured guests had been 'young Heinz – son of the famous Heinz food firm' and William Randolph Hearst Jr. Following the death of his father four years later, Hearst Jr took over the family business, becoming editor-in-chief of Hearst Newspapers.

Some young employees would even be invited to the Murdoch family home for grand and awe-inspiring dinners, complete with butlers, silverware and choice wines. After the elevated conversation over the meal, Keith would conduct a tour of his art and antique treasures before announcing on the dot of 9.30 pm, 'I suppose you will be needing your coats.'

One eminent physician friend of Keith's considered him a connoisseur, 'a collector of men and things'. For Keith the two passions combined in his fascination with and support of young artists.

It was not just the younger men at the start of their careers whom Keith sought to educate and elevate. He wanted to guide all sections and indeed ages of society. He wrote to Kenneth Clark, the world-famous English art critic asking whether he could find time to invite Robert Menzies, then on a visit to Britain, to his house '(no meal required)'. Keith explained that Menzies was 'terribly conservative – or wrong – in art matters ... such a nuisance to us with his views!' Half an hour, he thought, would be enough 'to educate Bob'.

Above all, Keith's ideal was to send his ablest young men to gain experience overseas. Mindful of the way his own career had been kick-started, he armed them with letters of introduction to the top newspaper proprietors and editors in London and New York. At the very outset of his career he had supported the idea of 'regular interchanges of journalists'. It was not only the young journalist at the heart of the exchange who reaped the benefit of this. One employee described Keith's 'marshalling of those battalions of friends who later became a great army in many parts of the world'. And the HWT-produced biography after Keith's death described another role for them: 'Working with him – however far-flung their postings round the world – they were at once the intelligence corps of his newspapers and the discoverers for him of new ideas, new features, new information links and new talent to join their band.' With time, many of Keith's protégés became important men, so that the global 'vast web of acquaintance' was 'still multiplying at his death'.

Beaverbrook preferred his 'young eagles' to fly free when sent out into the world, unencumbered by wives. But those favoured stars Keith planned to send were, if still unmarried, told to marry before heading off. Ignoring – or perhaps all too painfully aware – that he himself had been a globetrotting bachelor until the age of forty-two, Keith would stress, 'We don't approve of sending away young, single men.' In at least one instance, Keith insisted the young hopeful enter into a swiftly arranged marriage before departure.

Three exceptional men with international experience came to serve crucial roles during the last decade of Keith's life while Rupert was still in his teens. Two in particular helped lay the path for Rupert's own success.

Keith had spotted Colin Bednall at the outset of Bednall's career in the early 1930s, and later encouraged him to gain London experience, arranging a posting with the AAP wire service. Bednall was appointed to the assistant editorship of the *Daily Mail* in 1944, but Keith was able to persuade him to return to Australia as managing editor of his Queensland operations.

Randal Heymanson was working in London as the European correspondent for the HWT's Australian Newspaper Service when Keith decided in 1940 to install him in New York as manager and editor of the *Herald*'s new bureau. He soon proved his usefulness to Keith, arranging 'meetings with important people' and developing excellent contacts both in New York and in Washington.

Heymanson would lay the groundwork before Keith's visits, planning them with military precision. His list of people Keith met during his 1944 visit to Washington, headed by 'President Roosevelt and Mrs Franklin D. Roosevelt', and including senators, admirals and secretaries of state, ran to four close-typed pages. The list for New York was equally impressive, including Wendell Wilkie, Herbert Hoover, a couple of Rockefellers, more Roosevelts and Dr Gallup. From 1948 Heymanson would also run the American Australian Association.

Needless to say, Keith had London sewn up. In the late 1940s Rohan Rivett was 'Sir Keith's white-haired boy [of] the moment'. It perhaps helped that Keith knew his father Sir David Rivett through their association with the post-war reconstruction committee. Rivett was also a fellow member of the Eugenics Society of Victoria.

Impressed by Rohan's war reporting, Keith poached the tall, fair and handsome 29-year-old from the *Argus* in 1946. Two years later Rivett would be sent to the HWT's London office, from where he could keep a watchful eye on Rupert when he began his studies in Politics, Philosophy and Economics at Oxford. During Rupert's journey there through America, Heymanson would arrange for father and son to spend a Sunday with the Sulzberger family, the owners of the *New York*

Times and already good friends. (Arthur Sulzberger had in fact suggested the Murdochs stay with the family for the entirety of their trip but Keith had baulked at the commute this would entail.) Both Heymanson and Rivett would be tasked with helping plan the Murdochs' family holidays while optimising the chance for Keith to conduct meetings with the powerful. The usual tour sites would be on the wish list, though a typical European trip would give Rivett the headache of making additional arrangements to meet heads of government as well as the Pope.

In 1951 Rivett would be brought back to Australia to take up the crucial – for the Murdoch family's personal business interests – role as editor-in-chief of the Adelaide *News*. Rivett's devotion to Keith would prove total – he even named his second son after his employer. Rupert's devotion to the man his father handpicked as a guiding force and mentor for him would unfortunately prove less durable.

In the letter Rupert wrote to smooth the path of his takeover of Dow Jones and the *Wall Street Journal* in 2007, he not only cited his father's actions at Gallipoli but also stressed that News Corp was a family business:

> As a father myself, nothing makes me more proud than to see that my own children have inherited the passion that my father nurtured in me. They share with me a faith in the positive role that journalists play in society and in the future of newspapers to inform, educate and engage.

In later life Elisabeth said that Rupert's own children had been quite young when they were 'thrown in' to the newspaper business by their father. She stressed that, in doing this, Rupert had simply followed his father's example:

> Keith used to talk to Rupert a great deal when he was very young and it used to worry me. I thought he was too young to be [hearing] so much about all the financial side of it all. I remember saying to Keith when I think Rupert was sixteen or seventeen, 'It really worries me. I think Rupert's too young to be involved in all this.' And I remember Keith saying, 'Look, dear, I don't know how long I've got with him and I must do everything to try and prepare him, even if his interests do not turn out that way.'

But as Rupert would recall, his interest was set from childhood: 'I was brought up in a publishing home, a newspaper man's home, and was excited by that ... I saw that life at close range, and after the age of ten or twelve never really considered any other. Because if you're in the media, particularly newspapers, you are in the thick of all the interesting things that are going on in a community ... and I can't imagine any other life that one would want to dedicate oneself to.'

Rupert later observed that he had received little formal advice from his father on the newspaper business but that the daily dinner table discussions couldn't help but provide an insight:

He liked me to work hard and I think tried to instil always into me the high, moral *purpose* of newspapers . . . He was one of the great *journalists* of all time, a great builder, a creator of solid foundations. He had a high-minded idea of what a newspaper could do in society.

According to Tim McDonald, who first came to know Rupert at Geelong Grammar through the political club they set up together, Rupert 'followed what his father did very closely and was riveted on the publication of the *Herald* every day, picking up a copy and poring over it every afternoon'. Rupert would go through the paper, marking it up in pen, 'anticipating what his father would think of it; making comments such as, "There's an editorial on the front page – you can't have that!"' Rupert would refer to his father 'in reverential terms', but was 'completely disdainful' of the school hierarchy. (Rupert himself would tell his biographer William Shawcross of how he 'felt a loner at school, probably because of my father's position'. He had been bullied 'a lot' and feared his own children had likely experienced similar treatment. Rupert turned this ostracism to his advantage: 'It made me realise that if you're going to do your job as a publisher or a principal in the media, you've got to be your own person and not have close friendships which can compromise you. That philosophy just evolved, I think'.)

Looking back over the decades to their time at Geelong, Tim McDonald could only conclude that Rupert had been a 'complete loner' who 'never went with the prevailing culture. His eyes were instead always on the future'. So were those of his father.

Even when Keith took Rupert and some of his school friends for a fishing and camping trip on the pastoral property near Canberra he had bought as a handily located investment, politics and a lesson in networking followed. After writing to Elisabeth that they were 'comfortable and having a delightful liberty in clothing, movement and general thinking', Keith signed off with the information that he and Rupert were about to lunch at the American Embassy.

Keith was preoccupied with concerns for the future, eager for Dumas's view on the 'Brisbane show', as he termed it: the newspaper group that he hoped to hand on to his son. ('I am quite hopeful of Rupert being a good newspaper man!') Keith was buying up preference shares, conscious of the fact he was paying over the odds: 'But I want them to ensure control of the company after my death.'

As a backup to the 'Brisbane show', Keith had the Adelaide interests. At the start of 1949, though he was 'not in fine form', Keith told Dumas that he would be flying down to Adelaide to 'look over some News Ltd matters'. He added the qualifier, 'I want to bring Rupert.' A hotel suite would have to be booked, as Keith presumed his seventeen-year-old son, old enough to be introduced to the mechanics of the business world, would be 'too young for the Club'.

There was a pressing reason for Keith to be building up his personal holdings. By the late 1940s the HWT was slipping from his grip. Keith had come to bitterly regret having accepted £1,500 compensation from Baillieu and Fink in exchange for losing a significant number of his HWT shares – 'my right for doing all the work! . . . I was a fool and that's why I kept the shares for myself in the Brisbane show.' The power as well as wealth that shares with voting rights brought was a lesson learnt the hard way. Keith now appreciated the usefulness of guaranteeing board control even where a minority of the shares were held (a technique later employed to great effect by his son). Keith held the 'controlling interest' in the Brisbane paper and power over the nomination of the board.

A further indication of the type of shareholders and board Keith preferred is revealed in a letter to Dumas. The 'requirements of News Ltd' were 'non-interfering Directors who have touch with large sections of the community and are liberal minded but do not think they either own or run the newspapers'.

Now entering his mid-sixties and with his health failing, Keith was keen to concentrate his remaining energies in forming a legacy that could be passed on to Rupert. At the end of 1949 Keith made the momentous decision to retire from his role as managing director of the HWT. The year had proved additionally stressful as Keith had had to deal with the 'Coms and their fellow travellers' in the HWT office. He had suggested the office should 'get rid' of professed communists and their supporters, only to meet 'a complete wall of opinion' against him. Keith found his position with the journalists' union 'difficult': 'We are putting out the Coms in this place without telling them they are Coms.'

During Christmas 1949 Keith dictated a message to be circulated among the staff that though announcing his retirement, he would be often 'in the office as an active chairman'. This was no time to 'relax or reduce any of our standards'. Instead, with a rallying cry that harked back to his Editor's Notes of the 1920s, he looked to the future:

> We have to improve our products, extend our influence, increase our revenues and better our working lives. We have to examine everything we do, and see that it is modern in method and sound in result . . .

However, Keith soon had a secret plot under way – one that, had it worked, would have seen him leave the HWT entirely while securing personal control of the struggling *Argus*, before running it in competition with the *Sun News-Pictorial* and *Herald*.

The British Daily Mirror Newspapers group had bought the *Argus* in 1949, but had failed to make it profitable. Keith and the Mirror chairman, Northcliffe's nephew Cecil (Harmsworth) King, hatched a plan: the former would supply the management acumen and the latter the finance with the creation of a single media group centred on Queensland Newspapers, together with the Adelaide *News* and the *Argus*. The Mirror would finally turn a secure profit from its Australian adventure, while Keith would secure a 51 per cent controlling share of this new media empire for his family, and most specifically Rupert. Faced with the reality of the gamble, however, both parties pulled back from the deal. Keith was able to concentrate on his Brisbane and Adelaide interests but he also had a new worry on his mind.

Cecil King's business partner Hugh Cudlipp recalled that during the *Argus* manoeuvring Keith had taken him to Melbourne's war memorial (the design of which Keith had used to whip up the population and the *Herald*'s circulation three decades before):

> He was wearing a cloak, like Northcliffe's cloak and like Northcliffe's nephew's cloak. He affected the style and speech of the cultured English gentleman of standing; the corset of Australia's twentieth century respectability fitted him perfectly. 'I am worried about my son Rupert', he said. 'He's at Oxford and he's developing the most alarming Left-wing views.'

In his concern about Rupert, Keith was apparently forgetting his own deep sympathy for the working man when also first in Britain in his twenties. (Cudlipp later wrote that of course Keith needn't have worried: 'Young Rupert became the capitalist businessman *par excellence*, a newspaper operator as formidable as his father but on a world-wide scale.')

Though Keith may have baulked at young Rupert's politics, he nevertheless wanted to help him build connections, and saw hope for a later rightward shift such as he himself had experienced. In 1949 he wrote to Labor Prime Minister Ben Chifley – a man he privately regarded as 'a narrow bigot' – explaining that he had also meant to ask the prime minister 'to shake hands with my 18 year old student son who is at present a zealous Laborite but will I think (probably) eventually travel the same course of his father!' Chifley responded he would be 'very glad' to meet Rupert and was also 'glad to know that whatever may happen to him ultimately, at present he has some strong democratic tendencies'. The son of the media baron and the Labor prime minister developed a long-running correspondence, with letters musing on the political scene winging their way between Oxford and Canberra. Rupert expressed his admiration for socialism, set against his contempt for 'Tory quackery' and those who sought to curtail individual freedom with their plans to ban the Communist Party.

With an election imminent in early 1951, Rupert wished Chifley, now relegated to leader of the Opposition, 'every success in the coming struggle' against Prime Minister Menzies, adding wryly that he had been elected as: 'College Secretary of the British Labour Party! There's nothing like family tradition!' (Keith, a renowned prude who winced at his own very rare outbursts – one employee was amazed to hear his Chief provoked to the point of once saying, 'Why, the man is nothing but what you would call, I understand, a bum-licker!' – would have blushed at the cheeky slogan his son used in his campaign for secretary: 'Rooting for Rupert!') To a friend Keith expressed his concern that Rupert's interests were 'so scattered': he was not only on the executive of the Oxford University Labour Party but also the editor of its journal. Keith conceded, however, that he 'reads a diversified lot of stuff and on the whole I have cause to be proud and thankful about it'.

Rohan Rivett was certain of Rupert's prospects, assuring Keith that his son would 'make his first million with fantastic ease', while gaining 'enormous enjoyment out of everything'. But Keith cautioned that Rivett take care 'not to inflate Rupert':

> His prospects depend entirely on himself. I can assure him of a fine opportunity in the newspaper world, but it will be useless unless he has the right qualities and these are not easy to attain. By the time the Taxation Commissioner has finished with anybody these days, and he doesn't until you have been dead quite a time, there is not much money for anybody to inherit and I hope Rupert will earn whatever he gets. He is inclined to look forward with gusto to his opportunities. The real opportunity is that he makes himself a good man. I feel confident he will do so.

Tasked by Keith with arranging Rupert's first period of work experience in London during the university holiday, Rivett chose the *Chronicle*. Rupert excelled immediately and, Rivett reported, was already lunching with key figures and building 'up an amazing string of contacts' even in his few months in Britain.

Back in Australia Keith was trying to build up a viable empire to hand on to his son. He was keen to diversify and expand the reach of the family's media holdings. During 1951 he decided that News Limited should increase its shareholding in Southdown Press, the publisher of the national magazines *Life Digest*, *Adam and Eve* (incorporating *Movie Life*) and the then struggling *New Idea*. Described by its new owner as 'a charming little women's paper', *New Idea* received immediate cross-promotional boosts from Keith's related interests. Readers of the Adelaide *News* were presented with articles trailing the stories in this 'favorite women's weekly magazine' and instructed to ask their newsagents to stock the title. Keith's faith in *New Idea* was well placed. It later proved a key plank in the early expansion of Rupert's empire after he bought it back.

Keith Dunstan recalled the anger of his father William, general manager of the HWT from 1934, about the 'outrageous' way Keith had engineered favourable treatment from the company (HWT), particularly in terms of newsprint, for the *Courier-Mail* and the *News* in Adelaide.

Cecil Edwards described Keith's practice of selecting the cream of the HWT employees and transferring them to his own papers, titles that often 'seemed to get the better of deals' with the *Herald*. But the juggling act was proving stressful.

Though Keith had nominally relinquished executive power over the HWT he still continued almost fulltime in the office, pressing unwelcome advice onto his successor John Williams. The friction between them would cause tension and strain to both.

Keith wrote to Rupert updating him on 'our circulations', all of which were good. However, after a push spearheaded by Williams, Keith was unhappy with the appearance of the *Sun News-Pictorial*, describing it as 'vulgarised, crimey, badly printed and ill turned out'. Perhaps he recalled the Gun Alley sensation when he attributed the *Sun*'s spike in circulation that week to '(murder trial)'.

Thirty years earlier, Keith had declared to his mentor Northcliffe that the press baron's notes and letters were his 'bible'. Now Rivett assured the concerned father that his letters to his son were treasured along with their advice guiding him in the major steps Rupert faced: 'Your letters are – quite literally – his Bible.'

It was time for the father to hear directly how the experience of Oxford was shaping his son. Keith was becoming more and more concerned with Rupert's failure to write often enough. Keith's health issues and enforced hospital stays only compounded his concern. A ray of hope would soon come though. As Keith gleefully told Rivett, Rupert was 'writing letters at last – he has broken his ankle and can't do anything else!'

In April 1951 Keith explained that Rupert was 'the main magnet' of his upcoming visit to London (paid for by Reuters as he would be attending its centennial board meeting). He wanted to spend some time with his son 'summing things up and taking him to the Continent'. And so in the northern summer of 1951 Keith joined Rupert, a couple of his university friends and his tutor, the historian Asa Briggs, on a road trip across Europe.

They went as far as Yugoslavia, and Keith was fascinated by his first direct experience of a 'communised country'. (In Australia the Menzies government was struggling with its unconstitutional, ill-fated bill to ban the Communist Party: a move to which Keith controversially gave his full 'emotional backing'.) They had met Marshal Tito, the country's prime minister and shortly to be its president, and the visit had confirmed for Keith that 'complete socialism' was doomed to fail. He believed that 'the American foundation of competition protected by stern anti-trust administration is the best, although state competition should not be ruled out'. He had also been concerned to see how 'man's capacity is still terrific for much profit taking and soulless greed'. The lesson was clear: 'We must preach and teach!'

The father–son trip through Europe had heartened Keith. Rupert was 'blooming ... twice the man he was when he left Oxford'; but his rash handling of the big Rover on hairpin bends was a point of paternal concern. Leaving the party, Keith had urged Rupert to take the car straight by ship to Istanbul rather than 'risk the horrible journey up through Greece and over Gallipoli-way'.

Keith was following a risky course himself. His financial situation was perilous. In his anxiety to secure outright control of the Adelaide and Queensland holdings, in readiness to hand on to Rupert, he had overextended himself. In mid-1950 Keith would confide to a friend in England that though the wool clip from his pastoral property was excellent, he had 'a whale of a mortgage on it just now to help me pay for News shares'. By June 1951 Keith would write to Elisabeth from New York, assuring her that despite their financial concerns he was not afraid of the future. He promised not to sell the large home in the city until Elisabeth herself agreed, 'after Anne has been launched and Rupert is married'. And as late as 18 September 1952, though burdened with a significant overdraft, Keith instructed an Adelaide sharebroker that he would offer a shilling more than the market price for any News shares – up to 10,000 of them, in fact. But racked by ill health, Keith had also been on borrowed time for the last two decades.

In 1919 Keith had written that his only certainties had been that 'money will never be a principal objective, but independence in the use of power will be one'. He had also wanted to develop 'as a leader of men' through his writing. Over the years, however, Keith had warmed to the pursuit of wealth. Indeed, one of his editors, C. R. Bradish, believed Keith had 'missed some of the simple beauties of life by devoting so much of his time to securing his degree with honours in the dismal science of making money'. From his private conversations with Keith, Bradish felt he had gained 'peeps into the worries and apprehensions of a singularly sensitive man', a man who had a 'compelling terror' that a violent shift to the left 'might yet rob him of much of the wealth he had acquired' and destroy the capitalism that 'he adored'.

But the business of business took its toll on those at the top. A concerned Keith was moved to write to one of his stressed managers with some advice: 'We big executives go through the strain of consistent heavy routine without understanding the demand that it is making upon us. We only get the problems to deal with – the simple stuff flows over other desks – and it is the problems that put their weight on our shoulders . . .'. Keith continued to add to the weight. After each health setback, an encouraging doctor's report would embolden him to expand his dealings again in the fields of press, politics, industry and art.

One art historian has pointed out that much of what Keith chose to invest in – furniture, silverware, porcelain – consisted of 'objects, useful and realisable', while noting the elevation of status Keith's collection gave him: if he could not be an aristocrat by birth, 'he could at least imitate the Rockefellers'.

There is no doubt, however, that the works of art Keith gathered around him were cherished for more than their base value. As his health deteriorated they gave succour to his spirit and reminded him of his life, its achievements and his loves.

When Keith underwent a risky operation to remove cancer of the bowel he asked for his favourite pictures to be hung in his hospital room. They included his Augustus John painting of the head of a Canadian soldier, 'a trusty fellow to go into hard times with'; a landscape, 'for the outback' and a 'truly noble' fifteenth-century Adoration of the Christ child with the holy family. 'They just about kept me alive.'

But art could also provide a sharp reminder of actions regretted or better left unexamined. The Labor politician Arthur Calwell claimed to have witnessed Keith apparently lost in contemplation while studying the portrait of Joseph Lyons in Parliament House, Canberra: in Calwell's words, 'the man he had made, and the man who had tried to escape from his toils by showing some independence'. Sensing Calwell's presence, Keith turned and stared 'with eyes of hate'. Neither spoke.

Art also provided a link to the future. In August 1952 Rohan Rivett had taken the initiative and opened an art exhibition in Adelaide. Though Keith acknowledged this as a brave step, he feared it was 'a terrible affair' featuring the work of the 'old "stodgepots"' who were too commonly accepted in Australia; he was glad to see it 'soundly traduced' by the *News*'s own art critic.

And in echoing the contents of Henry Wellcome's 1909 booklet, art provided a bridge to the very origins of civilisation and the history of the media itself. Keith's *Courier-Mail* arranged for a gift to be sent to his 'good friend' Arthur Hays Sulzberger in America, publisher of the *New York Times*. In a ceremony overseen by Randal Heymanson, two stone reproductions made from tracings of rare Aboriginal cave paintings were presented to Sulzberger to be housed in the New York Times Museum of the Printed Word. The *Courier-Mail*'s write-up explained that the museum 'traces the story of communications from the earliest wall inscriptions to the modern newspaper'.

In mid-1952 Keith and Elisabeth travelled to Surfers Paradise in Queensland to allow Keith to recover from another operation, this time on his prostate gland. Reinvigorated by the immensity of ocean and beach and the uplifting spectacle of the healthy bodies of young bathers, Keith thought the name Paradise well suited: 'it really may be like it!' He could never entirely relax, however: too much needed to be done in this 'drifting country'. Keith felt that Robert Menzies as prime minister was not sufficiently aware of the fact that America was key to Australia's future. Half a century after his crisis of faith in London, Keith was now revelling in a new faith. Only very slowly was he 'getting into the minds' of the unions. 'But the American faith goes a great deal further. It connects work with a man's inner balance and completeness. There is almost a religious aspect in this.' Keith's son, however, was not yet a disciple of capitalism.

As 1951 drew to an end, Keith had been excited to report he was bringing Rupert back from Oxford to Australia for Christmas. With paternal pride and more than a little relief, he added to Heymanson that Rupert had 'attained to the position of some stability in his College, and, I think, will finally be a credit to it'. The trip would give Rupert the chance to see his sisters 'during a period of charming growth', which Keith, painfully conscious of the march of time, stressed 'can never be repeated and which it would be a pity for him to miss'. Keith was consoled by the fact that the trip would also mean his son, now making a success of himself on the other side of the world, would 'see his country and get his feet more firmly attached to the Australian soil'. The holiday was a great success, with Keith rejoicing in how 'very charming' it was to be 'all together again' as a family, Cruden Farm proving 'a paradise' in the fine weather. It would be Keith's last Christmas.

Keith had a further reason for delight and contentment that Christmas at Cruden: a new generation had been added to the family. Just a couple of months earlier Helen, now married to Geoffrey Handbury, had given birth to a son. The happy parents had named him Matthew Keith. Rupert and Miss Kimpton, the governess, were the godparents.

Even after Rupert returned to Oxford, the reinvigorated family ties were evident. In March 1952 Keith tasked Heymanson with getting hold of a copy of a book made up of examples of 'good reporting'. Rupert's sisters wanted to have it sent to him as a present for his twenty-first birthday. Keith wanted one too – in fact, he suggested to Heymanson that he should buy a dozen for all young reporters of promise.

While Rupert continued his studies, Keith was communicating much of his advice and skill to Rivett, now back in Adelaide and in charge of the *News*. In early 1952, three decades after he took Northcliffe's advice and mounted beauty competitions in the pages of his papers, Keith wrote to Rivett of his dislike for 'this obsession which we have at present in Melbourne led by the *Argus* or perhaps by our own *Sun*, of semi-nude women who have no beauty about them'. As Keith was at pains to stress, beauty was key. 'Of course, a pretty woman will always make a pretty picture particularly in a bathing dress. You would know that better than I being your own age.' Keith had urged a further note of caution to his newspaper's new editor-in-chief, warning Rivett that most of the *News*'s features were 'middle-class reading . . . not every man and woman's reading'. It was important that at least one of the double-page features should be 'thoroughly exciting and readable'. It would be Keith's son who would within twenty years perfect the art of supplying the exciting everyman read, spiced with semi-nude titillation, in his own *Sun*.

Three decades after Keith accompanied the then Prince of Wales on his tour, he suggested Rivett take and rework the front-page article on the now Duke of Windsor from one of the London Sunday papers he was sending, as it would make 'quite good reading out here'. (Keith had previously fought to obtain the serialisation rights for the second instalment of the Duke's memoirs, sure it would prove a 'sensational volume' as it covered the abdication period and 'Mrs Simpson story'. He had kept his business head firmly on, though, telling Dumas that, as well as of course wanting them for the Melbourne *Herald*, he 'would like to have them cheaply for Adelaide and/or Brisbane' – his personally owned holdings.) In a scrawled postscript, Keith pointed to two further attention-grabbing topics to rework from the Sunday papers: the series of articles on Stalin by his nephew, and the 'latest on flying saucers'.

In guiding Rivett's revitalisation of the *News*, Keith recalled his own circulation battles when he had first been editor of the *Herald*. He admitted he had 'used many devices – even a beauty competition' and 'full reports of sensational events', though he did not mention the name Colin Ross or the location of Gun Alley. Writing again to Rivett on 7 July 1952, Keith couldn't conceal his delight at some exciting news: 'Rupert has been expelled from the Labor Club!!' The news seemed to lift a weight from Keith's shoulders. One employee, writing the following day to Heymanson in New York, observed how Keith was looking very fit again: '[he] says he is going to take a much more active part in things than he has recently, and has made up his mind that he is good for another twenty years.' But time was about to run out.

Keith's attention extended much further than Adelaide. He was always eager for Heymanson in New York to update him on the latest media news and technological advances in communication. In the early 1950s TV was taking off in America. 'What interesting stuff you sent me about the television development. This is unavoidable. We must make the best of it. Like many of these things it is a great service to mankind and must be welcomed. But man must be guided to use it well.' For the last few years of his life, through his newspapers, Keith would urge the government into action to help television develop in Australia. Under him, the HWT acquired the large site in Melbourne on which 'he could foresee, in good time, the *Herald* television station rising'.

As well as the age of television, this was the 'Atomic Age'. For Keith it was the age 'not only of atomic energy but of atomic time. Things are moving very fast.' In America Keith had attended a private screening of the first films showing the atom bomb explosions at Bikini Atoll. The excitement was infectious. He signed a letter to his daughter Anne by adding 'two atomic bombs of kisses and hugs'.

As October 1952 began Keith was considering how his newspapers should best cover the news of the first British atomic bomb test, due to take place in the Montebello Islands off Western Australia. The 'A-bomb' exploded at 8.00 am local time on 3 October. The correspondents in the small port of Onslow about 110 kilometres away saw a brilliant flash followed by a huge grey cloud shaped like a ragged letter Z.

In New York Heymanson wrote to Keith, imagining how exciting he must have found the news that the explosion had proved a success. Keith never read the letter.

Keith Murdoch suffered a heart attack and died in his sleep on 4 October 1952. Two days before, one very important and long-awaited letter had arrived. Keith read Rupert's more objective, journalistic account of a Labour Party conference and exclaimed, 'Thank God, the boy's got it.' Elisabeth felt the letter was 'heaven-sent': Keith was happy, believing that Rupert 'was going to develop into the useful sort of person [his father] hoped he would be'.

For those closest to Keith his passing left a void: incredulity that the whirl of his activity and his great energy were now absent. His trusty secretary Eileen Demello cabled Heymanson in New York, the shock at Keith's sudden death still raw three weeks later: 'HE ALWAYS SEEMED SO FULL OF VIGOR THAT WE THOUGHT HIM ALMOST IMMORTAL.'

The obituaries were varied. *The Times* described Keith as 'Northcliffe of Australia'. A letter to the editor a few days later noted that 'from A to Z, the politicians, right and left: officials, journalists, high and low: the lot came to his table and were as fascinated by him as he by them'. The commemoration booklet published by the HWT summed up the contradictions of his personality, describing him as a 'revolutionary conservative'. The US State Department declared, 'He was a great and abiding friend of the United States.' And Prime Minister Robert Menzies, whose relationship with Keith had been variable, stated cryptically that he had 'left us in his debt.'

Others summed up Keith's legacy in less circumspect terms. The left-wing poet David Martin published a 'Dirge For a Press Lord', its lines beginning:

> The Lord of lies has gone to his last rest,
> Mourn him with hymns, all who hold falsehood dear;
> Silence your rotaries and bid your presses hush,
> And let four lies stand guard around his bier.

For Martin, the four brother lies of the unnamed Press Lord were those of 'war', 'human baseness', 'slanderer of those who toil', and lastly the 'lie that perverts the young'.

Douglas Brass, long-standing editor-in-chief of News Limited, would later write of how throughout his life Keith Murdoch's 'campaigning and politicising' was driven by his belief in what was 'best for Australia'. While Keith's methods may sometimes have 'raised eyebrows among the sensitive', for Brass it was 'not wrongheadedness' but patriotism that ultimately lay at the heart of it all.

Views poles apart perhaps, but the truth of the enigma that was Keith Murdoch lies somewhere in between.

14 THE SON RISES

– His methods are probably suitable for the times in which we live . . . He's probably a modern edition of his father.

ELISABETH *describing her son Rupert*

On 12 April 2012 Keith Rupert Murdoch submitted his witness statement to Britain's Leveson Inquiry into 'the culture, practice and ethics of the press'. Its opening lines stressed that his grandfather had been a Presbyterian minister and supporter of the free press. Rupert then quoted a section of Keith's will in which his father laid down his expectations that his son 'should continue to express ideals of newspaper and broadcasting activities in the service of others and these ideals should be pursued with deep interest'. The will, setting out Keith's hope that his son should have the 'great opportunity' of 'ultimately occupying a position of high responsibility' in the field of the media, was dated 21 January 1948. It had been written when Rupert was still at school, aged just sixteen.

Though it had pained him, Keith Murdoch had rebelled against his own father's hopes and plans for his career, believing the press was where he could serve his most 'useful' purpose. Keith's own son, however, would follow his father's wishes. The intensity with which Rupert has pursued – and achieved – success on an unheralded global level is something that as a proud father Keith could only have dreamt of.

In October 1952, Elisabeth had given Rupert's tutor at Oxford, Asa Briggs, the task of telling Rupert his father had died. Deeply shocked, Rupert returned to Melbourne as soon as he could, though unfortunately not soon enough to attend the funeral. Elisabeth, in her grief and shock, could only go along with the plans by the HWT and those powerful friends of Keith's who wished to give him a grand, public and prompt send-off commensurate with his standing in Australia.

When Rupert arrived back there was at least some time for private grief with his mother and sisters before he had to undertake the difficult tasks of understanding Keith's financial affairs and resolving the inheritance. It was decided that News

Limited should be retained, while the interest in Queensland Newspapers would ultimately be sold to the HWT. An auction sale of the exceptional collection of art and antiques would help discharge further debts and death duties. Rupert would return to Oxford to complete his studies before coming back to Australia to take up the reins. There was another, less tangible, inheritance, however. Keith's influence and the network of contacts he had laid down around the world would live on beyond him, as Rupert would soon discover.

Even the route of Rupert's journey back to Oxford via America provided an opportunity for Keith's satellites there to help distract him from his grief and cement professional and political links. At the end of 1952 it was election time in America and Keith's close friend the *Herald*'s New York bureau chief Randal Heymanson tried to get Rupert into one of the rallies 'which will doubtless increase his prestige with his Oxford pals'. (In what proved to be his last letter to Heymanson, Keith had asked for copies of the presidential campaign speeches of Democrat Adlai Stevenson to be sent to 'my neo-journalist son Rupert at Oxford.') With the young Rupert in town Heymanson also organised an American Australian Association luncheon at which tributes were paid to his father by the assistant secretary of state and Australia's own minister, Richard Casey.

As a family friend, Richard, later Baron Casey, believed Rupert had 'inherited a great deal from his father'. Just a year before his death, Casey would still be sending letters of recommendation on Rupert's behalf in 1975, emphasising that he was 'the son of the late Sir Keith Murdoch', to eminent Americans – including Nelson Rockefeller, the forty-first vice-president of the United States and grandson of the Standard Oil founder.

As Rupert returned to America at the end of 1952, back in Canberra preparations were being made for the construction of the American Memorial. A money-raising campaign driven by the Australian American Association had been topped up with funds by the Australian government. Keith, a major force behind the project, had foreseen 'something soaring, something standing apart in lonely grandeur'. Just over a year later the 73-metre octagonal aluminium column surmounted by a brutalist American eagle with sharp wings aloft in the V of Victory was complete.

The knowledge held by two towering figures in Keith's life would also be passed on to Rupert. The well-worn bundle of 'notes from the Chief' had a new owner. The collection of advice that Northcliffe had lent to Keith and that became his prodigy's 'bible' had never been returned. Now the notes were being read by the next generation. And during the round-the-world dash home three days after his father's death, Rupert had written a letter to Lord Beaverbrook.

After thanking Beaverbrook for his 'most generous and kind' leader about his father in the *Daily Express*, Rupert explained he was going to Australia to do what he could for his mother and sisters and to help in settling 'all the necessary matters'. He was unsure when he would be able to return to Oxford to finish his degree, or, whether he would ask for 'further much needed training' in Fleet Street.

All I know is that I am faced with much responsibility at an extremely early age, and it would be a great relief if I could feel – as I know I can – that I could rely on you for occasional and sympathetic advice. Again many thanks for all your kindnesses.

In his reply Beaverbrook overwrote his secretary's typewritten address of 'Mr Murdoch' with 'Dear Rupert'. He assured the 21-year-old of 'any assistance' he could give 'at any time' in the task that lay before him: 'I shall always be only too willing to help you in any direction in which my activities may be of value to you.'

Beaverbrook had already written personally to Elisabeth, emphasising that 'here in London we grieve for [Keith] deeply'. He had 'lost an honoured and trusted friend' and would miss Keith's 'wise advice, his independence, his quiet humour, his instinctive championship of freedom'. His friend had 'built well, and he built for the future. His name and fame will long endure.' Elisabeth responded by saying that the warm reception her husband always received in Fleet Street had been 'a great satisfaction' to him: 'even a few days in and around that part of the world stimulated and impressed him to work harder and harder for the higher purposes of Journalism'. Some, however, would question the purposes Beaverbrook's own journalism served and the example his career set.

Walter Murdoch, Keith's uncle who had inspired him to pursue journalism and later supported him during the difficult first year in London, had developed an increasingly critical view of Beaverbrook and the trajectory of the British press over the previous three decades. Reviewing Beaverbrook's self-help book *Success* (written 'for the young men of the new age' seeking 'the upward track') in 1923, Walter noted that the son of a minister who extolled his Presbyterian upbringing had nevertheless embraced wealth as 'an end to itself, the only conceivable end'. He quoted Beaverbrook's edict that '[t]he money brain is, in the modern world, the supreme brain'. Dismissing the artistic or altruistic ambitions of 'dreamers', Beaverbrook, writing from what he termed 'the golden pinnacle of success', had addressed instead the 'young men who want to succeed in business and to build up a new nation'. Walter thought Beaverbrook's message of a world being laid out for the taking was nothing new: after all, it had 'a very distinguished predecessor' in the Devil's temptation of Christ in the desert.

Visiting London again a few years later, Walter had been struck by the 'ominous . . . deterioration of the British newspaper . . . and the debauching of the public mind by the Beaverbrook and Rothermere Press. Fed on these newspapers the Englishman is in danger of becoming childish.' The country seemed to be losing its ancient wisdom in treating serious things lightly and light things, such as sport, seriously.

By 1936 Keith himself, at least in public, was sharing his uncle's concern about the apparent direction of the British press. The trip during which Keith had first exposed the young Rupert to the world had allowed him to observe that despite its 'circulation and technical excellence' the popular press had developed a much more strident tone:

> In more than one instance this stridency becomes outright hysteria. This section of the Press goes for an exploitation of people's private lives that has never before been known in England.

In private too, Keith had been scathing. He told Rohan Rivett he did not like the 'Daily Express types' among the compositors. He later deplored the 'doctoring or "jerking" of items to give them false interest'. This was 'downright sensationalism and is practised in the London *Daily Express* office'. However, despite his concerns, Keith retained his friendship with Beaverbrook and chose him as the man under whom Rupert should be blooded. Success was the key determinant. After all, the *Express* was the most successful daily newspaper in the world, its circulation by 1950 more than four million.

In early 1953 Rupert was continuing his Oxford studies. From his Worcester College address he wrote to Beaverbrook, taking him up on the offer of assistance, and seeking – as had his father forty-five years earlier – the stimulation and training of Fleet Street. Turning to wider business strategy and keenly mindful of his inheritance, Rupert also wished to discuss 'the Australian newspaper position' with the old hand.

The young Rupert was invited to Beaverbrook's flat in the glamorous, modernist block just behind the Ritz. (Later, Rupert chose this same prized St James's location for his own London base, his penthouse just yards from Beaverbrook's original and sharing the same panoramic view across Green Park and over the roofs of Buckingham Palace.) The meeting appears to have gone well with the old 'Demon Beaver' instructing Edward Pickering, the deputy editor of the *Daily Express*, to take Rupert under his wing and 'make sure he learns something of the trade'. One account has Beaverbrook saying: 'Take care of him, Pick, you never know where he might end up.' (Working on the sub-editor's bench of the *Express*, it was claimed Rupert was the only one of his colleagues who would head home to the Savoy at the end of his night shift.) Pickering would become Rupert's 'great mentor', who was later invited to become an independent director and then executive vice-chairman of The *Times* after the turbulent Murdoch takeover in 1981. In mid-1953 Beaverbrook wrote to Elisabeth to relay a report he had received about Rupert's progress: 'He is a most likeable, lively, attractive young man and in my view will go far in his profession.' Elisabeth assured him that she was delighted that Rupert had been 'able to do what his father would have wished'. When he returned to Australia, Rupert was soon forging ahead in his career. Keith needn't have worried. Rupert's young radical days were quickly put behind him after he finished his degree at Oxford and took up the reins in Adelaide. (Rivett confided to friends that 'the metamorphosis of the young left-winger, in the space of just four weeks, to a right-wing, hungry, self-seeking conservative was the most remarkable thing he ever witnessed. He didn't realise that a grub could turn into a moth so quickly.')

But as the decade progressed Rupert would revert to Beaverbrook for advice when needed.

On 4 October 1957, five years to the day after Keith's death, the history of communication took a great leap forward, one heralding the technology that Rupert would later exploit in order to extend his global power and influence. Standing with her son on the grass tennis court at Cruden Farm, Elisabeth recalled, 'We looked up into the night sky together and there was this white light passing overhead. It was the first satellite.' In Shakespeare's imagination, Puck had put a girdle round about the earth in forty minutes. Sputnik I, 'the simplest kind of baby moon', was now orbiting the earth in a little over an hour and a half. 'Rupert pointed the light out to me and said that this was one of the most exciting indications of what lay ahead for the future.'

At the outset of his career, frustrated by his inability to follow his own father and preach from the pulpit, Keith had determined that journalism, rather than the priesthood or representative politics, would be his means to exert an influence and 'be really useful in the world'.

The timing of Keith's choice of career coincided with the rise of the modern press. Keith was a central character in the power play that saw the first media barons Lords Northcliffe and Beaverbrook flex their muscle against elected government. Keith, later himself dubbed 'Lord Southcliffe', was a confidant of both. World War I had provided fertile ground for the development and refinement of propaganda and public relations techniques. Keith had forged his own role as a political agent, blurring the demarcation between press and politics, truth and propaganda. The will to influence and shape public opinion and political outcomes would continue.

A further lifelong obsession with business and technological development in the media industry, drawn from numerous research trips to America and Britain, informed the expansion and formation of Australia's first media conglomeration. Its multimedia, synergistic and syndicated character foreshadowed the worldwide model of the later News Corporation. By Rupert's birth in 1931 this included embracing not only newspapers, to which most previous accounts of Keith's life restrict their focus, but also wireless stations and talkie newsreels.

While Rupert has remained a self-avowed newspaperman and defender of the press, this Murdoch identification with other forms of media continues through the business passions of Keith's grandchildren, particularly Lachlan, James and Elisabeth. A belief in standing up for commercial interests in the face of state-funded models also directly and remarkably echoes their grandfather's early battles with the ABC.

Keith's early recognition of the ascendancy of the media to its position of pivotal power in the modern world was inspired. His decision to pursue a career in journalism and to wield power as a self-appointed gatekeeper of public discourse and opinion was his most important decision. It is also Keith's greatest legacy. His embrace of this concept, *not* the single Adelaide newspaper willed to his son on his death, as is the romanticised view, was Rupert's key inheritance. It explains the trajectory of this remarkable media dynasty, and its sense of duty to act through, but also its entitlement to possess and wield, the power of the media.

EPILOGUE

A NEW INHERITANCE

– 'I have always kept in mind very much the legacy of my father and the influence he had on me. I have his picture prominently on the wall of my study at home. We do feel – I feel – that's a family obligation.'

RUPERT MURDOCH

With the support of his mother and sisters, Rupert began a meteoric rise. He expanded News Limited aggressively, acquiring suburban and provincial newspapers throughout Australia, moving into Sydney and in 1960 securing the prize of the tabloid *Daily Mirror* there – the paper Keith had described as 'a rubbishy sheet, but there are a great many rubbishy minds in Sydney'.

Rupert's appetite for newspaper control was now voracious. Hugh Cudlipp recalled that when he first saw Rupert in the early 1950s, learning the trade from the sub-editors' bench at Beaverbrook's *Express*, he had thought him 'rather shy, rather charming, rather nice. When I saw him ten years later, one rather felt that he looked at one with all the sincerity of a boa constrictor contemplating his next meal.'

In 1964 Rupert achieved an ambition of his father's by launching the country's first national daily, *The Australian*. From 1968, however, his attention increasingly turned overseas, with acquisitions first in Britain and from 1973 in the United States.

In 1985 Rupert became an American citizen, enabling him to expand his American operations and develop the Fox Network. Sentimental family ties and business opportunity coincided a year later back in Australia, however. With his mother at his side, Rupert announced the successful takeover of the HWT. The subsidiary has remained closest to the family's heart, chaired initially by Rupert's sister Janet Calvert-Jones and since 2013 by her daughter, Keith's granddaughter, Penny Fowler.

Rupert's first marriage to Patricia Booker brought him a daughter, Prudence, born in 1958. His second marriage in 1967 to Anna Maria Torv, an Estonian-Scottish journalist who worked for his titles, proved more enduring, with three children: Elisabeth (born 1968), Lachlan Keith (born 1971) and James Rupert (born 1972).

Rupert's divorce from Anna in 1999 laid bare a dynastic struggle. Anna agreed to the terms of the financial settlement on condition that the four children would be the sole beneficiaries of the Murdoch family trust and its significant holding of voting shares in News Corporation. Rupert's controversial third marriage to Wendi Deng from 1999 to 2013 produced two more daughters, Grace Helen (born 2001) and Chloe (born 2003). In 2006 Rupert revealed that his two youngest daughters would receive equal shares in the family trust but would have no voting rights. All six children were given US $150 million each in cash and stock.

Though Prudence has never actively worked in the business her husband Alasdair MacLeod was with News Corporation for twenty years and served as managing director of a News Limited subsidiary, the Community Newspapers Group, and then Nationwide News until his resignation in 2010.

Elisabeth gained early experience with News Limited before working in News Corporation's television interests in America and the United Kingdom. After a fractious period with BSkyB she struck out on her own, founding the production company Shine in 2001. Elisabeth sold the company to News Corporation in 2011 but declined an invitation to join the corporation's board.

Lachlan cut his commercial teeth at Queensland Newspapers. Groomed by Rupert as heir apparent, he rose through News Limited to become deputy chief operating officer of News Corporation but, apparently frustrated by challenges to his authority, resigned in 2005. He had led the doomed purchase of One.Tel, though time would view News Limited's 2000 investment in the real estate website REA more kindly.

Insistent that he would not return to News Corporation, Lachlan based himself in Sydney, developing media interests through his Illyria investment vehicle. In 2007 he joined forces with his friend and fellow media dynasty heir James Packer in failed bids to take over Consolidated Media Holdings. The pair also joined forces to invest in the struggling Ten Network, which Lachlan would later chair. Lachlan's purchase of the Daily Mail Group's Nova radio network has proved more prudent and profitable.

James, initially regarded as the rebellious black sheep of the family, returned to the fold with international roles at Star TV in Asia and then BSkyB and News International in London. Following Lachlan's resignation, his primacy in the succession seemed assured. From 2011, however, the fallout from the revelations of phone hacking by the *News of the World*, a practice that had in part taken place on his watch, appears to have undermined his prospects. An in-depth *New York Times* investigation has since claimed James stayed with the company due to a sense of dynastic obligation and a need to prove himself to his father. He apparently told a friend during the hacking scandal: 'I can't leave . . . I was brought up to do this.'

Having served as the family matriarch for over eight decades, Dame Elisabeth Murdoch died in 2012 at the age of 103, leaving seventy-seven living descendants and a legacy of dedicated support for the arts and other causes. Explaining her particular passion for the Murdoch Children's Research Institute and its world-leading work on uncovering the genetic basis of childhood diseases and conditions, Elisabeth said she had 'always been tremendously interested in genetics' since her time with Keith and their attempts to breed prize cattle. The Institute continues to make breakthroughs in the field, including into the genetic causes of the most severe forms of speech impediment and stammering.

Keith's memory is kept alive through the News Awards' highest honour, the Sir Keith Murdoch Award for Excellence in Journalism. At the 2018 ceremony, Lachlan delivered a speech that paid tribute to Keith as well as Rupert, who attended. The Awards had been conceived, Lachlan stressed, as a way 'to celebrate our company's culture' and 'collective values as journalists'. Once again, the myth of Keith's Gallipoli letter and how it had 'changed history' through 'the power of fearless truth telling' was trumpeted. 'It was a lesson not lost on Sir Keith's son, who has lived a life defined by the deepest love of journalism, ultimately to build the world's most successful company devoted to news and information.' Lachlan concluded: 'Dad, all of us here tonight thank you for your lifelong tireless investment in our journalism and for your truly inspiring leadership.' (The Keith Murdoch Award for Excellence in Journalism that night was handed to the political editor of one of the Murdoch tabloids for her scoop revealing the deputy prime minister had a love child.)

The 2013 rebranding of News Corporation following the global division of newspaper and entertainment interests, saw a formal switch to its more personable, informal name: News Corp. Even more significantly, the Murdoch family heritage was re-emphasised with the font of the fresh logos for both the main company and its subsidiaries – News Corp Australia and News UK – being based on a composite of Rupert's and Keith's handwriting.

In 2014 those questioning the Murdochs' ability to maintain control of two multi-billion-dollar global corporations as effectively family businesses were confounded. Lachlan returned to active involvement as non-executive co-chairman of News Corp and 21st Century Fox and James was appointed co-chief operating officer of 21st Century Fox. On 1 July 2015 James became chief executive of Fox when his father stepped down, Rupert remaining as executive chairman with Lachlan his executive co-chairman. But at the end of 2017 Rupert announced he would be selling the bulk of Fox's television and film holdings to Disney. The wily old operator had confounded everyone again. One person was particularly worried about what the sale might mean for Fox News. Donald Trump phoned Rupert seeking his assurance that the channel's support for his presidency would not change. His fears calmed, the 'deal-maker' President duly let it be known that he had congratulated Rupert, though Trump's claim that the deal would be 'a great thing' for jobs rang rather hollow.

In March 2019, following the sale of 21st Century Fox, Lachlan became Chairman and CEO of the slimmed down FOX Corporation, its focus, in a retrograde move, now refined back to news, US broadcasting and suitably enough, sports betting. Meanwhile, having lost out to Disney in the fight for 21st Century Fox, the US cable giant Comcast settled for securing control of the Murdochs' holdings in Sky. Rupert remained Executive Chairman of News Corp, the company left holding those assets closest to his heart: the newspapers – from the red-topped tabloids to the broadsheet papers of record – whose value increasingly seems more political than commercial.

While Lachlan appears to share his father's political views, James duly stepped away from the business, turning instead to entrepreneurial interests and philanthropy with a socially liberal and environmental slant outside of the Murdoch empire. James had previously managed to convince his father of the threat posed by climate change. In 2007 Rupert announced that News Corp would become carbon neutral with positive messaging on the need to act for the planet woven into its content. But as James' star faded, so too it seemed did Rupert's resolve on the defining issue of our time. (Ironically, a few months before his death, Rupert's own father asked to be sent a copy of *Our Plundered Earth*, a book that was one of the first to warn of environmental collapse, while stressing 'these things are important'.)

In contrast to the indebted estate that Rupert inherited on the death of his father, he has already made his six children independent billionaires, with each gaining a cash and stock inheritance estimated at $2 billion. But without that impetus of needing to fight to make their own way and prove rivals and the establishment wrong, will this next generation inherit the same drive that made him want to create and succeed? Perhaps the model is broken; perhaps after all, in the words of the president Murdoch made, there is, and can but ever be, 'only one Rupert'.

SELECTED READING

'Keith Murdoch: The Man in the Paper Mask', in Hetherington, John, *Australians: Nine Profiles*, Halstead Press: Sydney, 1960.

McKnight, David, *Rupert Murdoch: An investigation of political power*, Allen & Unwin, Sydney, 2012.

Monks, John, *Elisabeth Murdoch: Two Lives*, Pan Macmillan: Sydney, 1994.

Munster, George, *A Paper Prince*, Viking: Ringwood, Vic., 1985.

Murdoch, Keith, *The Gallipoli Letter: The letter that changed the course of the Gallipoli campaign*, Allen & Unwin: Crows Nest, NSW, 2010.

Sayers, Charles E., 'K.M. – A Life of Keith Murdoch, Newspaper Reporter', unpublished manuscript, *c*.1970, MS2823/11, NLA.

Serle, Geoffrey, 'Murdoch, Sir Keith Arthur', *Australian Dictionary of National Biography*, Volume 10, Melbourne University Press: Melbourne, 1986.

Shawcross, William, *Rupert Murdoch: Ringmaster of the Information Circus*, Chatto & Windus: London, 1992.

Wolff, Michael, *The Man Who Owns the News: Inside the Secret World of Rupert Murdoch*, Broadway Books: New York, 2008.

Younger, Ronald M., *Keith Murdoch: Founder of a Media Empire*, HarperCollins: Sydney, 2003.

Zwar, Desmond, *In Search of Keith Murdoch*, Macmillan: South Melbourne, Vic., 1980.

A NOTE ON SOURCING

As well as an extensive range of secondary source material, including the key works listed in the Selected Reading above, the author consulted contemporary newspapers and periodicals reporting the events detailed, and the diaries, correspondence and memoirs, both published and unpublished, of the figures that feature in this story. These Papers and their repositories are detailed below. Two collections should be emphasised as their extensive contents underpin much of this book: the Keith Murdoch Papers and the Lloyd Dumas Papers, both held at the National Library of Australia. Both provide exceptional, candid insight into the life and business dealings of Rupert's father and the origins of the Murdoch empire.

While constraints of space mean a full detailing of each reference is not possible, an indicative list of the key sources, as they first appear, for each chapter follows. The author, via the publisher, will be happy to answer specific queries relating to any particular reference and its source.

ARCHIVES AND PAPERS

(via the Australian Joint Copying Project)
The Papers of Andrew Bonar Law (M1123); David Lloyd George (M1124-5); and Ellis Ashmead-Bartlett (M2582)

Australian National University Archives
The Frederic Eggleston Papers (ANUA 107); and *Australian Dictionary of Biography* file for Sir Keith Murdoch (ANUA 312)

Australian War Memorial
Papers of Charles Bean (AWM38 3DRL/606); William Birdwood (AWM 3DRL/337); Keith Murdoch (AWM 3DRL/2925 and AWM 419); and George Pearce (AWM 3DRL/2222)

British Library
The Northcliffe (Alfred Harmsworth) Papers (62203); and George Riddell Diaries (62979)

Herald & Weekly Times Archives (Melbourne)
Company Minute Books and the full run of *House News*

National Archives (UK)
Records of the Colonial Office; Commonwealth and Foreign and Commonwealth Offices; and Cabinet Office, including First World War Memoranda (CAB 24)

National Library of Scotland
The Elibank (Arthur C. Murray) Papers

Parliamentary Archives (UK)
The Beaverbrook Papers (BBK); and Andrew Bonar Law Papers (BL)

Mitchell Library, State Library of New South Wales
Papers of Florence James (MLMSS 5877); George Ernest Morrison Papers (MLMSS 312) and Sydney Ure Smith (MLMSS 31)

National Archives of Australia
Papers of Richard Casey (M112); Joseph Lyons (CP103 and CP30); the Malcolm Shepherd Memoirs (A1632); and Defence AIF Papers

National Library of Australia
Papers of Lloyd Dumas (MS 4849); Andrew Fisher (MS 2919); Randal Heymanson (MS 7999); William Hughes (MS 1538); Keith Murdoch (MS 2823); John Monash (MS 1884); Ronald Munro Ferguson alt. Novar (MS 696); and Rohan Rivett (MS 8049)

State Library of Victoria
Papers of Charles Goddard (MS 13106); and Charles Sayers (MS 10600)

University of Melbourne Archives
Theodore Fink Papers (1997.0127)

Other archives consulted
BBC Written Archives Centre; British Pathé Archive; Churchill Archives, Churchill College, Cambridge; Imperial War Museum Archives; Liddell Hart Centre for Military Archives; London School of Economics Archives; National Portrait Gallery Archives; MacArthur Memorial Archives; Reuters Archive (London); The Tate Gallery Archives; and UCLA Film & Television Archive – Hearst Metrotone News Collection

SELECT REFERENCES

Introduction
Moulding a myth

Australian Dictionary of Biography file for Sir Keith Murdoch; Eggleston Papers; Sayers Papers; Hetherington, *Australians: Nine Profiles;* Younger, *Keith Murdoch: Founder of a Media Empire;* Zwar, *In Search of Keith Murdoch.*

1 Rosehearty

James Fagan, *The Earth: A Modern Play in Four Acts*, T. Fisher Unwin: London, 1909; Thomas H. Hardman, *A Parliament of the Press: the First Imperial Press Conference*, Horace Marshall & Son: London, 1909; Charles Masterman, *The Condition of England*, 1909 as republished with an introduction and notes by J.T. Boulton, Methuen & Co: London, 1960.

2 American Immigrant

Henry S. Wellcome, *The Evolution of Journalism Etcetera: Souvenir of The International Press Conference London, 1909*, Burroughs Wellcome & Co: London, 1909.

3 Finding his voice

David Day, *Andrew Fisher: Prime Minister of Australia*, Fourth Estate: Sydney, 2008; Fisher Papers.

4 'Murder, history, war'

Ian Hamilton, *Gallipoli Diary*, Vol. II, George H. Doran Company, New York, 1920; Ashmead-Bartlett Papers; X, *My Journey Round the World 1921–22*, John Lane: London, 1923; John Avieson, 'The Reporter Who Stopped a War', unpublished manuscript, *c.*1986, copy held by the author; C. E. W. Bean, *The Official History of Australia in the War of 1914–18,* Angus and Robertson: Sydney, 1937; Pearce Papers; Morrison Papers; Eric Andrews, *The Anzac Illusion: Anglo-Australian Relations during World War I,* Cambridge University Press: New York, 1993; *The Times History of The War,* Vol. VI, *The Times:* London, 1916; Les Carlyon, *Gallipoli,* Pan Macmillan: Sydney, 2001; Jenny Mcleod, *Reconsidering Gallipoli,* Manchester University Press: Manchester, 2004; Aubrey Solomon, *The Fox Film Corporation, 1915–1935: A History and Filmography,* MacFarland & Company: Jefferson, NC, 2011.

5 Hearts and minds . . . and bodies

A.J.P. Taylor, *Beaverbrook,* Hamish Hamilton: London, 1972; Louis Raemaekers, *Kultur in Cartoons,* New York: The Century Co., 1917; J. Lee Thompson, *Politicians, the Press, & Propaganda: Lord Northcliffe & the Great War, 1914–18,* Kent State University Press: Kent, Ohio, 1999; Joachim Neander and Randal Marlin, 'Media and Propaganda: The Northcliffe Press and the Corpse Factory Story of World War I', *Global Media Journal – Canadian Edition,* Vol. 3, No. 2, 2010, pp.67–82; Malcolm Shepherd Memoirs; Keith Murdoch (ed.), *"The Day" – And After: War Speeches of the Rt. Hon. W. M. Hughes,* Arranged by Keith A. Murdoch, With an Introduction by The Rt. Hon. D. Lloyd George, Cassell and Company: London, New York, Toronto and Melbourne, 1916; Keith Murdoch, *The Australians at Bullecourt,* Williams Brooks & Co.: Sydney, 1917; Hughes Papers; Bean Papers; Birdwood; Murdoch Papers (AWM 3DRL/2925 and AWM 419); Lloyd George Papers; Monash Papers; Geoffrey Serle, *John Monash: A Biography,* Melbourne University Press in association with Monash University: Melbourne, 2002; Roland Perry, *Monash: The outsider who won a war,* Random House: Milsons Point, NSW, 2004; Peter Putnis, 'Keith Murdoch: wartime journalist, 1915–1918', *Australian Journalism Review,* Vol. 33, No. 2, 2011, pp.61–70; John Connor, *Anzac and Empire: George Foster Pearce and the Foundations of Australian Defence,* Cambridge University Press: Cambridge, 2011; Anne Chisholm and Michael Davie, *Beaverbrook: A Life,* Pimlico: London, 1992; Maxwell Aitken, *Politicians and the Press by Lord Beaverbrook,* Hutchinson & Co.: London, 1926; Charles Montague, *Disenchantment,* Brentano's: New York, 1922.

6 A romance into air

Morrison Papers; Ralph Adams, *Bonar Law,* Stanford University Press: Stanford, 1999; Robert Blake, *The Unknown Prime Minister. The Life and Times of Andrew Bonar Law, 1858–1923,* Eyre & Spottiswoode: London, 1955; Malcolm Booker, *The Great Professional: A study of W.M. Hughes,* McGraw Hill: Sydney, 1980; Frederick Sykes, *Aviation in Peace and War,* Edward Arnold: London, 1922; Frederick Sykes, *From Many Angles: An Autobiography,* Harrap: London, 1942; Eric Ash, *Sir Frederick Sykes and the Air Revolution, 1912–1918,* Frank Cass: London, 1999.

7 The Prince and the pressman

Kevin Fewster, 'Politics, Pageantry and Purpose: The 1920 Tour of Australia by the Prince of Wales', *Labour History,* No. 38, May 1980, pp.59–66; F.D. Ward and R. Godfrey, *Letters from a Prince: Edward, Prince of Wales to Mrs Freda Dudley Ward, March 1918–January 1921*, Little, Brown & Company: London, 1998; [By Authority], *Crossing the line with His Royal Highness the Prince of Wales in H.M.S. Renown, Friday–Saturday, April 16–17, 1920*, Sydney: Angus and Robertson, 1920; Novar Papers; British Pathé Archive; Piers Legh, (ed.), *With the 'Renown' in Australasia: The magazine of HMS Renown, December 1919 to October 1920*, Melbourne: Australasian Publishing Co., 1920; Philip Ziegler, *Personal Diary of Admiral the Lord Louis Mountbatten, Supreme Allied Commander, South-East Asia, 1943–1946*, Collins: London, 1988.

8 Lessons from a madman's bible

Don Garden, *Theodore Fink: A Talent for Ubiquity*, Melbourne University Press: Melbourne, 1998; John Kirwan, *My Life's Adventure*, Eyre & Spottiswoode: London, 1936; J. Lee Thompson, *Northcliffe: Press Baron in Politics 1865–1922*, John Murray: London, 2000; Stephen Koss, *The Rise and Fall of The Political Press In Britain*, Fontana Press: London, 1990; Iverach McDonald, *The History of The Times: The 150th Anniversary and Beyond, 1912–1948*, Vol. IV, Part II, *The Times* Office: London, 1952; Max Pemberton, *Lord Northcliffe: A Memoir*, Hodder and Stoughton: London, 1922; Tom Pocock, Tom, *Rider Haggard And The Lost Empire*, Weidenfeld and Nicolson: London, 1993; Claude McKay, *This is The Life*, Angus and Robertson: Sydney, 1961; Northcliffe Papers; Paul Ferris, *The House of Northcliffe: A Biography of an Empire*, World Publishing: New York, 1972; James Weber Linn, *James Keeley, Newspaperman*, Bobbs-Merrill Co: Indianapolis, 1937; Reginald Pound and Geoffrey Harmsworth, *Northcliffe*, Cassell & Company: London, 1959; Tom Clarke, *My Northcliffe Diary*, Victor Gollancz: London, 1931; T.C. Brennan, *The Gun Alley Tragedy: Record of the Trial of Colin Campbell Ross,* Fraser & Jenkinson: Melbourne, 1922; Kevin Morgan, *Gun Alley: Murder, Lies and Failure of Justice*, Simon & Schuster: Pymble, NSW, 2005; C. R. Bradish, 'Back Seat At The Circus: Reminiscences of a Veteran Newspaperman', Melbourne *c.*1950, unpublished manuscript held by the British Library, BLL01000447929; Hugh Cudlipp, *Walking on the Water*, The Bodley Head: London, 1976.

9 Healthy competition

James Murdoch, 'The Absence of Trust', The 2009 Edinburgh International Television Festival, MacTaggart Lecture, 28 August 2009; Peter Putnis, 'Lord Northcliffe, Keith Murdoch, and the development of the Melbourne Herald in the 1920s', *Australian Journal of Communication*, Vol. 38, No. 2, 2011, pp. 71–8; Matthew Engel, *Tickle the Public: One Hundred Years of the Popular Press*, Victor Gollancz: London, 1996; Peter Chippindale and Chris Horrie, *Stick It Up Your Punter! The Uncut Story of the* Sun *Newspaper*, Simon & Schuster: London, 1999; Diana H. Wyndham, *Eugenics in Australia: Striving for National Fitness*, Galton Institute: London, 2003; Ross L. Jones, 'Skeletons in Toorak and Collingwood cupboards: Eugenics in educational and health policy in Victoria, 1910 to 1939', PhD thesis, 2000, Monash University; Ross L. Jones, 'The Master Potter and the Rejected Pots: Eugenic Legislation in Victoria, 1918–1939', *Australian Historical Studies*, Vol. 30, No. 113, 1999, pp.319–42; Ann Blainey, *I am Melba*, Black Inc.: Melbourne, 2008; John Hetherington, John, *Melba*, F.W Cheshire: Melbourne, 1967; Joan Lindsay, *Time*

Without Clocks, Ringwood Vic.: Penguin, 1976; Elisabeth Murdoch, Elisabeth (Dame) interviewed by John Farquharson, 20 February 1995, transcript, National Library of Australia Oral History Project, 2077994; ORAL TRC 3194.

10 Kingmaker

Dumas Papers; Peter Yule, *William Lawrence Baillieu: Founder of Australia's Greatest Business Empire*, Hardie Grant: Richmond, Vic. 2012; Hugh Cudlipp, *The Prerogative of the Harlot: Press Barons & Power*, Bodley Head: London, 1980; Bridget Griffen-Foley, *Changing Stations: The Story of Australian Commercial Radio*, University of New South Wales Press: Sydney, 2009; Sally Young, *Paper Emperors: The Rise of Australia's Newspaper Empires*, NewSouth Publishing: Sydney, 2019; Peter Fitzsimons, *Charles Kingsford Smith and Those Magnificent Men,* HarperCollins: Sydney, 2010; Anne Henderson, *Joseph Lyons: The People's Prime Minister*, NewSouth: Sydney, 2011; John Faulkner and Stuart Macintyre (eds), *True Believers: The Story of the Federal Parliamentary Labor Party*, Allen & Unwin: Crows Nest, NSW, 2001.

11 Media empire

Lyons Papers; Ken Inglis, *This is the ABC: The Australian Broadcasting Commission, 1932–83*, Black Inc.: Melbourne, 2006 edition; Mark Scott, 'Why Public Broadcasting Matters More Than Ever', CBA Lecture 2009; 'Countries: Australia. Thomas Bearup 1936–45', BBC Written Archives Centre; Eileen Chanin and Steven Miller, *Degenerates and Perverts: The 1939 Herald Exhibition of French and British Contemporary Art*, Miegunyah Press: Melbourne, 2005.

12 A girdle round about the Earth

Cecil Edwards, *The Editor Regrets*, Hill of Content: Melbourne, 1972; Clem Lloyd and Richard Hall (eds), *Backroom Briefings: John Curtin's War*, NLA: Canberra, 1997; Norman E. Lee, *John Curtin, Saviour of Australia*, Longman Cheshire: Melbourne, 1983; J. R. Hay, 'The institute of public affairs and social policy in World War II', *Australian Historical Studies*, 20: 79; MacArthur Memorial archive; Geoffrey Blainey (ed.), *If I Remember Rightly: The Memoirs of W.S. Robinson 1876–1963*, Cheshire: Melbourne, 1967.

13 By phone and clone

Keith Dunstan, *No Brains At All*, Penguin: Ringwood, Vic., 1990; Michael Keon, *Glad Morning Again*, Imprint: Watsons Bay, NSW, 1996; Kenneth Clark Papers, Tate Gallery Archive; Rivett Papers; Ure Smith Papers; Heymanson Papers; Tom Pocock, *Alan Moorehead*, The Bodley Head: London, 1990; Humphrey McQueen, *The Black Swan of*

Trespass: The Emergence of Modernist Painting in Australia to 1944, Alternative Publishing Cooperative: Sydney, 1979.

14 The son rises

Casey Papers; Beaverbrook Papers; Lord Beaverbrook, *Success*, Stanley Paul & Co: London, 1921; Michael Leapman, *Barefaced Cheek: The Apotheosis of Rupert Murdoch*, Hodder & Stoughton: London, 1983.

Epilogue

A new inheritance

Paul Barry, *Breaking News: Sex, Lies and the Murdoch Succession*, Allen & Unwin: Crows Nest, NSW, 2003; Rod Tiffen, 'Fraying Empire', 9 April 2019, *Inside Story*.

ACKNOWLEDGEMENTS

During the years of researching the Murdoch family and their media empire I have been lucky enough to receive the help of many people. Prime among these are Professor Bridget Griffen-Foley and Emeritus Professor Murray Goot who supervised my doctoral research at Macquarie University on Sir Keith Murdoch. Following completion of my thesis, I was extremely fortunate to gain a brave publisher in Alexandra Payne at UQP, and a superb editor in Jacqueline Kent. Further luck came when the subsequent book, published in Australia as *Before Rupert: Keith Murdoch and the Birth of a Dynasty*, was awarded the country's National Biography Award in 2017. The prize fund, generously supported by the State Library of New South Wales and Michael Crouch AC, enabled me to undertake the further research and writing that has resulted in *The Making of Murdoch*. Tomasz Hoskins and his team at I.B. Tauris/Bloomsbury, as well as Sara Bryant and Merv Honeywood have been brilliant in helping bring the story up to date and to an international readership, even as developments — both political and business — continue to unfold.

Over the years, many individual librarians and archivists around the world have aided me in the great task of locating and gaining access to elusive records and I thank all of them. I am also grateful for those who agreed to speak to me and kindly shared their memories of Sir Keith and the young Rupert, including Phillip Knightley, Sir Alcon Copisarow, Tim McDonald and George Masterman.

It seems apt that in the process of researching a tale focused on the origins of a family dynasty I was to become indebted to the help of the family members and descendants of those associated with the early development of the Murdoch family's media empire. I am extremely grateful to Bunty Avieson, daughter of John; Mark Logue, grandson of Lionel; Jessie Serle, widow of Geoffrey; Helen Marshall, granddaughter of Charles Sayers; and Rhyll Rivett who granted permission for me to access the closed files of the Rivett Papers. Though unfortunately Dame Elisabeth Murdoch was unable to respond to my approach, her daughter Janet Calvert-Jones very kindly answered my questions regarding her father and helped arrange access to the HWT minute books and to the full run of *House News*.

Finally, I thank my own family and Tim, as ever, for their support. This book is dedicated to Theo, Joss and Nella in the hope that the future remains bright for them and their generation.

INDEX